MAGIC

The Cookbook of the Junior League of Birmingham, AL.

This MAGIC collection has been tested by Junior League members, their families, and friends, and represents their favorite choices.

Copies of MAGIC may be obtained from:
The Junior League of Birmingham, Inc.
2212 Twentieth Ave. South
Birmingham, AL 35223

$10.95 per copy $1.50 postage and handling Ala. residents $.77 tax

Proceeds from the sale of MAGIC are returned to the community through the projects of the Junior League of Birmingham, Inc.

First Printing	Feb., 1982	10,000
Special Printing	Aug., 1982	5,000
Second Printing	Oct., 1982	15,000
Third Printing	Nov., 1984	15,000

Library of Congress Catalog Card Number 81-85953
International Standard Book Number 0-9607810-0-5

Printed by
Kansas City Press, Inc.

THE COOKBOOK PEOPLE
Olathe, Kansas
800/821-5745

Contents

COOKBOOK COMMITTEE

Chairman Kim Ryne Hazzard

Assistants Carolyn McDavid Ray
Karen Valentine Sanders

Publishing
Lee McLaughlin Gewin
Jean Qualman Ager

Finance
Kathy Johnston Myatt
Connie Strickland Frazier

Creative
Olive Gaines Arant
Jeanne Edwards Rogers
Ashley Wiltshire Spotswood

Marketing
Kate Johnson Nielsen
Murray Spencer South
Eleanor Bridges Griffin

Food Editors

Kay Shumate Reed
Pat McCabe Forman
Caroline Johnson Abele
Cathy Criss Adams
Dorothy Rosamond Christian

Carol King Nolen
Adele Williamson Scielzo
Millymac Jenkins Shackelford
Genie Brooks Wilson
Jan Roby Wofford

Sustainer Advisor Jean Riley Tomlinson

Typists

Margaret Parker Moor
Nancy Freeman Denson

Beth Hazelrig Yoe
Wendy Wall White

Illustrations Olive Gaines Arant

BIRMINGHAM *The Magic City*

Birmingham has always been called "The Magic City". Perhaps, to those of us who live here, our rolling hills, the dense pine forests which surround us or our long, brilliant springs with their profusion of blooming azaleas, mountain laurel and dogwood are enough to explain the name. But Birmingham's nickname actually has its roots in Birmingham's history—a history that is as flamboyant and intriguing as "Magic City" implies.

Birmingham was not born as most cities are, slowly, over a period of years. It erupted onto the landscape at a time when the whole country was still reeling under the devastation of the War Between the States. Poverty, despondency and chaos were the watchwords of the entire South. Thousands of veterans returned to farms which had lain fallow for years or towns dead from lack of normal trade. What little industry there had been in the South before the war was at a standstill. Recently freed slaves who now needed jobs poured into cities that were already bankrupt. To all of these men and women, the future must have looked bleak, indeed.

But, unknown to them, the seeds of birth for the South's first great industrial city had already been sewn in the imaginations of a few visionary men back before the war began. These men knew that in the rugged foothills of north Alabama there were vast deposits of iron ore. One of them had spent nearly two years on horseback surveying the region before the war broke out. From his reports, they knew that in addition to an almost incalculable amount of iron ore, there was also a wealth of limestone and coal—the three basic ingredients necessary to make pig iron and steel.

But there were problems. The very mountains of iron which were so enticing, effectively cut the region off from the rest of the state. Just to get men and supplies into the area meant a railroad would have to be built—relaying the tracks which had been destroyed during the war and cutting through the mountains to lay new ones. Where was capital to be found for such an enormous project? How would men home from a long war react to the prospect of such a back-breaking task which would require them to leave home once again with no guarantee that the venture would even succeed?

Despite all these uncertainties, Birmingham's founding fathers did not hesitate. They not only pooled all their captial and resolutely went ahead with their pre-war plans to develop the minerals of this region, they laid out a great city, complete with schools, churches and parks, in a beautiful valley they found cradled among the northern hills of Alabama. Officially, they named this city "Birmingham", after England's great industrial city. And, as word of this incredible undertaking spread, it lit a spark of hope in the hearts of thousands of men and women. To them this unborn city, with its promise of work, homes for their families, and the chance to prosper, became known as "The Magic City".

With the help of nothing but gunpowder, nitroglycerin, picks and shovels, 1500 men dug their way seventy feet straight down through a solid mountain of limestone to cut Brock's Gap and open the valley where Birmingham was to lie. At that time, it was the deepest man-made gap in the world.

Through this gap and down the valleys from the north poured hungry, nearly desperate settlers—not just from the South, but from all over the United States and from abroad as well. Every imaginable nationality, religion and occupation was represented. All of them had heard the whispers of a "Magic City" that was going to rise like a phoenix from the ruins of war. They brought with them their own unique heritages of custom, dress, language, art, music and cuisine. So from her earliest days, Birmingham was a wild and colorful blend of peoples, a rugged, Western-style, boom-town in the middle of the "Old" South.

In this boom-town atmosphere, land prices sky-rocketed. Lots in the center of town which sold originally for $100 were sold and resold a dozen times, so fast the deeds were not even registered. Fortunes were made overnight. The Magic City was magic indeed.

Of course, there were bad times, too. There were depressions and cholera epidemics. But young Birmingham survived because her supporters were fiercely loyal. They never lost faith in their vision of Birmingham as a great city. In the final analysis, the people themselves became the "magic" that made Birmingham special and guaranteed Birmingham's place in history as the first great industrial city in the South, and later as a highly diversified city of commerce and banking, educational, medical and cultural activities as well.

As Southern cities go, Birmingham is still young. And reminders of our not-so-distant past still surround us, including our wild and colorful mixture of peoples and cultures. It is from this happy mixture that we have developed our eclectic cuisine which defies any simple labeling. Our tastes are not limited to traditional Southern cooking—though who among us does not love spoonbread, our grandmother's pound cake, turnip greens and fried chicken! But Birminghamians also embrace with equal fervor pasta dishes from Italy, the phyllo of Greece, and paella from Spain. They are, after all, a familiar part of our culinary heritage.

The women of the Junior League of Birmingham have done an outstanding job of capturing this variety, originality and plain old deliciousness in this sampling of Birmingham cooking. The recipes range in nature from simple to sophisticated, from down-home Southern to exotic foreign fare, but they all have several things in common. Each recipe was prepared and sampled by other excellent cooks. Then each was carefully written so that even amateurs like myself could prepare them confidently.

This cookbook is, then, just one more example of that special "Birmingham Magic"—a pinch of this and a pinch of that which adds up to an exciting, delectable and unique whole! Happy eating.

Julia Coley Duncan
Author, *Halfway Home*

BEVERAGES, SOUPS, SANDWICHES

Beverages, Sandwiches, Soups

Mocha Milkshake

Can be used as an elegant dessert.

Mocha base serves 22

1 (2 ounce) jar instant coffee granules
¼ cup hot water
1 (16 ounce) can chocolate syrup
1 cup rum
1 tablespoon vanilla
Vanilla ice cream
Milk

In mixing bowl combine coffee granules and water. Stir until dissolved. Add chocolate syrup, rum, vanilla, and stir. Store mixture in covered container in refrigerator. It keeps for months.
To serve: Use 2 tablespoons of mocha base and 1 scoop ice cream for each serving. Put base and ice cream into blender and blend. Add milk to desired consistency. One blender container of mocha milkshakes makes 6 easy, delicious desserts. Serve in tall bubble wine glasses with a chocolate curl on top.

Barbara Scott Sandner

Brandy Alexander

Serves 2

2 ounces whipping cream
1 ounce creme de cocoa
2 ounces brandy
2 scoops vanilla ice cream

Mix in blender about 10 seconds.

Adele Redditt Williamson
BATON ROUGE, LOUISIANA

Brandy Milk Punch

A delicious drink

Yield: 1 generous drink

1½ ounces brandy or bourbon
1½ ounces half-and-half
1 generous scoop vanilla ice cream
Vanilla to taste
1 teaspoon sugar
Nutmeg for garnish

Mix ingredients in blender. Pour into 16-ounce glass and garnish with nutmeg if desired.

Robert Washington
MOUNTAIN BROOK CLUB

Freezer Frozen Dacquiris

Can be made ahead and kept in freezer as long as you can keep nippers out of it.

Serves 20

1 (46 ounce) can pineapple-grapefruit juice
1 (6 ounce) can limeade concentrate, thawed
1 (6 ounce) can lemonade concentrate, thawed
1 (750 ml.) bottle light rum

Combine all ingredients in a large plastic container. Stir well. Cover tightly and put in freezer. As liquid begins to freeze, stir occasionally until all liquid is frozen. Makes a potent slush that is enough for 20 drinks. *Serve in small glasses with spoons or straws, a smile, and a warning.*

Belle Sumter Roberts Hazzard

Matthews' Freeze

Serves 20

6 (6 ounce) bottles 7-Up
3 (6 ounce) cans frozen lemonade concentrate
2 cans water to each can of concentrate
1 (750 ml.) bottle vodka, gin, or light rum
Maraschino cherries
Orange slices

Stir all ingredients together. Put in large plastic container and freeze. Serve in clear, tall glasses with a straw, spoon, cherry, and orange slice. *This is a great summer drink to have in your freezer, but only serve 2 per person!*

Jeanie Jemison Matthews

Pisco Sours

Serves 6

6 ounces Pisco
1 (6 ounce) can limeade, undiluted
1 egg white
4-5 ice cubes
Crushed ice
2-3 drops bitters

Put Pisco, limeade, egg white, and ice cubes in blender. Blend. Pour over crushed ice in wine glass. Add dash of bitters.

Nicholas Henry Scielzo

Whiskey Sour

Yield: 5 cups

1 (6 ounce) can frozen pink lemonade
1 lemonade can bourbon
Ice (about 4 cups of cubes)

Place lemonade, bourbon, and ice in blender. Liquefy. Serve in whiskey sour glasses or deep wine glasses.

Mildred Cotten Knight

Pink Delight

Yield: 1 drink

1½ ounces undiluted frozen pink lemonade
1½ ounces rosé wine
Crushed ice
Strawberry, cherry, or lemon slice for garnish

Place all in blender with enough ice to make mixture frothy, as a frozen dacquiri. Serve in champagne glass, and garnish with strawberry, cherry, or slice of lemon.

Elizabeth Nesbitt Simpson

Champagne Punch

Yield: 2 gallons

4 (6 ounce) cans frozen lemonade
1 (750 ml.) bottle brandy
½ pint light Jamaican rum
3 (750 ml.) bottles champagne

Make lemonade according to directions. Pour into punch bowl over block of ice. Add brandy and rum. Stir mixture and at the last minute, add the champagne slowly. *This is very potent.*

William Floyd Williamson, Jr.
BATON ROUGE, LA.

Dan's "Boot Leg"

For children, leave out alcohol and call it "BOOT-ADE".

Serves 12

1 double old-fashioned glass filled with mint leaves

¾ pound sugar

12 ounces lemon juice (about 12 lemons)

Vodka, rum, or gin

Soda water

Combine mint, sugar, and lemon juice in blender to make a green syrup. Take 1 jigger of syrup per 1 jigger of alcohol. Fill tall glass with ice. Add syrup, alcohol, and fill with soda water.

Marsha Gear Oliver

Party Pink Punch

30 servings

1 (46 ounce) can pineapple juice

1 (6 ounce) can frozen lemonade

1 cup sugar

1 (48 ounce) bottle cranberry juice

2 (1 quart) bottles ginger ale, chilled

Blend first 4 ingredients. Freeze. Take out of freezer two hours before serving. As it softens, break into mush. Add chilled ginger ale at last minute, so that it does not get flat. *May be frozen in a ring mold to float in a punch bowl.*

Jane Henderson McDonald

Hot Rum Cider

Serves 12

8½ cups apple cider
2 teaspoons pumpkin pie spice
2-3 cups light or dark rum, to taste
12 cinnamon sticks
12 whole cloves
12 slices lime

In large saucepan, bring apple cider and pumpkin pie spice to a boil. Remove from heat and add rum. Ladle into mugs and add a cinnamon stick and a whole clove to each. If desired, add a slice of lime to each mug. Serve at once.

Caroline McCall Graves

Charleston Wassail

A delicious Christmas beverage

Serves 12-15

2 quarts apple juice
2 cups orange juice
¾-1 cup fresh lemon juice
1 (18 ounce) can pineapple juice
1 stick cinnamon, about 4 inches long
1 rounded teaspoon whole cloves
¼ - ½ cup sugar, optional

Place all ingredients in large saucepan and bring to boil. Reduce heat, partially cover pot, and simmer for 1 hour. Serve hot. May be prepared ahead. Reheat slowly before serving.

Ginna Henking Lowry

Neptune's Fire

Yield: 1 Drink

1½ ounces Tequila
5 ounces Clamato juice
½ teaspoon cream style horseradish, or more to taste
Worcestershire sauce to taste
Celery salt to taste
Shrimp or lemon slice for garnish

Combine ingredients and add ice. Frappé in blender. Garnish with a whole shrimp or lemon slice.

Kay Shumate Reed

Magic Marys

Serves 6-8

1 teaspoon celery salt
1 teaspoon salt
1 teaspoon garlic salt
1 tablespoon black pepper
3 ounces Worcestershire sauce
6 ounces sweet and sour mix
32 ounces tomato juice
Gin or vodka to taste

Mix all ingredients except liquor and let marinate at least overnight. Add gin or vodka to taste.

Mrs. Alvin A. Biggio

Iced Mint Tea

Yield: ½ gallon

½ gallon water
¾ cup sugar or 1½ teaspoons Sweet and Low
3 lemons, juiced
6 tea bags
1 cup fresh mint leaves

Bring water to boil. Add ingredients and steep for 10 minutes. Strain and refrigerate.

Jody Hamre

Watercress Soup

Serves 12

4 cups diced potatoes
1 cup diced leeks or onions
1 stick butter
1¼ cups water
2 bunches watercress, washed and drained and chopped coarsely (all stems removed)
3 cups milk
1 cup whipping cream
3 cups chicken stock
1 tablespoon salt
¼ teaspoon white pepper
Watercress for garnish

Combine potatoes, leeks, butter, and water in a large heavy saucepan. Bring to a boil. Cover and simmer about 20 minutes or until vegetables are quite tender. Add chopped watercress and cook gently until just wilted. Add milk. Place in blender, a little at a time. Blend until almost smooth. Add cream, chicken stock, salt and pepper. Chill. Serve cold. Garnish with sprigs of watercress.

Josephine Harris Wasson

Cucumber Soup

Summer appetizer or lunch

Yield: 4 cups

2 medium cucumbers
2 cups chicken broth
2 tablespoons chopped onion
½ cup watercress leaves
Sprig of parsley
½ teaspoon salt
¼ teaspoon pepper
¼ teaspoon dry mustard
1-2 teaspoons dry dill weed
2 cups yogurt

Peel and seed cucumbers, then cut into strips. Should yield 2 cups. Cook in broth with onion, watercress, and parsley. Simmer until tender. Pour mixture into blender and purée. Add salt, pepper, mustard, and dill to taste. Chill. Stir in yogurt and chill thoroughly before serving. *Better if made a day ahead.*

Gail Andrews Trechsel

Cream of Crécy With Dill

Serves 6-8

½ stick butter
1 large onion, chopped
2 pounds carrots, sliced
4 cups chicken broth
¼ teaspoon cayenne pepper (or less)
2 tablespoons dill weed
3 drops of lemon juice
Salt to taste
2 cups milk or half-and-half

Sauté onion in butter until soft. Add carrots and onion to chicken broth. Cook until carrots are very tender (about 20-30 minutes). Purée in food processor or blender in batches. Strain if any lumps appear (this is usually not necessary). Return to saucepan. Season with cayenne pepper, dill weed, lemon, and salt. Heat thoroughly. Add milk. *Wonderful hot and good cold.*

Jean Qualman Ager

Cold Zucchini Soup

Serves 6-8

6-8 zucchini, unpeeled
1 onion
1 carrot
4 slices raw bacon
3 cups chicken broth
1½ teaspoons salt
1 teaspoon basil
¼ teaspoon pepper
Parmesan cheese, grated

Cut vegetables and bacon in large pieces. Mix all ingredients, except cheese, and cook in saucepan about 30 minutes. Remove bacon and pour into blender. Blend for a few seconds only. Mixture should not be puréed. Serve cold with fresh Parmesan cheese on top.

Kay Luckie Shackelford

Curried Zucchini Soup

Serves 8

5-6 zucchini
1 large onion, thinly sliced (1 cup) or 1 bunch green onions, sliced
1½ teaspoons curry powder
3 cans chicken broth
1½ cups half-and-half
Salt and white pepper to taste

Rinse zucchini and pat dry. Trim ends. Cut half of 1 zucchini into thin matchsticks, blanch, and set aside. Slice remaining zucchini and place in pan. Add onion and sprinkle with curry, stirring to coat pieces. Add broth; boil and simmer covered, 45 minutes. Spoon into blender and purée. Add half-and-half, salt and pepper. Add reserved zucchini strips, chill and serve.

Carolyn Markstein Frohsin

Gazpacho

Serves 6

1 cup peeled, chopped tomatoes
½ cup chopped green pepper
½ cup chopped celery
½ cup chopped cucumber
½ cup chopped carrots
¼ cup chopped onions
2 teaspoons snipped parsley
1 teaspoon snipped chives
2 tablespoons olive or vegetable oil
1 small clove garlic, minced
1 teaspoon salt
2-3 tablespoons wine vinegar
¼ teaspoon ground pepper
½ teaspoon Worcestershire sauce
2 cups tomato juice
Croutons to garnish

Combine all ingredients. Cover and chill thoroughly for at least 4 hours. Serve in chilled cups. Top with croutons. *Keeps in refrigerator for days.*

Alpha Johnson Goings

Tomato Lemon Consommé

Serves 6

1 cup beef consommé
2 cups tomato juice
2 cups orange juice
½ cup lemon juice
Celery salt to taste
Watercress to garnish

Blend consommé and juices together and season with celery salt. Serve hot or cold garnished with watercress.

Elizabeth Locke Schuler

Potage de Tomates

Serves 6-8

1 large onion, chopped
4 tablespoons butter or margarine
3 pounds ripe tomatoes, peeled and chopped or 2 (1 pound 12 ounce) cans whole peeled tomatoes, drained and chopped
½ teaspoon thyme
1 teaspoon basil
Salt and pepper to taste
1 teaspoon sugar
3 tablespoons tomato paste
2-3 cups chicken broth
¾-1 cup half-and-half
2 tablespoons butter (optional)
2 tablespoons sour cream
2 ounces vermouth, optional
Lemon slices and parsley for garnish

In a large saucepan, sauté onion in butter until tender. Add tomatoes, herbs, salt and pepper, sugar, and tomato paste to onions. Simmer 10 minutes. Add 2 cups broth and simmer 30 minutes more. Remove soup from heat. Purée in batches, adding more broth if needed, to produce desired consistency. Reheat, stir in sour cream, half-and-half and butter. Garnish each serving with a thin slice of lemon sprinkled with parsley. *This soup is great hot or cold.*

Sam Franks

Fresh Mushroom Soup

Good and pretty first course

Serves 6-8 for first course

½ stick butter
1-2 cloves of garlic, minced
12 ounces fresh mushrooms, sliced
3¾ tablespoons flour
2 cups chicken broth
2 cups milk
½ cup parsley
Grated nutmeg to taste
Salt and pepper to taste
3 tablespoons vermouth, optional

Heat butter in saucepan. Sauté garlic and mushrooms in butter for 5 minutes, stirring continuously. Stir in flour, blending well. Slowly add the broth, followed by the milk. Bring to a boil, stirring continuously. Turn heat down and simmer for 5 minutes. Add the nutmeg, parsley, salt and pepper. Add vermouth, if desired. *May be prepared a day ahead.*

Tandy Sweeney Graves

Beef Soup

Serves 4

1½ pounds beef, cubed
1 teaspoon salt
½ teaspoon pepper
2 bay leaves
Basil to taste
Oregano to taste
4-5 carrots, sliced
½ cup chopped onions
1 cup chopped cabbage
1 (28 ounce) can tomatoes
1 teaspoon Worcestershire sauce
1 bouillon cube

Cover meat with cold water in a covered 4-quart saucepan. Add salt, pepper, bay leaves, basil, and oregano. Let mixture come to a boil. Turn heat down to low and add vegetables. Simmer at least 2½ hours. Add tomatoes, Worcestershire, and bouillon cube. Simmer ½ hour more. Remove bay leaves before serving. *May be prepared ahead and frozen.*

Wendy Wall White

Cream of Cauliflower Soup

Serves 4-6

4 cups milk
1½ cups vegetable stock or water
1 cauliflower, cut into flowerets
4 tablespoons butter
4 tablespoons flour
Salt and pepper to taste
Chopped parsley for garnish

Mix milk and stock (or water) and boil. Add cauliflower and cook until tender. Pureé the cauliflower with the liquid. In large saucepan, melt butter, stir in flour, and cook for 2 minutes. Slowly pour in cauliflower mixture, stirring constantly until smooth. Add salt and pepper to taste and cook at least 10 minutes longer. Garnish with chopped parsley.

Serena Casey Vann

Cream Of Split Pea Soup

Serves 6

1 (1 pound) package dried split peas
1 cup sliced carrots
1 cup chopped onions
2 teaspoons celery salt
1 cup diced celery
1 cup celery tops
2 cups cubed ham
1 ham bone, if available
Salt and pepper to taste
1 teaspoon dried tarragon
1 pint half-and-half

Pour 8 cups water into heavy pot and add all ingredients except half-and-half. Cook slowly, stirring occasionally, for about 2 hours. Soup should be quite thick. Remove from heat and purée in blender or processor. Adjust seasoning. When ready to serve, add half-and-half. *This may be served chilled or hot.*

Cream of Broccoli Soup

Serves 6-8

4 cups water
2 cups chopped broccoli, fresh or frozen
2 cups chopped cooked ham
1 medium onion, chopped
1 medium potato, chopped
3 tablespoons margarine or butter
1 teaspoon basil
¾ teaspoon pepper
1 chicken bouillon cube
¼ teaspoon thyme
½ teaspoon salt
1 cup milk
Grated Parmesan cheese for topping

Combine all ingredients except milk and cheese in a Dutch oven and bring to a boil. Reduce heat and simmer 30 minutes, stirring occasionally. Let cool. Purée in batches, blending about 20 seconds. Pour mixture back into Dutch oven. Stir in milk and simmer 20 minutes. Garnish each serving with cheese. *Recipe may be halved.*

Senate Bean Soup

Hot hearty soup for a chilly winter lunch!

Serves 8

2 cups dried Great Northern Beans
1 package smoked ham hocks
1 medium potato, diced
1 cup diced celery
1 clove garlic, minced
2 onions, diced
Salt to taste
Pepper to taste
Chopped parsley for garnish

Soak beans overnight in 2 quarts of water. Drain, saving liquid. Add enough water to liquid to make 2 quarts. Place liquid, beans, and ham in Dutch oven. Simmer for 2 hours, covered. Add potato, celery, garlic, and onions. Simmer 1 hour, uncovered. Remove ham from bone, dice it and return to soup. Discard bone. Season to taste and garnish with parsley.

Elizabeth Ennis Hillhouse

Tamale Soup

Nice change from chili

Serves 4

1 pound ground beef
1 medium onion, chopped
1 green pepper, chopped
1 (16 ounce) can stewed tomatoes
2 (16 ounce) cans pinto beans, undrained
1 (16 ounce) can creamed corn, yellow or white
1 (10¾ ounce) can beef bouillon
2 jars Derby hot tamales or 2 (16 ounce) cans any brand, sliced

Brown beef, onion, and green pepper. Add other ingredients, except tamales, and simmer for at least 1 hour. Add tamales before serving. *Better the second day as time improves flavor.*

Margaret Kirby Hall
SHERMAN, TEXAS

Greek Lemon Soup

Serves 6-8

6 cups chicken broth
⅓ cup long grain rice
1 tablespoon chopped onion
1 teaspoon salt
3 eggs
¼ cup lemon juice
1 slice lemon per serving for garnish

Combine broth, rice, onion, and salt. Bring to a boil. Reduce heat, cover, and simmer until rice is tender, about 15 minutes. Beat eggs until fluffy and pale yellow, then beat in lemon juice. Slowly stir 2 cups of hot broth into egg mixture, then add egg mixture to remaining broth. Whisk until slightly thickened. Cool, then chill until icy cold. Taste for seasoning when cold. Garnish with lemon slices. *May also be served hot.*

Irene Johnson Botsford

The Green Door Basic Bean Soup

Serves 6

3 tablespoons olive oil
1 clove garlic
1 onion, chopped
1 carrot, chopped
5 cups water
½ teaspoon cumin
¼ teaspoon thyme
1 teaspoon Brewer's yeast, celery flavored
1 cup beans (soybeans, chick peas, navy beans, etc. or a combination of split peas and barley, red beans and brown rice)
2 teaspoons miso (soybean paste)
3 tablespoons tamari (zesty soy sauce)
½ teaspoon vegetable sea salt

Heat olive oil in soup kettle. Add garlic, onion, and carrot and sauté 5 minutes. Add water, cumin, thyme, and yeast and bring to boil. Add remaining ingredients and cook until tender. (Soybeans take the longest to cook). Process in small batches in food processor or blender until puréed. *To make bean dip, cut the liquid in half.*

East Indian Mulligatawny Soup

Serves 8-10

2 medium green peppers, coarsely chopped
2 medium carrots, coarsely chopped
2 medium onions, coarsely chopped
1 stick butter
2 ribs celery, chopped
3 medium apples, pared and sliced
2 cups cooked chicken breasts, cut into medium pieces
6 cups chicken stock (or consommé)
1 tablespoon cornstarch
¼ cup cold water
2 teaspoons salt
½ teaspoon cayenne pepper
2 teaspoons curry powder
¼ teaspoon mace
¼ teaspoon ground cloves
2 cups cooked tomatoes
2 sprigs fresh parsley, minced

Cook green peppers and carrots in water until softened. Drain and set aside. Using low heat, sauté onion in butter in Dutch oven (uncovered). Remove from stove and add cooked green peppers and carrots, celery, apple, and cooked chicken. Set aside. Heat stock to boiling point. Make a smooth paste of cornstarch and water. Add to stock, stirring constantly until stock returns to boil. Add to ingredients in Dutch oven. Add salt, cayenne pepper, curry powder, mace, cloves, and tomatoes. Simmer, covered, ½ hour. Serve hot. Garnish with minced parsley.
May be prepared ahead.

Josephine Harris Wasson

Grand Central Station Oyster Bar Stew

Serves 2

Celery salt to taste
Salt to taste
Pepper to taste
Paprika to taste
½ teaspoon Worcestershire sauce
2 tablespoons butter
1 pint oysters, drained, liquid reserved
1 pint half-and-half
2 pats of butter
Cayenne pepper

In a double boiler combine celery salt, salt, pepper, paprika, Worcestershire, butter, and oyster liquid. Allow to simmer a few minutes over boiling water. Add half-and-half. Let soup become very hot and then add oysters. Remove from heat as soon as oysters are heated because you want them to remain plump and juicy. Top each serving with a pat of butter and a dash of cayenne pepper.

Marjorie Longenecker White

She-Crab Soup

Quick and easy

Serves 6

2 cups milk
¼ teaspoon ground mace
2 pieces lemon peel
1 pound white crabmeat
½ stick butter
1 pint half-and-half
Salt to taste
Pepper to taste
¼ cup cracker crumbs, finely crushed
2 teaspoons sherry

In *double boiler* over direct heat, combine milk, mace, and lemon peel. Let simmer 7 minutes. Add crabmeat, butter, and half-and-half, stirring carefully. Heat over boiling water for 15 minutes. Season to taste. Remove lemon peel and add cracker crumbs. Stir in sherry and serve.

Susie Hand Denson

New England Clam Chowder

A meal in itself on winter nights

Serves 4

3 slices bacon
1 cup finely minced onion
2 cups potatoes, peeled and cubed
1 teaspoon salt
Pepper to taste
Tabasco to taste
1 cup water
2 (6½ ounce) cans minced clams or 1 pint fresh shucked clams
½ cup clam liquid
1 pint half-and-half
2 tablespoons butter

Cut bacon into small pieces and sauté in large kettle until almost crisp. Add onion and cook for 5 minutes. Add potato, salt, pepper, Tabasco, and water. Cook until potatoes are tender. Drain clams reserving ½ cup clam liquid. Chop clams coarsely. Add clams, clam liquid, half-and-half, and butter to mixture. Stir and heat on low about 10 minutes. Do not boil.

Kathryn D. Keys

Pickwick's Crab Gumbo

Serves 6-8

2 onions, finely chopped
2 green peppers, finely chopped
1 stalk celery, finely chopped
½ stick butter
1 (16 ounce) can tomatoes
1 (16 ounce) can okra
1 quart soup stock
1 pound fresh crabmeat, flaked
2 cups cooked rice
1 tablespoon gumbo filé
Salt and pepper to taste

In large soup pot, sauté onions, peppers, and celery in butter until clear. Add tomatoes, okra, and soup stock. Simmer 15 minutes. Add crabmeat, rice, and gumbo filé. Cook 15 minutes longer. Add salt and pepper to taste.

Pickwick Restaurant
MONTGOMERY, ALABAMA

Seafood Chowder

Serves 8-10

⅓ cup sliced carrots
1 cup diced potatoes
½ cup minced onion
⅓ cup sliced celery
3 tablespoons chopped green pepper
6 tablespoons butter
1 cup tomatoes and juice
2 tablespoons parsley
1 tablespoon vinegar
1 bay leaf
2 teaspoons salt
½ teaspoon pepper
¼ teaspoon thyme
1 teaspoon Tabasco sauce
1 cup water
6 tablespoons flour
6 cups milk
1 pound crabmeat, lump or claw
3 pounds raw shrimp, peeled

Sauté first 5 ingredients in butter until tender. Add tomatoes, parsley, vinegar, seasonings, and water. Heat to boiling point. Remove from heat and slowly add flour. Add milk and stir until thickened. Stir in seafood, return to heat, and simmer for 20 minutes.

Dana Blair Davis

Shrimp Soup

Serves 4

1 carrot, sliced
1 onion, chopped
1 bay leaf
1 tablespoon chopped parsley
2 tablespoons celery leaves
3 tablespoons butter, divided
4 cups chicken broth
¼ cup uncooked rice
1 pound raw shrimp, peeled and deveined
½ cup white wine
Salt and pepper to taste

In large saucepan, sauté carrot, onion, bay leaf, parsley, and celery leaves in 2 tablespoons of butter until limp. Add 3 cups of broth and bring to a boil. Add rice and simmer until tender. In separate pan, cover shrimp with wine and remaining chicken broth. Cook for 5 minutes. Drain shrimp, adding liquid to broth mixture. Reserve 8 cooked shrimp for garnish. Finely chop remaining shrimp and add to vegetables and broth. Purée mixture. Before serving, reheat, add 1 tablespoon butter, and season with salt and pepper. Cut up the 8 remaining shrimp and garnish the soup.

Ann Adams Pritchard

Gumbo

Serves 8

6 Polish sausages
¾ cup flour
¾ cup oil
1 onion, chopped
2 celery stalks, chopped
1 green pepper, chopped
4 green onions, chopped
30 ounces canned okra
¾ cup tomato paste
3 quarts water
1 pound shrimp or may use 8 broken crab with ½ pound shrimp
1 pound crabmeat
1 teaspoon thyme
1 tablespoon Worcestershire sauce
¼ teaspoon Tabasco
¼ teaspoon red pepper
1 teaspoon salt
1 teaspoon basil
3 bay leaves
2 tablespoons parsley
2 cloves garlic
½ teaspoon pepper

Chop sausage and brown in large skillet. Add flour and oil to make a roux. Stir constantly 45 minutes. Add onion, celery, green pepper, and green onion. Cook 30 minutes longer. Put all of the above ingredients into your largest soup pot and add the remaining ingredients. Cook over medium heat the rest of the day.

Kathy Watkins Broughton

Oyster Loaf

Serves 4

1 (1 pound) loaf French bread
1 stick butter, melted
2 dozen select oysters, drained
Salt to taste
Pepper to taste
Cayenne pepper to taste
2 eggs, beaten
2 tablespoons milk
1 cup cracker crumbs
Cooking oil for frying
½ cup tartar sauce
1 cup shredded lettuce
1 large tomato, sliced thinly

Slice bread in half horizontally and hollow out both halves. Brush the inside and the edges of both halves with melted butter and toast under broiler until lightly browned. Sprinkle oysters with salt, pepper, and cayenne pepper. Combine eggs and milk and mix well. Dip oysters in egg, then crumbs; *repeat*. Fry oysters in 1½ inches of hot cooking oil until golden brown, about 2-3 minutes. Drain on paper towels. Spread tartar sauce inside both bread halves. Sprinkle lettuce on the bottom, top with tomato slices and oysters. Replace top of bread and cut loaf into 4 pieces.

Anne Armstrong Reynolds

Cheese Vegetable Sandwich

Serves 6

½ cup minced cabbage
½ cup minced carrots
½ cup minced green pepper
½ cup minced celery
½ cup minced radishes
½ cup minced red onions
6 cups grated Cheddar cheese
½ cup beer
White pepper
Cayenne pepper
6 slices white bread or whole wheat
Butter

Combine vegetables in a bowl. In top of double boiler over simmering water, melt cheese with beer, stirring constantly. Season sauce with white and cayenne pepper to taste. Lightly toast and butter bread. Spread each slice with ½ cup vegetable mixture. Place on baking sheet. Pour cheese sauce over sandwiches and broil 3 minutes or until lightly browned. Serve hot.

Perry Davis Hotel
PETROSKEY, MICHIGAN

Grilled Pineapple Sandwich

Serves 4

1 (8½ ounce) can pineapple slices
French dressing
1 cup shredded Cheddar cheese
¼ cup finely chopped green pepper
¼ teaspoon chili powder
2 tablespoons mayonnaise
4 slices bread
Butter
4 slices baked or boiled ham

Drain pineapple. Brush slices lightly with French dressing. Combine cheese, green pepper, chili powder, and mayonnaise. Butter bread and lightly toast. Arrange on baking sheet. Top with ham and pineapple slices. Spread cheese mixture over each sandwich. Broil until topping is melted and golden brown, being careful not to burn.

Corned Beef for Reubens

Serves 10

1 whole corned beef
1 bell pepper, sliced
2-3 stalks celery
Cracked black pepper to taste
1 (12 ounce) can beer
1 onion, sliced
1 clove garlic, optional

Put all of the above ingredients in a large pot and cover with water. Bring to a boil, then turn heat to simmer for about 40 minutes per pound. Chill. Butcher will slice thinly for sandwiches. To assemble sandwiches: Melt butter in skillet. Put rye bread slices in skillet. Top bread with Swiss cheese, corned beef, sauerkraut, and your favorite mustard. Cover with other bread slice. Grill turning once.

Ellis Parsons Bynum

Bacon-Asparagus Rollups

Yield: about 60

1 (8 ounce) package cream cheese, softened
6 slices cooked bacon, crumbled
1 tablespoon chives
1 cup mayonnaise
1 loaf white bread, crusts removed
1 (15 ounce) can asparagus spears, drained
1 stick butter, melted

Preheat oven to 400°. Combine cream cheese, bacon, chives, and mayonnaise. Beat at medium speed 1 minute. Spread mixture on each slice of bread. Roll 2 asparagus spears in each slice of bread and cut into 3 bite-size rolls. Arrange on greased cookie sheet, putting seam side down and brush with melted butter. Bake for 12 minutes. *May be prepared ahead and frozen before baking.*

Linda Etten Vann

Bacon and Chutney Rollups

Yield: about 4 dozen

6 slices bread
1 (10 ounce) jar chutney
1 pound bacon

Preheat oven to 350°. Trim crusts from slices of bread and cut each slice into 9 cubes. Put some chutney on each cube and wrap a section of bacon (about ⅓ slice) around each. Do not use a toothpick. Bake for 15-20 minutes. Watch so it doesn't burn. May use a broiler pan.

Libby Forman Norwood
ROCKVILLE, MARYLAND

Beef and Rye Bites

Try for a teenage party.

Yield: 70-80

1 pound lean ground beef
1 pound sausage
Salt to taste
Pepper to taste
Seasoned salt to taste
1 small onion, finely chopped
1 (8 ounce) box Velveeta cheese, diced
2 loaves Pepperidge Farm party rye

Preheat oven to 375°. Mix ground beef, sausage, salt, pepper, and seasoned salt. Add onion to mixture and brown in skillet. Pour off grease. Remove from heat and stir in cheese until melted. Spread bread with meat and cheese mixture. Freeze or bake immediately for 8-10 minutes.

Sara Jane Tackett

Ham Delights

Yield: 36 Rolls

1½ pounds Cure 81 ham or similar cooked ham
¾ pound Swiss cheese
1 medium onion, quartered
2 sticks margarine, softened
3 tablespoons prepared mustard
1 teaspoon Worcestershire sauce
1½ tablespoons poppy seeds
3 packages party rolls (Pepperidge Farm Party or Finger Rolls)

Using steel blade of food processor, chop ham finely. Remove to bowl. Chop cheese finely and set aside. Combine onion, margarine, mustard, and Worcestershire. Process. Add poppy seeds and process. Split the whole package of rolls as one large roll. Spread both insides with onion mixture. Sprinkle ham and cheese on 1 side of rolls. Put rolls together in original container and cut out individual rolls. May return to original plastic bag cover, and freeze. When ready to serve, preheat oven to 375° and heat rolls for 15-20 minutes. Serve hot.

Trudy Rogers Evans

Cream Cheese and Bacon Delights

Serve at teas, luncheons, or in lunch boxes.

Yield: 4 dozen party sandwiches

2 (8 ounce) packages cream cheese
¼ cup grated onion
4 strips crisp bacon, crumbled
Mayonnaise to make spreadable
1½ loaves whole wheat bread, crusts removed

Combine first 4 ingredients in food processor. Process until mixture is blended. Make sandwiches and cut each sandwich into 3 strips.

Mary Leary McDavid

Cheese Puffs

Yield: 3½-4 dozen

1 loaf unsliced French bread
¼ pound sharp Cheddar cheese, grated
1 (3 ounce) package cream cheese
1 stick margarine
2 egg whites

Remove crusts from bread and cut into 1-inch cubes. Melt cheeses and margarine in boiler stirring often until thick and creamy. Remove from heat. Beat egg whites until stiff. Add to cheese mixture. Dip bread cubes into mixture and dry on baking sheet lined with waxed paper. Freeze the cubes by placing baking sheet into freezer for 30 minutes. Cubes may then be placed in plastic bags and stored in the freezer until needed (will keep up to 1 month). When ready to use, place frozen cubes on baking sheet, let thaw 30 minutes, and bake in 450° oven for 5-10 minutes until very lightly browned. Serve hot.

Carol Lukens Hall

Highland Meat Spread

1 pound *smoked* sausage
½ small onion
2 hard boiled eggs
5 small, whole sweet pickles
¼ cup prepared mustard
½ cup mayonnaise

Cut sausage into pieces. Process sausage, onion, egg, and pickles in food processor or blender. Add mustard and mayonnaise to mixture. Serve on rye bread or crackers.

Irma Frech St. John

Tomato Cheese Spread

Yield: 6-cup mold

½ cup chopped celery
1 (2 ounce) jar pimientos, drained and chopped
½ cup finely chopped green pepper
5 small green onions, chopped (tops included)
1 (10¾ ounce) can tomato soup
1 (8 ounce) package cream cheese
1 (3 ounce) package lemon Jello
½ cup mayonnaise

Mix celery, pimiento, green pepper and onion in large bowl. Heat soup until bubbly and melt cheese in it, stirring frequently. Add Jello and stir until dissolved. Add vegetables to soup mixture, then stir in mayonnaise. Chill covered in a bowl or oiled mold. Serve on party bread slices.

Mrs. F. Lynn Tankersley
PELHAM, ALABAMA

Butifarra

Serves 24

½ cup finely sliced onions
1 cup water
Salt and pepper to taste
¼ cup vinegar
¼ cup shredded chilies
¼ cup diced radishes
1 tablespoon oil
1 teaspoon lemon juice
24 pieces of lettuce leaves (Boston or Leaf)
24 small slices roasted pork
24 party rolls

Slice onions and place in a bowl with water and salt. Rub onions gently with your hands. Drain. Add vinegar to onions. When it turns a rosy color, add chilies, radishes, oil, lemon juice, salt and pepper. Let marinate 5 minutes or so. To assemble: Place lettuce leaf, slice of pork, and onion sauce on each roll.
Can be big sandwich on onion roll or cocktail sandwich.

Carmela B. de Lino
LIMA, PERU

APPETIZERS

Appetizers

Shrimp Dip

Make 1 day ahead

Serves 10-12

1 (8 ounce) package cream cheese, softened
Juice of 1 lemon
½ cup mayonnaise
¼ cup catsup
½ cup chopped celery
¼ cup minced onion
Tops of 2 green onions, chopped
5 drops Tabasco
White pepper to taste
1 pound cooked shrimp, cut into small pieces

Combine all ingredients. Chill in refrigerator. Serve with crackers. *May be doubled.*

Oyster and Green Onion Dip

Serves 12

3 bunches green onions, chopped
Minced garlic to taste
1 stick butter
1 quart oysters, finely chopped
Salt and pepper to taste
4 slices toast, crushed into crumbs

Sauté onions and garlic in butter for about 10 minutes or until tender. Add oysters and simmer about 1 minute. Season with salt and pepper. Before serving, heat mixture and add bread crumbs. Serve in chafing dish with your favorite cracker.

Dorothy Weston Robinson
PAST PRESIDENT

Mushroom-Clam Dip

1 pound fresh mushrooms, finely chopped
2 tablespoons butter
1 (8 ounce) package cream cheese, softened
5 green onions, finely chopped, using some of tops
1 (6½ ounce) can minced clams, drained
1 teaspoon Accent
Juice of ½ lemon
1 teaspoon soy sauce
Sugar to taste

Sauté the mushrooms in butter. Beat cream cheese, add onion and mushrooms. Add all other ingredients and mix well. Heat immediately before serving in a chafing dish with your choice of crackers. *Freezes beautifully.*

Mike McCarren
GROSSE ILE, MICHIGAN

Arizona Dip

Serves 6-8

2 (8 ounce) packages cream cheese, softened
4 tablespoons milk
5 ounces dried chipped beef
⅓ cup chopped green pepper
1 (8 ounce) carton sour cream
4 tablespoons minced onion
1 cup chopped pecans

Preheat oven to 350°. Combine all ingredients except pecans, mixing by hand until well blended. Place in a shallow baking dish. Top casserole with chopped pecans. Bake for 20 minutes or until bubbly, but *not* boiling. Serve hot with crackers. *This recipe may be doubled or halved. It may also be frozen.*

Patti O'Neill Rust
PAST PRESIDENT

Spinach Dip

1 (10 ounce) package frozen, chopped spinach, thawed and drained
1 cup mayonnaise
1 (8 ounce) carton sour cream
1 package Knorr's vegetable soup mix
1 can water chestnuts, drained and chopped
¼ teaspoon grated onion

Mix all ingredients well and chill. Good as a dip with vegetables or corn chips. Also may be served in the center of hollowed pumpernickle bread or on party sandwiches. *Serving suggestion:* Cut cocktail tomatoes in half and scoop out center. Drain on paper towels. Spoon spinach mixture into each half and serve as hors d'oeuvres.

Louise McKinley Cooper

Relish Dip

Serves 8

3 small tomatoes, peeled and chopped
4 green onions, chopped
1 (7¾ ounce) can pitted black olives, chopped
1 (4 ounce) can green chilies
3 tablespoons olive oil
1½ tablespoons vinegar
1¼ teaspoons garlic salt
Pepper to taste
Taco chips

Mix all ingredients except taco chips together. Let set overnight. Drain. Serve as dip for taco chips.

Anna Eleanore Simmons

Artichokes With Red Caviar Dip

4 artichokes
1 teaspoon salt
Boiling water
1 tablespoon lemon juice

To prepare artichokes: Cut off stems at base and remove small bottom leaves. Trim top of remaining leaves with kitchen scissors. Stand artichokes upright in deep saucepan. Add salt and 2-3 inches boiling water. Add lemon juice. Cover and boil gently for 30 minutes. When cooked, gently spread leaves and remove choke (thistle portion) from center. Chill and fill with dip.

Red Caviar Dip

1 pint sour cream
1 (8 ounce) package cream cheese
½ teaspoon lemon juice
2 teaspoons grated onion
Tabasco to taste
1 (8 ounce) jar red caviar

Blend the first 5 ingredients. Carefully add the caviar, reserving a little for garnish. Do not crush eggs. Pour dip into center of artichoke and top with reserved caviar. Chill in refrigerator and serve cold. Red Caviar Dip is also good served with chips or crackers.

Helene Elkus

Hot Crabmeat Dip

Serves 12

1 pound fresh crabmeat, cleaned
1 (8 ounce) package cream cheese
1 cup mayonnaise
1 (8 ounce) carton sour cream
1½ teaspoons salt
1 teaspoon onion juice
2 teaspoons lemon juice
1 teaspoon Accent
Grated onion to taste
Tabasco to taste
1 teaspoon curry powder, optional

Mix all ingredients together and heat, but do not boil. Serve warm in a chafing dish as a dip with melba toast rounds or in patty shells. If dip is too stiff, add more sour cream.

Deedee Tomkins Cowin

Hummus

2 cloves garlic
⅓ cup tahini (sesame seed paste)
¼ cup water
3 tablespoons olive oil
6 tablespoons lemon juice
1 (19 ounce) can chick peas, drained
½ teaspoon cumin
1 teaspoon coriander
¼ teaspoon cayenne pepper
Salt and pepper to taste

Chop garlic in food processor or blender until fine. Add tahini, water, olive oil, and lemon juice, blending until smooth. Add remaining ingredients and process until puréed. Add salt and pepper. If mixture is too thick, add additional water. Spread in a flat plate and garnish with parsley. Serve with Melbarized Pita, see page 259.

Sharon Pierce
VANCOUVER, B.C.

Brie en Croute

So easy and so elegant

1 (4½ ounce) package Brie cheese
1 individual Pepperidge Farm patty shell

Preheat oven to 450°. Thaw individual patty shell without removing "top." Roll out with rolling pin until large enough to cover cheese. Carefully pull dough over top, sides, and some of the bottom of the cheese, tucking in the pastry on the bottom. Put on a cookie sheet and bake until brown, about 15 minutes. Serve with crackers.

Sandra Jones Thomasson

Layered Camembert

Serves 8

1 (4½ ounce) round of Camembert cheese
4 ounces cream cheese, softened
1 tablespoon dry sherry
2 tablespoons sliced almonds
2 tablespoons sliced grapes, peeled and seeded

Cut Camembert in half lengthwise. Blend cream cheese with sherry; add almonds and grapes. Reserve 1 tablespoon cheese mixture and spread rest on bottom layer of cheese. Place top on filling and garnish with reserved mixture. Serve with crackers.

Anne Starnes Finch

Herb Parmesan Rounds

Nice substitute for cheese straws

Yield: 48 biscuits

1¼ cups freshly grated Parmesan cheese
1 cup flour
1 stick unsalted butter, room temperature
¾ teaspoon marjoram
¾ teaspoon oregano
¾ teaspoon basil
½ teaspoon Worcestershire
2-3 tablespoons dry white wine

Blend cheese, flour, butter, marjoram, oregano, and basil to a coarse meal. Add Worcestershire and wine to form a ball. Roll into log 1½-inch diameter. Wrap in plastic wrap and chill for 1 hour. Slice into ¼-inch slices. Arrange slices ½ inch apart on baking sheets. Bake in a preheated 400° oven for 12-15 minutes.

Agnes Payne Perry

Mushroom Hors D'Oeuvres

Yield: 40 canapes

10 bread slices
1 stick butter, softened
1 (3 ounce) package cream cheese, softened
1 egg yolk, hard boiled
1 (8 ounce) can mushrooms sliced
Garlic salt to taste

Cut bread into fourths. Toast on 1 side in the oven. Beat butter and cream cheese until smooth. Add egg yolk and mix well. Stir in mushrooms and season with garlic salt. Spread on untoasted side of bread. Broil until bubbly. *Mushroom mixture will keep in refrigerator for about a week.*

Kathy Dorlon Anderson

Chutney Glazed Cheese Paté

Serves 18

6 ounces sharp Cheddar cheese, softened and shredded
1 (8 ounce) package cream cheese, softened
¾ teaspoon curry powder
3 tablespoons *dry* sherry
¼ teaspoon salt
1½-2 cups chutney
1½-2 cups finely chopped green onion

In a bowl, beat together cheeses, curry powder, dry sherry, and salt. Spread mixture ½-inch thick on a serving dish. Cover and chill until firm. At serving time, spread top with chutney and sprinkle with finely chopped green onion. Serve with bland crackers.

Nancy Vail McNair

Consommé Paté Mold

Yield: 2½-cup mold

1 (10¾ ounce) can beef consommé, heated
1 tablespoon unflavored gelatin
¼ cup sherry
1 (8 ounce) package cream cheese, softened
½ cup chicken liver paté or 1 can paté
Salt to taste
Lemon juice to taste

Soak gelatin in sherry, then dissolve it in hot soup. Pour into mold and let set. When jelly is firm, cover it with cream cheese mixed with paté and seasoned with salt and a dash of lemon juice. Let mold set overnight. Turn mold onto serving plate and serve with wafers. *May be prepared 24 hours ahead.*

Patricia Smith Nebergall

Mushroom Liver Paté

Yield: 2 cups

3 tablespoons oil
1 medium onion, finely chopped
1 pound chicken livers, cut into small pieces
½ pound fresh mushrooms, sliced
¼ cup dry sherry or wine
3 tablespoons minced parsley
2 garlic cloves, pressed
2 tablespoons butter or margarine, softened
Salt to taste
Pepper to taste
Nutmeg to taste

Heat oil in large skillet over medium heat. Add onions and sauté 2-3 minutes. Add livers and mushrooms and cook until livers are no longer pink. Transfer with slotted spoon to blender, food processor or meat grinder in small batches and process into a paste. Add remaining ingredients, season to taste, and mix thoroughly. Refrigerate 1 hour or more.

Jean Bissell Willcox

Chicken Liver Paté

Yield: 1 cup

½ pound chicken livers
1 teaspoon salt
Cayenne pepper to taste
1 stick butter, softened
¼ teaspoon nutmeg
1 teaspoon dry mustard
⅛ teaspoon ground cloves
2 tablespoons minced onion
1 tablespoon sherry or cognac

Pour water over chicken livers until barely covered and bring to a boil. Simmer, covered, 15-20 minutes. Drain and finely chop the livers in food processor or blender. Combine remaining ingredients with liver and process again. Pack into crock or mold and refrigerate.

Marinated Raw Mushrooms

Must be prepared 2 days ahead.

Serves 8

1 pound small fresh white mushrooms
1 red onion, sliced into rings
⅔ cup white vinegar
¼ cup water
1 clove garlic, minced
2 tablespoons olive or salad oil
1½ teaspoons salt
¼ teaspoon ground pepper

Combine all ingredients in a bowl, cover, and refrigerate 2 days before serving. 55 calories per serving. *Can be used for cocktails or as a salad.*

Carol Perkins Poynor

Vegetable Mold

Serves 20

2 envelopes gelatin
1 pint mayonnaise
1 teaspoon salt
Finely chop and drain:
- **2 tomatoes**
- **1 small onion**
- **1 cup celery**
- **1 bell pepper**
- **1 cucumber**

Dissolve gelatin in ¼ cup cold water. Add ¼ cup boiling water and mix well. Add mayonnaise and salt and mix well. Add the chopped vegetables and mix. Grease a 6-cup ring mold with mayonnaise. Pour mixture into mold, cover with plastic wrap and refrigerate at least 6-8 hours. Unmold onto curly lettuce and garnish. Serve with rye crisp or your favorite cracker. *This can be used as a spread on party sandwiches.*

Judith Luks Wearb

Marinated Crabmeat

Serves 12 as appetizer; 4-6 as first course

1 cup mayonnaise
2 teaspoons capers and juice
2 tablespoons Worcestershire sauce
Tabasco to taste
1 teaspoon black or white pepper
2 tablespoons lemon juice
1 pound lump crabmeat
Paprika, optional

Mix first 6 ingredients to make marinade. Carefully fold in cleaned lump crabmeat. Refrigerate. Serve on lettuce with parsley, decorated with a little paprika, in an avocado half, or with pumpernickel bread.

Rosalind Weil Markstein

Caviar and Egg in Aspic

Serves 8

2 envelopes unflavored gelatin
1 cup water
2 cans consommé
2 tablespoons sherry
1 tablespoon lemon juice
Salt
4 eggs, hard boiled
1 (2 ounce) jar caviar
1 teaspoon green onion, chopped
1 tablespoon mayonnaise

Soften gelatin in water and stir over heat. Remove from heat. Stir in consommé, sherry, lemon juice, and salt. Spoon 2 tablespoons of this mixture into 8 oiled molds. Chill until firm. Keep remaining mixture at room temperature. Halve eggs lengthwise, remove yolks. Put some of the caviar in each egg white. Mash 2 of the yolks. Blend in onion and enough mayonnaise to be spreadable. Spread over each egg cavity to seal in caviar. Place filled egg whites face down on gelatin. Cover with remaining gelatin. Refrigerate. To serve as a main dish, surround with avocado slices and shrimp.

Beverly White Dunn
PAST PRESIDENT

Shrimp Mold

Serves 20

1 (10¾ ounce) can cream of shrimp soup
1 (8 ounce) package cream cheese
1½ envelopes gelatin
1 pound shrimp, cooked and diced
½ cup chopped celery
½ small onion, chopped
1 cup mayonnaise
Seasonings to taste:
Diced parsley
Garlic powder
Onion salt
Lemon juice
Salt
Tabasco
Worcestershire sauce

Heat soup and add cream cheese, stirring until melted. Add gelatin and stir until thickened. Add other ingredients and seasonings to taste. Pour into 1-quart greased fish-shaped mold. Serve on red leaf lettuce with assorted crackers.

Elsie Barnes Cothran

Horseradish Mold

Serves 16-20

1 (6½ ounce) package lemon Jello
1 cup boiling water
1½ tablespoons unflavored gelatin
3 tablespoons cold water
1 (8 ounce) carton sour cream
1 cup mayonnaise
1 (5 ounce) jar plus 2 tablespoons horseradish

Dissolve the lemon Jello in boiling water. Soak the unflavored gelatin in the cold water. Add gelatin mixture to the Jello mixture. Add sour cream, mayonnaise, and horseradish to the mixture. Pour into greased 1-quart ring mold and set in refrigerator. When set, serve with crackers.

Virginia Batton Browne

Sherry Mold With Caviar

Serves 20

2 cups sour cream
2 cups creamed cottage cheese
Tabasco to taste
2 teaspoons Worcestershire
1 clove garlic, pressed
Salt to taste
1 tablespoon plus 1 teaspoon gelatin
½ cup sherry
Caviar

Mix together first 6 ingredients. In separate bowl, soak gelatin in sherry. After the gelatin expands, dissolve it over hot water. Add gelatin to cheese mixture and pour into greased mold. Use a fish mold if possible. Refrigerate overnight. Unmold and ice with caviar. Serve with crackers.

Virginia Batton Browne

Carolina Crabmeat

Make 24 hours ahead to blend flavors.

Serves 8

2 (8 ounce) packages cream cheese, room temperature
¼-⅓ cup minced onion
1 tablespoon Worcestershire sauce
1 tablespoon mayonnaise
½ teaspoon garlic juice or powder
1 pound fresh crabmeat or 2 (7½ ounce) cans crabmeat, drained thoroughly
1 (12 ounce) bottle chili sauce
Fresh minced parsley

Mix cream cheese, onion, Worcestershire, mayonnaise, and garlic juice. Place in flat 9-inch serving dish. Smooth mixture flat and even. Spread crabmeat over cheese mixture. Cover with chili sauce. Prior to serving, garnish heavily with fresh parsley. Serve with favorite crackers. *Its festive red color makes this a natural for Christmas parties, especially served on a white dish.*

Helen Buchanan Monson

Salmon Mousse

May be prepared a day before serving but do not freeze.

Serves 5 for luncheon,
15-20 as appetizer

1 (16 ounce) can Pink Beauty Salmon
1¾ cups liquid, water and salmon liquid
2 envelopes unflavored gelatin
1 cup Kraft mayonnaise
2 tablespoons lemon juice (fresh)
2 teaspoons horseradish (drained)
½ teaspoon paprika
½ cup diced celery
¼ cup chopped pimiento-stuffed green olives
1 small to medium white onion, chopped
½ teaspoon Tabasco
½ cup heavy cream, whipped

Drain salmon, reserving liquid. Remove skin and large bones; flake salmon. Add cold water to reserved liquid to equal 1¾ cups. In saucepan soften gelatin in salmon liquid. Stir over low heat until gelatin is dissolved; cool slightly. Blend together mayonnaise and next 3 ingredients; gradually stir in cooled gelatin mixture. Chill until partially set. Fold in salmon, celery, olives, onion, and Tabasco. Whip cream until soft peaks begin to form; fold into mixture. Turn mixture into a 5½ cup fish mold. Chill until firm (2-3 hours). Turn out onto a large glass platter. Trim with fresh parsley sprigs. Sprinkle with more paprika for added color. Use olive slices for eyes. *Serves 5 for luncheon but is at its best used as cocktail fare served with an unsalted cracker.*

Lee Skilling Marcus

Crab Stuffed Mushrooms

Yield: 20 appetizers

20 large mushroom caps
Italian dressing
1½ cups fresh crabmeat or 1 (6½ ounce) can flaked crabmeat
¾ cup fresh breadcrumbs
2 eggs, beaten
¼ cup mayonnaise
¼ cup minced onion
1 teaspoon lemon juice

Preheat oven to 375°. Marinate mushroom caps in Italian dressing about 10 minutes; drain. Combine crabmeat, ½ cup crumbs, eggs, mayonnaise, onion, and lemon juice; fill mushrooms. Top with remaining crumbs. Bake mushroom caps for 15 minutes.

Mushrooms With Shrimp

Serves 18

1 pound large mushrooms
1 cup fresh lemon juice
1 pound cooked shrimp, shelled and deveined
¼ cup bottled Italian dressing
6 ounces cream cheese, softened
½ cup chopped chives

Remove stems from mushrooms. Place caps in bowl, cover with lemon juice, and set aside. Place shrimp in another bowl, add Italian dressing, cover, and refrigerate several hours. Mix cheese and chives until smooth and creamy. Drain mushrooms and shrimp. Fill each cap with 1 tablespoon cheese mixture and top with a shrimp.

Grace Brady Bentley

Shrimp Spread

Serves 10-20

2½ pounds shrimp
1 small onion
2 hard boiled eggs
1 cup pecans
2 cups chopped celery
¼ cup pickle relish
2 cups mayonnaise
2 tablespoons sherry

Boil shrimp in salted water 5-7 minutes until shells become transparent. Peel shrimp. Coarsely grind shrimp, onion, eggs, and pecans. Combine with remaining ingredients. Serve with crackers.

Lorene Daugherty Dorlon

Cheese Spread

1 pound sharp Cheddar cheese, grated
1 cup mayonnaise
1 cup chopped pecans
1 small onion, grated
4 teaspoons Worcestershire sauce
Tabasco to taste
Cayenne pepper to taste

Mix all ingredients. Use as a sandwich spread or on crackers as an appetizer.

Millie Elmore Hulsey

Rye Rounds

Yield: about 60

⅓ cup Parmesan cheese
¾ cup mayonnaise
½ cup chopped onion
Worcestershire sauce to taste
2 loaves rye bread, cut into 2-inch circles

Mix ingredients together and spread on rye rounds. Broil until brown. *May be doubled and made up to 2 days ahead.*

Mary Sanford Allen

Ham Puffs

Yield: 24

1 (8 ounce) package cream cheese, softened
1 egg yolk, beaten
1 teaspoon onion juice
½ teaspoon baking powder
Salt to taste
¼ teaspoon horseradish
¼ teaspoon hot sauce
24 small bread rounds
2 (2¼ ounce) cans deviled ham

Blend together the first 7 ingredients. Toast bread rounds on one side. Spread untoasted side with deviled ham and cover each with a mound of the cheese mixture. Place on a cookie sheet and bake at 375° for 10-12 minutes or until puffed and brown. Serve hot.

Frances Enloe Phillips
SHERMAN, TEXAS

Onion Delight

Yield: 24 cocktail party appetizers

2 Vidalia sweet onions
½ cup sugar
1 cup apple cider vinegar
2 cups water
½ cup Hellman's mayonnaise
½ teaspoon dill seed
1 (3 ounce) package cream cheese, optional
½ box Ritz crackers

Chop onions. Mix sugar, vinegar, and water with onions. Marinate overnight or at least 4-6 hours. Before serving, mix mayonnaise, dill seed, and drained onion mixture. Spread on crackers. Variation: spread crackers with cream cheese first and then onion mixture.

T. Cullen Gilbland

Shrimp Hors D'Oeuvres

Serves 4

1 pound shrimp, cooked and peeled
1 onion, chopped
2 cups mayonnaise
2 cups Parmesan cheese
Minced parsley
Small biscuits or patty shells

Put shrimp through processor or chop fairly fine. Mix all ingredients. Spread on small biscuits and run under broiler until hot and bubbly, or serve in oven-proof dish with small patty shells.

Chollet Perry Still

Spanakopita

Serves 15-20

5 (10 ounce) packages frozen leaf spinach, thawed overnight
1 bunch parsley, chopped
2 bunches green onions, chopped
5 eggs, slightly beaten
½ teaspoon salt
White pepper to taste
1 cup Parmesan cheese
1 pound feta cheese, crumbled
2 tablespoons Uncle Ben's rice
3-4 sticks butter or margarine, melted
1 pound phyllo leaves, defrosted overnight in refrigerator

Drain spinach thoroughly in colander. Pat dry and chop with knife. Mix spinach with all ingredients except butter and phyllo leaves. Brush each of 9 phyllo leaves with melted butter and place in bottom of 10" x 15" pan. Keep unused leaves covered with damp towel. Pour in filling and top with 9 more sheets brushed with butter. Cut into servings with sharp knife and bake at 375° for 15 minutes, then 350° for 45 minutes. *This pie may be made in 2 smaller pans. Cook 1 and freeze the other for later.*

Dorothy Sarris McDaniel

Mezza *(Lamb appetizers)*

This is unusual and delicious.

Yield: 20 Hors d'Oeuvres

½ pound lean ground lamb
½ cup bulghur, soaked 20 minutes in water then squeezed dry (whole wheat bread crumbs may be substituted)
½ teaspoon salt
½ teaspoon allspice
½ teaspoon cinnamon
1 pinch of saffron or cumin
2 tablespoons dried currants
1 clove garlic, crushed
1 small onion, finely chopped
Salt to taste
Pepper to taste
¼ cup olive oil
1 pound phyllo, cut in 4″ x 5″ rectangles

Preheat over to 400°. Mix lamb and bulghur (or bread crumbs) with all the remaining ingredients except olive oil and phyllo. Cook mixture in olive oil over medium heat for 5 minutes. Cool slightly. Place 1 tablespoon of mixture on each phyllo piece. Turn shorter sides in slightly and starting with long side roll as for a jelly roll. Place seam side down on ungreased cookie sheet. Bake at 400° for 10 minutes or until slightly browned. May be frozen and cooked while still frozen adding 5 minutes to cooking time. There will be some phyllo left over. Wrap tightly and freeze for later use.

Lee McLaughlin Gewin

Tiropetes

Yield: 80-100

4 eggs, well beaten
1 (8 ounce) package cream cheese
1¼ pounds feta cheese, crumbled
1 pound phyllo
1 pound melted butter

Mix eggs and cream cheese and beat until smooth. Add feta cheese and mix gently on low speed with mixer or by hand. Cut phyllo pastry into 5 equal parts before unfolding. Take 1 part at a time and unfold. Keep remaining phyllo wrapped in wax paper and a damp tea towel so that it will not dry out. Take 1 piece of phyllo and brush with melted butter. Place teaspoonful of mixture in left corner. Fold flag style and brush with butter. Bake immediately or freeze in airtight container with wax paper between layers. Bake at 375° for 15-20 minutes. *It is not necessary to thaw before baking.*

Dorothy Sarris McDaniel

Sausage Paté en Croute

Good as a main dish

Serves 6-8

Paté

1 pound hot sausage
3 eggs
2 tablespoons Calvados or cognac
Thyme to taste
¼ cup bread crumbs
1 egg
1 teaspoon milk

Preheat oven to 350°. Grease loaf pan. Mix together first 5 ingredients. Turn paté into pan and bake 45 minutes. Beat egg with milk and brush over sausage mixture. Cool to room temperature.

Pastry

2 cups sifted flour
½ teaspoon salt
⅛ teaspoon sugar
1 stick chilled butter, cut into ½-inch pieces
3 tablespoons shortening
5 tablespoons cold water

Increase oven temperature to 375°. Place all ingredients except cold water into processor and blend. If you do not have a processor, use pastry cutter. Add cold water and blend until ball is formed. Refrigerate dough until firm. Roll pastry ¼-inch thick. Wrap paté with the pastry and decorate with leaves and flowers from leftover pastry rolled ⅛-inch thick. Brush again with egg mixture. Bake for 40 minutes. This may be frozen. To reheat, wrap in foil and heat 30 minutes or longer at 375°.

Martha Ellis Carraway

Gourmet Patė

Serves 12

1 recipe pâte brisée or favorite pastry dough
8 tablespoons butter, divided
2 large onions, finely chopped
Salt and pepper to taste
½ pound fresh mushrooms, chopped
1½ tablespoons fresh parsley
1 teaspoon dried thyme
1 teaspoon dried chervil
1½ cups R.M. Quiggs Paella Rice, cooked
12-14 canned artichoke hearts, chopped
1 tablespoon flour
¼ cup whipping cream
½ teaspoon dill weed
1 teaspoon vinegar
½ pound ham, diced

Make pastry dough and chill. Sauté onions in 4 tablespoons of butter until soft. Season with salt and pepper. Purée in blender or food processor and set aside. In clean skillet sauté mushrooms in 2 tablespoons butter. Add herbs and salt and pepper to taste. Add rice, mix thoroughly and set aside. In a clean skillet, sauté artichoke hearts in 2 tablespoons butter, sprinkle with flour and cook slowly for 4 minutes. Add cream and stir constantly until mixture is thick and smooth. Stir in seasonings, vinegar, and ham, and mix thoroughly. Cool. Roll pastry dough into 2 rectangles, 7″ x 13″. Put 1 on a greased cookie sheet. Spread half the mushroom mixture on pastry, leaving a 1-inch border on all sides. Cover with artichoke mixture, then onion mixture and the remaining mushrooms. Put other rectangle of pastry over all and crimp edges together with fork dipped in water. Trim edges. Slash top in 2 or 3 places and decorate with fancy shapes of pastry scraps. Chill for at least 25-30 minutes. Preheat oven to 375° and bake 30-40 minutes or until golden. Cool at room temperature and transfer to serving platter. Serve at room temperature with crackers.

Sausage-Mushroom Log

Serves 8-10

2 pounds bulk sausage
6 tablespoons unsalted butter
2 tablespoons oil
2 pounds mushrooms, finely chopped
¼ cup finely chopped onion
2 tablespoons minced parsley
Salt and pepper to taste
2 (8 ounce) packages cream cheese, softened
8 sheets phyllo pastry
¾ cup unsalted butter, melted
1 cup bread crumbs

Sauté sausage until it loses its pink color. Drain and crumble. Set aside. Melt butter and oil together and sauté mushrooms and onions until moisture has evaporated and pieces separate. Add parsley, salt, and pepper. Combine sausage, mushrooms, and cream cheese. Lightly dampen a tea towel and place 1 sheet of phyllo on it. Keep remaining sheets covered while working with pastry. Brush sheet with melted butter, then sprinkle with bread crumbs. Top with second sheet, buttering and sprinkling with crumbs. Repeat, using 4 sheets in all, but do not put crumbs on top layer. Leaving a 2-inch margin on all sides, spoon half sausage mixture along narrow edge of pastry. Fold in margins and roll pastry, lengthwise, into log. Lift log onto a buttered baking sheet, brush with melted butter. Repeat procedure, making a second log with remaining phyllo sheets and sausage filling. Bake at 400° for 20 minutes. Can be wrapped and frozen before cooking. Defrost and cook as above.

Marjorie Harris Johnston

Mushrooms in Bread Cups

Yield: 36

18 slices white bread
½ pound chopped, fresh mushrooms
3 tablespoons finely chopped green onions
½ stick butter
2 tablespoons flour
½ pint whipping cream
½ teaspoon salt
¼ teaspoon cayenne pepper
1 tablespoon chopped parsley
5 teaspoons frozen chopped chives
1 teaspoon lemon juice
Parmesan cheese

Bread Cups

Preheat oven to 350°. Roll bread slices to flatten. Use small biscuit cutter to cut 2 circles from each bread slice. Press into small muffin pan. Bake until toasted, about 10 minutes. Remove to cookie sheet.

Filling

Sauté onions and mushrooms in butter for 10-15 minutes. Sprinkle in flour. Stir. Add cream, and stir at low boil until mixture thickens. Remove from heat. Add herbs and seasonings. Spoon mixture into bread cups. Sprinkle with Parmesan cheese. Bake at 350° until bubbly. To freeze: Leave cup on cookie sheet and put in freezer. When frozen, remove from cookie sheet and place in plastic bags. Return to freezer. Reheat frozen cups 10 minutes at 350°. *Bread cups can be filled with a variety of mixtures—sausage and cream of mushroom soup, pimiento cheese, jelly.*

Shelley Gearhart Lindstrom

Champignons Farcis *(Stuffed Mushrooms)*

Yield 12-15 mushrooms

12-15 large mushrooms
2-3 tablespoons melted butter
Salt and pepper to taste
2 tablespoons minced shallots
2 tablespoons butter
½ tablespoon flour
½ cup whipping cream
3 tablespoons freshly minced parsley
Salt and pepper to taste
¼ cup grated Swiss cheese
1-2 tablespoons melted butter

Remove mushroom stems and reserve. Wash and dry caps, brush with melted butter, and arrange hollow side up in shallow baking dish. Season lightly with salt and pepper. Wash and dry stems, and mince. Twist stems in corner of towel to extract as much juice as possible. Sauté with shallots in butter 4-5 minutes until pieces separate. Lower heat, add flour, and stir for 1 minute. Stir in cream and simmer until thickened. Stir in parsley and seasonings. Fill mushroom caps with mixture, top each with 1 teaspoon of cheese and dribble with melted butter. Set aside until ready to cook. Bake 15 minutes in upper third of 375° oven, until caps are tender and light brown.

Gordon Jackson McWhorter

Artichoke Nibbles

Yield: 80 squares

2 (6 ounce) jars marinated artichokes
1 onion, finely chopped
1 clove garlic, minced
2 tablespoons butter
4 eggs
¼ cup fine cracker crumbs (Ritz)
¼ teaspoon salt
⅛ teaspoon pepper
⅛ teaspoon oregano
⅛ teaspoon Tabasco sauce
½ pound shredded sharp Cheddar cheese
1 tablespoon dried parsley

Drain and chop artichokes. Sauté onion and garlic in butter until tender. Cool. Beat eggs and stir in cracker crumbs, salt, pepper, oregano, Tabasco, cheese, and parsley. Add chopped artichokes, blending well. Then add onion mixture, mixing thoroughly. Spread in a greased 8″ x 10″ pan. Bake 30 minutes at 350°. Cut into 1-inch squares. *May be frozen, thawed, and reheated for 12 minutes at 350°.*

Jean Riley Tomlinson

Artichoke Balls

Yield: 3-4 dozen

1 egg
1 (14½ ounce) can artichoke hearts packed in water, drained and mashed
¾ cup grated Romano or Parmesan cheese
¼ cup olive oil
Progresso seasoned bread crumbs

Preheat oven to 350°. Mix together egg, artichoke hearts, cheese, and olive oil. Shape small amounts of mixture into balls and roll in Progresso bread crumbs. Bake for 35 minutes.

May be prepared ahead and frozen.

Sarah Scruggs Estes

Spinach Balls

Nice change from cheese and dips

Yield: 5-6 dozen

1 (10 ounce) package frozen chopped spinach
1½ cups Pepperidge Farm herb stuffing mix
½ cup finely chopped onion
3 eggs, beaten
½ stick butter, melted
¼ cup Parmesan cheese
½ teaspoon pepper
¾ teaspoon garlic salt

Preheat oven to 325°. Cook spinach. Drain well, squeezing out excess liquid. Add all other ingredients, mixing well. Form into small balls and place on lightly greased cookie sheet. Bake 15 minutes. Do not overcook. *May be prepared ahead and frozen before baking.*

Kay Luckie Shackelford

Ham Balls

Yield: 4 dozen for cocktails
12 for main dish

1½ pounds ham
½ pound lean pork or veal
2 slices bread
1 cup milk
1 egg
1 teaspoon salt

Sauce

1 cup light brown sugar
1 tablespoon dry mustard
½ cup vinegar
½ cup water
1 teaspoon cornstarch

Preheat oven to 325°. Have butcher grind meats together. Soak bread in the milk until soft. Add egg and salt. Mix bread mixture and meat together. Shape into balls, packing lightly. Place in casserole and cover with sauce, basting often. Bake 1 hour. *These are good as an hors d'oeuvre or as an entrée, so adjust the size of the balls accordingly.*

Hazel Terrell Gentry
MONTEVALLO, ALABAMA

Marinated Sausage Balls

Yield: 6 dozen

2 pounds hot sausage
½ cup catsup
½ cup wine vinegar
1 tablespoon soy sauce
½ teaspoon ginger
½ cup brown sugar

Preheat oven to 375°. Form sausage into small balls about the size of a walnut. Bake on broiler pan 20-30 minutes or until brown. Do not overcook. Combine remaining ingredients, and heat to boiling point. Pour sauce over sausage balls. Cover and refrigerate overnight. Serve in chafing dish with toothpicks. *May be frozen.*

Mrs. Alvin A. Biggio

Seasoned Sausage

Serves 12

2 pounds ground chuck
1 pound bulk pork sausage
1 teaspoon mustard seed
1 teaspoon coarse ground pepper
3 tablespoons Morton's tender quick salt
½ teaspoon garlic powder
1 tablespoon liquid smoke
¼ teaspoon red pepper
1 cup water

Mix all ingredients well. Roll into 3 (12-inch) rolls. Wrap in wax paper and then foil. Refrigerate 24 hours. Unwrap and bake on broiler pan at 300° for 1½ hours. Turn once during cooking. Slice and serve.

Margaret Kirby Hall
SHERMAN, TEXAS

Cocktail Party Beef Tenderloin

Serves 25-30 for cocktails

1 beef tenderloin, 5-7 pounds

To cook beef tenderloin: Preheat oven to 500°. Cook beef tenderloin in pyrex dish (uncovered). Cook 3 minutes per pound (and count the ounces, too). Cook tenderloin only to medium rare point. Turn stove off and leave until cool.

Marinade

1 cup dry red wine
1 tablespoon Worcestershire sauce
2 teaspoons freshly ground pepper
Juice of one lemon

At this point, marinate tenderloin at least 12 hours. Slice tenderloin in ¾-inch slices and cut slices into ¾-inch cubes.

Sauce

½ cup chopped shallots
3 tablespoons butter
⅔ cup cognac
¼ cup dry red wine
½ teaspoon salt
1 teaspoon freshly ground pepper
2 teaspoons Worcestershire sauce
¾ cup beef bouillon

To prepare sauce: Brown shallots in butter over medium heat, being careful not to burn. Add rest of ingredients and simmer. Place tenderloin cubes in chafing dish and pour the hot sauce over them. Serve with toothpicks or on French bread or small rolls. Keep tenderloin over low heat in chafing dish. *May be prepared ahead.*

Yates Middleton Amason

Eggplant Derbigny

Also good as an entrée

Serves 8

¼ cup oil (½ olive oil if desired)
1 large eggplant, peeled and diced
1 medium onion, finely chopped
¼ cup finely chopped green pepper
1 clove garlic, crushed
2 teaspoons finely chopped parsley
2 stalks celery, finely chopped
1 small bay leaf
1 pound shrimp, shelled and cut in pieces (not too small)
½ pint box fresh mushrooms, cut in pieces (not too small)

To Taste:
Salt
Pepper
Cayenne
Thyme
Marjoram

Sauté eggplant, onion, green pepper, garlic, parsley, celery, and bay leaf until coated with oil, stirring constantly. Cover with tight lid and cook over low heat until soft, about 10 minutes. Add shrimp and mushrooms and cook another 5 minutes. Season with remaining ingredients to taste. Stir occasionally while cooking and mix well. Remove the bay leaf and pour into a large casserole. Bake for 30 minutes at 350°. When ready to serve, place casserole over candle warmer and serve with either tiny pastry shells or toast rounds. Mixture may be spread on crackers and run under the broiler until hot and bubbly. *This is even better the second day.*

Helen Byrd

EGGS, CHEESE, GRAINS, PASTA

Eggs, Cheese, Grains, Pasta

Creole Stuffed Eggs

A tasty deviled egg variation

Yield: 16 halves

8 eggs, hard boiled and halved lengthwise
2 tablespoons minced green pepper
2 tablespoons minced spring onions, with some green parts
2 tablespoons minced celery, using a few tender leaves
2 tablespoons minced fresh parsley
¼ teaspoon salt
¼ teaspoon cayenne pepper
Juice of 1 lemon
Black pepper to taste
Mayonnaise to bind, about 3 tablespoons
Paprika

Scoop out yolks and mix with remaining ingredients, using processor if available. Refrigerate. Scoop mixture into halves of eggs and sprinkle with paprika before serving.

Glenda Huff Johnson
NEW ORLEANS, LOUISIANA

Scrambled Egg Casserole

Prepare ahead and chill overnight.

Serves 12-14

1 cup cubed ham or Canadian bacon
¼ cup chopped green onions
3 tablespoons melted margarine
1 dozen eggs, beaten
1 (4 ounce) can sliced mushrooms, drained
Cheese sauce
¼ cup melted margarine
2 cups soft bread crumbs
⅛ teaspoon paprika

Sauté ham and green onions in 3 tablespoons margarine in large skillet until onion is tender. Add eggs and cook over medium high heat, stirring to form large, soft curds. When eggs are set, stir in mushrooms and cheese sauce. Spoon eggs into greased 13″ x 9″ x 2″ baking pan. Combine ¼ cup melted margarine and crumbs, mixing well. Spread evenly over egg mixture. Sprinkle with paprika. Cover and chill overnight. Uncover and bake at 350° for 30 minutes or until heated thoroughly.

Cheese Sauce

2 tablespoons margarine
2½ tablespoons flour
2 cups milk
½ teaspoon salt
¼ teaspoon pepper
1 cup (4 ounces) shredded cheese

Melt margarine in a heavy saucepan over low heat; blend in flour and cook 1 minute. Gradually add milk; cook over medium heat until thickened, stirring constantly. Add salt, pepper, and cheese, stirring until cheese melts and mixture is smooth.

Frances Lauer Falvey
OCALA, FLORIDA

Girlette's Party Strata

Serves 10-12

2 (10 ounce) packages chopped frozen spinach or broccoli
1 tablespoon butter
2 tablespoons chopped onion
½ teaspoon black pepper
18 slices of day-old bread, crusts removed
12 slices sharp American cheese or Swiss cheese (1¼ cups)
2 cups diced or cubed ham or any leftover meat, hamburger or lamb
6 eggs, slightly beaten
3½ cups milk
¼ cup grated or shredded Parmesan, Swiss, or Gruyère cheese

Cook and drain spinach and season with butter, onion, and black pepper. Cover bottom of 9″ x 13″ Pyrex dish with 6 slices of bread and top with 6 slices of cheese. Next add half spinach mixture and sprinkle with 1 cup diced ham. Repeat layers of bread, cheese slices, spinach, and ham. Gently pat down with hand. Take 6 bread slices and cut diagonally into halves and arrange 12 triangles in two overlapping rows on top of strata. Combine eggs and milk and pour on top of entire dish. Cover and let stand refrigerated several hours or overnight. Bake at 325° for 45 minutes. Remove from oven and sprinkle with grated cheese. Return to oven and bake for 15 minutes more.

Girlette Warner
ANTIGUA, WEST INDIES

Sunday Night Skillet Supper

The children will ask for seconds!

Serves 6

4 tablespoons margarine
1 (16 ounce) package frozen hash browns
⅓ cup finely chopped onion
⅓ cup finely chopped green pepper
Salt and pepper to taste
4 eggs, beaten
1 (12 ounce) package bulk sausage, cooked, crumbled, and drained
½ cup shredded Cheddar cheese

Melt margarine in skillet on low heat. Add potatoes, onion, and green pepper. Sprinkle with salt and pepper. Cover and cook over low heat 15-20 minutes. Pour eggs over potatoes. Arrange sausage over eggs. Cover and cook until eggs are set, about 15 minutes. Sprinkle with cheese. Cover and heat until cheese melts. Cut into wedges to serve.

Cynda Mathis Screws

Foolproof Cheese Soufflé

A nice change from baked potatoes.

Serves 6

12 ounces sharp Cheddar cheese, grated
10 slices of buttered, crustless bread
4 eggs
2 cups milk
1 teaspoon salt
½ teaspoon dried mustard

Using metal blade of food processor, add half of each of the ingredients to work bowl and mix well. Pour this mixture into greased 1½-quart soufflé dish. Repeat with the other half of the ingredients. Bake at 350° for 1 hour. Can be prepared a day ahead and refrigerated, or may be frozen!

Julia May Webb Hoke

Cheese Soufflé

Serves 4

4 tablespoons butter
2 tablespoons flour
½ teaspoon salt
½ teaspoon dry mustard
⅛ teaspoon cayenne
⅛ teaspoon nutmeg (fresh grated is best!)
1 cup milk
1 rounded cup grated extra sharp Cheddar cheese
⅛ teaspoon cream of tartar, optional
5 large eggs, separated

Melt butter in saucepan or iron skillet. Remove from heat and add flour, salt, mustard, cayenne, and half of nutmeg. Blend. Stir in milk slowly and cook over medium low heat, stirring often until mixture thickens. Gradually add cheese until all is melted. Remove from heat. May be prepared ahead to this point. Beat egg whites and cream of tartar until whites are very stiff. Blend yolks into cheese sauce, then fold cheese sauce into egg whites and pour into 1½-quart buttered soufflé dish. Sprinkle with remaining nutmeg and a few grains of cayenne and bake in 375° oven for 20 or 22 minutes. Straw will come out clean when done and soufflé will be lightly browned. Serve at once.

William Jackson Arant

John Wayne Casserole

Serves 6-8

A spicy cheese side dish

- **1 (4½ ounce) can chopped green chilies**
- **1 pound Monterey Jack cheese, grated**
- **1 pound medium sharp Cheddar cheese, grated**
- **4 eggs, separated**
- **⅔ cup evaporated milk**
- **1 tablespoon flour**
- **½ teaspoon salt**
- **⅛ teaspoon pepper**
- **2 tomatoes, sliced**

Preheat oven to 350°. Place chilies and cheeses in a 2-quart buttered casserole. Beat egg whites until stiff. Set aside. Combine egg yolks, evaporated milk, flour, salt and pepper. Fold in egg whites. Pour over cheese mixture and pierce with fork to allow liquid to absorb into cheese. Bake for 30 minutes. Put a layer of sliced tomatoes on top. Bake for additional 30 minutes. *Excellent side dish for steaks or barbequed chicken.*

Beth Ennis Hillhouse

Sausage and Cheese Grits Casserole

Serves 10

May be prepared a day ahead.

- **1 cup grits**
- **2 tablespoons butter**
- **2 cups grated sharp Cheddar cheese**
- **1 teaspoon garlic salt**
- **2 teaspoons Worcestershire sauce**
- **Pepper to taste**
- **1 egg, beaten**
- **¼ cup milk**
- **8 sausage patties, cooked and halved (12 ounces)**
- **Grated cheese for garnish**
- **Paprika for garnish**

Preheat oven to 350°. Cook grits as package directs. Add butter, cheese, garlic salt, Worcestershire, and pepper. Cool. Add egg and milk. Put a layer of sausage in bottom of casserole and cover with a layer of grits. Repeat. Sprinkle top with additional cheese and paprika. Bake for 30 minutes or until hot and bubbly.

Lucy Walter Burr

Cheese Grits

Wonderful with pork

Serves 6-8

1 cup quick grits
1 stick butter, cut into small cubes
½ pound extra sharp Cheddar cheese, cut into small cubes
½ roll nippy garlic cheese, optional
2 teaspoons Worcestershire sauce

Preheat oven to 350°. Cook grits according to package directions. While grits are still hot add butter, cheeses, and Worcestershire sauce. Stir until butter and cheeses are melted. Place in buttered 1½-quart casserole and bake for 20 minutes or until bubbly. Grits may be prepared a day ahead and refrigerated. If made ahead, pour a very small amount of milk on top and pierce grits with fork to allow milk to soak in.

Creagh McCollum Richardson

Gouda Grits

Serves 6

1 cup quick grits
1 stick butter
8 ounces Gouda cheese, grated
1 (5 ounce) can evaporated milk

Preheat oven to 350°. Cook grits according to package directions. Mix all ingredients and pour into 1½-quart casserole dish. Bake for 45 minutes to 1 hour. Garnish with paprika or grate more Gouda over top of casserole and run under broiler to melt.

Celeta Barnes Manley

Spinach Cheese Pie

A good light crust—nice and cheesy

Serves 8

4 frozen patty shells or 1 sheet frozen puff pastry dough
1 (10 ounce) frozen chopped spinach
1 (3 ounce) cream cheese, softened
6 eggs
¼ cup shredded sharp Cheddar cheese
2 tablespoons sliced green onion
1 tablespoon snipped parsley
½ teaspoon salt
Dash pepper
3 tablespoons Parmesan cheese
8 tomato wedges or 4 cherry tomatoes

Thaw pastry in refrigerator for 2 hours. Roll on floured surface to fit a 10-inch pie plate. Seal edge together and let rest 5 minutes. Place in pie plate and flute edges. Cook spinach according to package directions and drain well. Mix cream cheese with hot spinach. Combine eggs and shredded cheese; mix well. Stir in spinach, onion, parsley, salt and pepper. Pour in pie shell and top with 2 tablespoons Parmesan. Bake 15 minutes or until edges are set in preheated 425° oven. Remove and let stand 10 minutes. Before serving, top with tomato wedges and rest of Parmesan. Return to oven for 3-5 minutes. Pie can be assembled early in the day and refrigerated before baking. *The spinach mixture can be used as a stuffing for tomatoes or used in individual tarts.*

Angelia Pitts Brady

Spinach and Feta Cheese Quiche

Serves 6

4 ounces Feta cheese, well rinsed, patted dry, and crumbled
½ cup Parmesan cheese
½ cup chopped green onion
½ cup minced fresh parsley
¼ cup fresh bread crumbs
1 (10 ounce) package frozen chopped spinach, thawed and squeezed dry
1½ cups grated Monterey Jack cheese
1 9-inch deep dish pie shell
1 cup half-and-half
4 eggs
Parmesan cheese
Minced green onion
Minced fresh parsley

Preheat oven to 375°. Combine first 6 ingredients in mixing bowl and blend well. Sprinkle Monterey Jack cheese on pie shell. Spoon spinach mixture over top. Heat cream. Beat eggs and add warm cream, beating well. Slowly pour over spinach mixture, allowing spinach to absorb liquid before adding more. Sprinkle top with extra Parmesan, onion, and parsley. Bake about 1 hour. Let stand 5 minutes before serving.

Ginna Henking Lowry

Zucchini Pie

Serves 8

5 or 6 zucchini squash, very thinly sliced
1 onion, sliced
3 tomatoes, sliced
3 cups grated sharp cheese
Salt and pepper
¾ cup Bisquick
2 eggs
½ cup milk

Preheat oven to 400°. Place slices of zucchini in bottom of shallow buttered 3-quart baking dish. Add slices of onion. Place slices of tomato on top. Add salt and pepper. Top with grated cheese. Mix Bisquick with eggs and milk. Pour over the layers and bake for 30 minutes.

Adeline Williams

Football Brunch Spinach Quiche

Serves 8

1 9-inch pastry shell, unbaked
1 tablespoon margarine
½ cup minced onion
1 (10 ounce) package frozen chopped spinach, thawed
1 (15 ounce) carton cottage cheese
2 eggs, beaten
⅛ teaspoon pepper
Salt to taste
⅛ teaspoon ground nutmeg
¼ cup grated Parmesan cheese

Preheat oven to 400°. Prick pie shell all over with a fork and bake 15 minutes until lightly browned. In medium-sized skillet melt butter over moderate heat. Add onion and cook until soft, stirring occasionally. Press spinach in strainer to remove as much moisture as possible. Add spinach to onion and toss over heat until the liquid has evaporated. Remove from heat. Place remaining ingredients in large mixing bowl and mix well. Add spinach mixture. Pour into pie shell, reduce heat to 350°, bake for 40-45 minutes. Let cool 10 minutes before serving.

Debby Davis Denson

Artichoke Pie

A rich pie which can be served hot or cold.

Serves 6-8

1 (9 ounce) package frozen or 1 (14 ounce) can artichoke hearts
½ stick butter
½ cup chopped onion
1 tablespoon flour
½ cup half-and-half
4 eggs, beaten
½ cup sour cream
Salt, pepper, and nutmeg to taste
1 tablespoon chopped parsley
1 9-inch deep dish pie shell, unbaked
½ cup shredded Swiss or Monterey Jack cheese
¼ cup shredded Cheddar cheese
¼ cup grated Parmesan cheese

Preheat oven to 350°. If using frozen artichoke hearts, cook according to package directions. Drain artichokes and chop. Melt butter, add onion, and sauté until golden and tender. Blend in flour. Gradually add cream and cook over low heat, stirring constantly, until smooth and thickened. In a bowl combine eggs, sour cream, salt, pepper, nutmeg, and parsley. Add onion mixture to egg mixture. Place artichokes on bottom of pie shell. Sprinkle cheese over artichokes and pour egg mixture on top. Bake for 45 minutes or until set. Let stand 5 minutes before serving.

Sandra S. MacDonald

Blue Cheese Quiche

May be baked in individual tart shells as an appetizer.

Serves 4-6

3 ounces blue cheese
6 ounces cream cheese
2 tablespoons butter, softened
3 tablespoons whipping cream
2 eggs
Salt and white pepper to taste
Red pepper to taste
½ tablespoon fresh chives or ½ teaspoon minced green onion tops
8-inch pie shell, partially cooked

Preheat oven to 375°. Blend the cheeses, butter, and cream in processor or with fork. Beat in eggs. Force through sieve to remove lumps if necessary. Season with salt and peppers and stir in chives or onion tops. Pour mixture into partially cooked pastry shell. Set in upper third of oven. Bake for 25-30 minutes or until quiche has puffed and top has browned.

Lois Folmar Turnipseed

Mushroom Quiche

Serves 8-10

2 9-inch pie shells, unbaked
1 tablespoon butter, softened
2 cups whipping cream
4 eggs
1 teaspoon salt
½ stick butter, melted
½ pound fresh mushrooms, sliced
4 tablespoons minced green onion
¼ teaspoon salt
Pepper to taste

Preheat oven to 425°. Spread pie crusts with the softened butter. In medium bowl, beat cream, eggs, and 1 teaspoon salt with wire whisk until well blended. In melted butter, sauté mushrooms, green onion, salt and pepper. Cook until tender, about 5 minutes, stirring frequently. Add cream mixture to mushroom mixture. Pour into pie crusts. Bake 15 minutes at 425°; reduce heat to 325° and bake 35 minutes longer.

Pamela Allen DeBardeleben

Corn Quiche

Cinnamon and brown sugar give a different taste to corn.

Serves 6

1 9-inch deep dish pie shell
1 (12 ounce) can whole kernel white corn, drained
4 ounces Swiss cheese, shredded
3 eggs, beaten
1 cup half-and-half
½ teaspoon salt
⅛ teaspoon white pepper
⅛ teaspoon nutmeg
1½ tablespoons butter, melted
1½ tablespoons brown sugar
¼ teaspoon cinnamon

Preheat oven to 425°. Bake pie shell for 5 minutes. Reduce oven temperature to 350°. Place corn in pastry shell and sprinkle with cheese. Combine eggs, half-and-half, salt, pepper, and nutmeg and pour over corn and cheese. Bake for 30 minutes. Drizzle melted butter over top of quiche and sprinkle combined brown sugar and cinnamon on top. Return to oven for 5 minutes or until center is firm. Quiche can be made ahead and frozen by omitting topping and the last 5 minutes of baking time. Defrost and bring quiche to room temperature, add topping, and bake in preheated 350° oven for 15 minutes. *Delicious alternative to sweet potatoes or can be sliced into small wedges and served instead of bread with a meal.*

Susan Walter Rediker

Eggplant Quiche

Serves 6-8

2 9-inch pie shells, unbaked
1 small eggplant, peeled and cubed
¾ cup chopped onion
½ cup chopped green pepper
4 tablespoons butter
1½ tablespoons flour
1 (10¾ ounce) can cream of chicken soup
½ teaspoon salt
1 teaspoon sugar
⅛ teaspoon oregano
¼ teaspoon pepper
4 beaten eggs
1 tomato, peeled and chopped
1 cup grated sharp cheese
¼ cup grated Parmesan cheese

Preheat oven to 450°. Partially bake pie shells for 6 minutes. Reduce oven temperature to 350°. Cook eggplant covered in boiling, salted water for 8-10 minutes. Drain well. Sauté onion and green pepper in butter until tender. Blend in flour, soup, salt, sugar, oregano, and pepper. Heat until bubbly. Remove from heat and let cool. Stir in beaten eggs; fold in tomato, cheese, and eggplant. Pour into pie shells; sprinkle with Parmesan cheese. Bake for 30-35 minutes. May be prepared several hours before baking. *Variation:* Prepare in individual pastry shells.

Dorothy Simpson Bennett

Individual Shrimp Quiches

Yield: 12 small quiches

Pastry for 2 9-inch pies or 12 small pie shells
¾ cup chopped cooked shrimp
¼ cup sliced green onion
4 ounces Swiss cheese, shredded (1 cup)
½ cup mayonnaise
2 eggs
⅓ cup milk
¼ teaspoon salt
¼ teaspoon dried dill weed, optional
Cayenne pepper to taste

Preheat oven to 400°. On floured surface, roll half of pastry into 12-inch circle. Cut six 4-inch circles. Repeat with remaining pastry. Fit into twelve 2½-inch muffin pan cups. Fill each pastry with some shrimp, onion, and cheese. Beat remaining ingredients. Pour over cheese. Bake 15-20 minutes or until browned.

Cathy Criss Adams

Crab Quiche

Serves 4-6

½ cup mayonnaise
1 tablespoon flour
2 eggs, beaten
½ cup milk
½ pound crabmeat
½ pound Swiss cheese, grated
⅓ cup chopped fresh chives
Parsley for garnish
1 deep dish pie shell

Preheat oven to 350°. Mix mayonnaise, flour, eggs, and milk thoroughly. Stir in crabmeat, cheese, and chives. Spoon into pie shell. Bake for 30-40 minutes or until firm in center. Garnish with parsley.

Alice London Cox

Cheddar Jack Quiche

May be prepared 1 or 2 days ahead.

Serves 6-8

1 9-inch pie shell
1 cup sliced mushrooms
⅓ cup chopped onion
2 tablespoons margarine
2 tablespoons dry bread crumbs
1 cup (4 ounces) shredded Monterey Jack cheese
½ cup (2 ounces) shredded sharp Cheddar cheese
5 eggs
½ cup mayonnaise
½ cup whipping cream or half-and-half
2 tablespoons minced parsley
1 teaspoon Dijon mustard
1 jalapeño pepper, seeded and minced, optional
½ teaspoon salt
¼ teaspoon white pepper

Preheat oven to 425°. Bake crust for 10 minutes or until crust is lightly browned. Cool. Sauté mushrooms and onion in margarine until onion is tender and liquid is absorbed. Sprinkle bread crumbs in bottom of crust. Add cheeses and mushroom mixture. Mix remaining ingredients until blended; pour into crust. Bake at 375° for 30-35 minutes or until a knife comes out clean. May be frozen.

Alice Wildman Rogers

Risotto Milanese

Serves 8

1 stick butter, divided
½ cup minced onion
2 cups rice, uncooked
1 cup dry white wine
6 cups chicken broth, heated
¼ teaspoon saffron, optional
¼ cup Parmesan cheese

Sauté onion in ½ stick butter in a large heavy saucepan. Add rice, stirring until well coated with butter. Add wine and simmer until wine has evaporated. Add 1 cup of the chicken broth and simmer the mixture until the stock is almost absorbed. Reserve 1 tablespoon broth and add the remaining 5 cups broth, 1 cup at a time, letting the rice absorb each cup before adding more. Cook the rice an additional 15 minutes or until tender. Dissolve saffron in the reserved 1 tablespoon hot broth in a small dish and add to rice. Add Parmesan cheese and blend with a fork. *Best when prepared at the last minute, but can be done ahead and reheated.*

Allison Comer Murray

Baked Rice with Vegetables

Serves 12

2 cups long-grain rice
⅓ cup butter
4 cups liquid—3 (10 ounce) cans chicken broth or undiluted consommé
¼ teaspoon oregano
¼ teaspoon thyme
½ teaspoon salt
¼ teaspoon pepper
¾ cup coarsely ground carrots
¾ cup chopped celery
¾ cup chopped parsley (or 1 tablespoon dried)
½ cup chopped onion
2 cups fresh mushrooms, sliced

Preheat oven to 350°. Heat casserole dish in oven. Melt butter in skillet and brown rice. Heat liquid to boiling. Pour 3¼ cups liquid into casserole. Add rice, oregano, thyme, salt, and pepper. Cover and bake for 30 minutes. Add remaining heated liquid and vegetables to casserole. Stir well. Cover and cook 30 minutes longer.

Jean Qualman Ager

Baked Wild Rice

Delicious served with duck or game

Serves 12

2 tablespoons butter
1 cup wild rice
3 onions, chopped
3 stalks celery, chopped
1 teaspoon seasoned salt
1 quart chicken broth
Mushrooms, optional

Brown rice and onion in butter. Put rice in 2-quart casserole and add other ingredients. Cover and bake at 325° for 2 hours or until all liquid is absorbed. Sautéed mushrooms can be added.
Best if prepared ahead, refrigerated overnight, and warmed in a 300° oven for 30-40 minutes.

Fairfax Smathers Nabers

Tossed Wild Rice with Pecans

Serves 6-8

1 cup wild rice
Chicken broth
1 stick butter, melted
½ cup green onions, finely sliced
1 cup pecans

Toast pecans in flat pan at 200° for 20 minutes, stirring occasionally. Cook wild rice according to package directions, but substitute chicken broth for water. When rice is done, toss with butter, onions, and pecans. Serve while steaming hot! *Amount of chicken broth will vary according to brand of wild rice.*

Cindy Potts Bibb

Wild Rice and Sausage Supreme

Serves 8-10

2 boxes Uncle Ben's Long Grain and Wild Rice
2 pounds mild sausage
8 ounces fresh mushrooms
1 can cream of mushroom soup
1 soup can half-and-half
2 tablespoons Worcestershire sauce

Cook rice according to directions, but exclude butter, and remove from heat 5 minutes early. Drain rice. Cook sausage and drain. Sauté mushrooms in the same pan. Mix all ingredients and put in casserole dish. Cover and bake at 350° for 30-40 minutes.

Nancy Hamilton Bagby

Green Rice

Serves 16-18

2 cups rice
2 eggs, beaten
⅓ cup salad oil
⅓ cup olive oil
2 cups evaporated milk
2 cups grated sharp Cheddar cheese
3 medium onions, chopped
1 cup fresh parsley, chopped
2 green peppers, chopped
1 clove garlic, chopped
2 tablespoons salt

Cook rice according to package directions. Add other ingredients, mixing well. Put in a greased 3-quart casserole. Bake uncovered, 45 minutes at 350°.

Jane Clark Wilson
JACKSON, MISSISSIPPI

Apple Brown Rice

A tasty dish with game or fowl

Serves 6

1⅓ cups apple juice
1⅓ cups water
1 cup brown rice, rinsed 2 or 3 times
1 tablespoon margarine
1 tablespoon honey
1 teaspoon salt
2 medium red apples, coarsely chopped
¾ cup celery, thinly sliced
⅓ cup pecans or walnuts, chopped

Bring juice and water to a boil in a large saucepan. Add rice, margarine, honey, and salt. Cover tightly and cook over low heat until all liquid is absorbed, about 50 minutes. Stir in apples, celery, and nuts. Heat through.

Millymac Jenkins Shackelford

California Rice Casserole

Unusual and extremely tasty. Hot and spicy!

Serves 8

½ stick butter
1 cup chopped onion
4 cups cooked white rice
2 cups sour cream
1 cup cream style cottage cheese
1 large bay leaf, crumbled
½ teaspoon salt
⅛ teaspoon pepper
1 (4 ounce) can green chilies, drained and halved lengthwise, leaving seeds
2 cups grated sharp Cheddar cheese
Chopped parsley

Preheat oven to 375°. Lightly grease 12″ x 8″ x 2″ baking dish (2-quart). Sauté onion in butter until golden, remove from heat. Stir in rice, sour cream, cottage cheese, bay leaf, salt and pepper. Toss lightly to mix well. Place half the rice mixture in baking dish, add half of the chilies, and sprinkle with half the cheese. Repeat layers. Bake uncovered for 25 minutes or until bubbly hot. Sprinkle with chopped parsley.

Anne Starnes Finch

Homemade Pasta

3-4 persons	5-6 persons	7-8 persons
2 large eggs	3 eggs	4 large eggs
1½ cups flour	2¼ cups flour	3 cups flour

These are not inflexible proportions because eggs vary in size and flour absorbing qualities vary. If you find that the egg will take more flour, add it; but do not exceed 1 cup flour per egg. It is easier for beginners to work with less flour because the dough stays softer and easier to handle.

Pour flour onto work surface, shape it into a mound and make a well in the center. Put whole eggs in the well. Beat eggs slightly with fingers or fork. Start mixing the flour into the eggs with a circular motion, drawing the flour from inside wall of well. When eggs are no longer runny, toss rest of flour over them and mix eggs and flour until they are a somewhat crumbly paste. Knead dough until firm and smooth. Pull off a piece of dough about the size of an orange, keeping the rest covered between 2 plates. Set pasta machine rollers to widest setting (0). Pass the dough through widest setting, then pass it through increasingly narrow settings until it is the thickness you choose (4-6). The thinner the pasta, the lighter it will be. Dust with flour if it sticks to rollers. Pass the kneaded thin dough through the cutter. Hang to dry on a broom or golf club between 2 chairs. Store flat between sheets of wax paper. Cook in boiling salted water as you would commercial noodles.

Rose Anne Ferrante Waters

Spaghetti with Burnt Butter

This is an excellent side dish for veal or fish entrées.

Serves 6

1 (12 ounce) package vermicelli
2 garlic cloves (or more), cut in half
2 sticks butter

Cook vermicelli in boiling salted water for 8 minutes until al dente (just firm). Drain thoroughly in colander. While vermicelli is cooking, melt butter in small saucepan. Add garlic. Let butter and garlic brown slowly. Remove garlic as soon as it browns (about 4 minutes). Continue to brown butter, just to "burnt" stage. Immediately return vermicelli to pot in which it was cooked and pour butter over all. Mix gently but thoroughly. Allow to stand 1 or 2 minutes before serving. Serve while it's hot!

Laide Long Karpeles

Linguine

Serves 4

8 ounces thin spaghetti
3 tablespoons olive oil
1 heaping teaspoon salt
1 heaping tablespoon fresh parsley
1 teaspoon garlic powder or to taste
1 stick butter or margarine
1-3 tablespoons grated Parmesan cheese

Gently boil spaghetti in 1 quart boiling water with salt and olive oil for 8-10 minutes until cooked but still firm. Drain well and toss with remaining ingredients. *This is good served with Italian sausage and a tossed salad or with baked chicken and salad.*

James B. Knight, Jr.

Pasta Primavera

Serves 6-8

1 cup sliced zucchini
1½ cups broccoli flowerets
1 box frozen snow peas
1 cup baby peas
6 stalks fresh asparagus, sliced
1 pound linguine or spaghetti
12 cherry tomatoes, cut in half
3 tablespoons olive oil, divided
2 teaspoons minced garlic, divided
Salt and pepper to taste
¼ cup chopped parsley
10 large mushrooms, sliced
½ stick butter
½ cup Parmesan cheese
1 cup cream
⅓ cup chopped fresh basil
⅓ cup chicken consommé, optional
⅓ cup pine nuts, toasted

Blanch zucchini, broccoli, snow peas, baby peas, and asparagus until tender crisp—no longer. This can be done ahead of time. Cook pasta in boiling salted water until al dente (just firm). Drain. While pasta is cooking, sauté tomatoes in 1 tablespoon oil with 1 teaspoon garlic, salt, pepper, and parsley. Set aside. In another large pan with remaining oil, add second teaspoon garlic and all vegetables. Simmer a few minutes just until hot. Stir together butter, cheese, cream, and basil. Add pasta and cream sauce to vegetables. Toss. If sauce gets too thick, thin with consommé. Top with cherry tomatoes and pine nuts. Season to taste with more salt and pepper and Parmesan cheese. Serves 6 as entrée, 8 as a first course.

Rose Anne Ferrante Waters

Spaghetti Carbonara

Elegant use for leftover ham

Serves 4

1 (8 ounce) package spaghetti
½ stick butter
1 cup chopped ham or bacon
⅓ cup sliced onion
⅓ cup chopped green pepper
½ cup sliced mushrooms
Salt and pepper to taste
1 egg, beaten
½ cup half-and-half
½ cup Parmesan cheese

Boil spaghetti in large pot of salted water. Drain. Melt butter and sauté ham, onion, green pepper, and mushroom until tender. Add drained spaghetti. Salt and pepper to taste. Add egg beaten with cream. Toss in Parmesan cheese and stir until heated through. Remove from heat and serve.

Kacy Ireland Mitchell

Tortellini with Cream Sauce

Tortellini *(a horseshoe-shaped pasta stuffed with sausage)*
1 tablespoon oil
2 tablespoons salt

Bring 4 quarts water and oil to boil. Add salt, then tortellini. Cover and allow water to return to a boil, then cook 5 minutes.

Cream Sauce

1 cup half-and-half
3 teaspoons butter
⅔ cup freshly grated Parmesan cheese
White pepper to taste
Nutmeg to taste
Salt to taste

Simmer half-and-half and butter over medium heat for less than a minute until thickened. Turn off heat. When ready to serve, add rest of ingredients over low heat, stirring until smooth. Pour sauce over cooked tortellini.

Tandy Sweeney Graves

Linguini with White Clam Sauce

Serves 2

Pasta

4 ounces linguini
1 tablespoon butter

Prepare linguini according to package directions.

Sauce

⅓ cup olive oil
2 teaspoons fresh garlic, sliced
1 (16 ounce) can minced clams with broth
3 tablespoons finely chopped fresh parsley
Salt and pepper to taste
2 tablespoons white wine, optional
Parmesan cheese

While linguini is cooking prepare sauce. Heat oil over medium heat until a light haze forms (not smoking). Add garlic and cook until golden brown (about 2 minutes) being careful not to burn. Remove garlic. Add clams with broth to oil and cook over medium heat. Allow foam to subside, until liquid is reduced to about half the original volume. Add parsley. Remove from heat. Drain prepared linguini and toss with butter. Bring clam broth mixture to a rapid boil. Cook only until heated. Add salt, pepper, and wine. Pour over linguini. Serve topped with Parmesan cheese.

Charlotte Blackwell Coleman

Pasta Leon

A delicious creamy zucchini sauce for pasta

Serves 2

1½ cups grated raw zucchini
2 tablespoons grated onion
2 tablespoons butter
⅓ cup half-and-half
⅛ teaspoon dried dill weed or more to taste
¼ teaspoon garlic salt
Black pepper to taste
½ cup sour cream

Sauté zucchini and onion in butter over medium heat until golden. Add half-and-half, dill weed, garlic salt, and pepper. Stir constantly over low heat 1 minute. Stir in sour cream and heat to serve, but *do not boil*. Serve immediately over cooked pasta of your choice.

Shrimp and Pasta

Serves 6

6 slices bacon
1 stick butter or margarine
1 green pepper, halved and thinly sliced
5 or 6 green onions, thinly sliced
1 pound large shrimp, peeled
2 tablespoon vermouth, optional
1 (8 ounce) package vermicelli, cooked
½ cup grated Parmesan
½ cup half-and-half
½ cup toasted fresh bread crumbs
Salt and pepper to taste

Fry bacon until crisp and set aside. Pour bacon grease out of skillet. Add butter and sauté the green pepper and onions for 3 or 4 minutes. Add shrimp and cook until pink—about 5 minutes. Add vermouth and simmer about 3 minutes more. Toss the shrimp mixture with the cooked vermicelli. Add Parmesan cheese, cream, bread crumbs, salt and pepper. Toss again. Heat thoroughly and serve with bacon crumbled on top.

Lucinda Leeth Grissom

Fettuccini Alfredo

Serves 4-6

1 pound package fettuccini
1 tablespoon vegetable oil
2 tablespoons salt
1 stick butter (no substitute)
1 cup whipping cream
Freshly ground pepper
1 cup fresh Parmesan cheese, grated
Nutmeg, optional
Fresh parsley, chopped

Must have all ingredients ready. Work quickly and serve immediately. Cook noodles with oil and salt in boiling water according to package directions until tender but still firm. While noodles are cooking, melt butter in skillet and keep skillet warm. Drain noodles and toss with butter in skillet. Add cream and a lot of pepper. Stir gently until cream thickens. Add cheese, nutmeg if desired, and taste for salt. Garnish with parsley.

Fettucini with Prosciutto

Serves 4-6

1 pound fettucini noodles or green spinach noodles
1½ sticks butter
1 cup whipping cream
1 cup freshly grated Parmesan cheese
6 thin slices Prosciutto ham or any good thinly sliced ham, cut in julienne strips
Salt to taste
Freshly ground pepper
Extra Parmesan

Drop noodles into 6 quarts salted, boiling water and cook until al dente (still firm). While noodles are cooking, melt butter in a large skillet. Drain noodles, add to butter, tossing to coat. Add cream and cook over low heat until cream thickens. Stir in Parmesan and ham. Cook until cheese melts (does not take long). Season with salt and pepper and serve at once. Provide extra cheese and a pepper mill.

Alicia Weeks McGivaren

Stir-Fried Vegetables and Pasta

Serves 6

1 medium onion, sliced
1 stalk celery, sliced
1 green pepper, sliced
2 medium zucchini squash, sliced
3 tablespoons margarine
6 mushrooms, sliced
3 tomatoes, quartered
½ cup freshly grated Parmesan cheese
1 teaspoon dried oregano
½ teaspoon salt
¼ teaspoon pepper
1 (10 ounce) package spaghetti, cooked and drained

In a skillet or wok, sauté onion, celery, pepper, and zucchini in margarine for 2 minutes. Do *not* overcook; vegetables must stay crisp! Add mushrooms, tomatoes, cheese, and spices. Stir until thoroughly heated. Do *not* overcook. Serve immediately on hot buttered spaghetti; sprinkle with additional Parmesan cheese if desired.

Emily Chenoweth Major

Blender Pesto and Pasta

Good

Serves 4-6

2 cups *fresh* basil leaves
½ cup olive oil
2 tablespoons pine nuts
2 cloves garlic
½-1 teaspoon salt
½ cup grated Parmesan cheese
3 tablespoons butter, softened
2 tablespoons Romano or Parmesan cheese
1 pound cooked pasta, liquid reserved

Put first 5 ingredients in blender and purée. (This can be frozen until needed. Just thaw and continue with recipe.) Pour purée into bowl and beat in cheese and butter. If thinner consistency is desired, beat in 1-2 tablespoons hot pasta water and then toss in pasta. Sprinkle with remaining 2 tablespoons Parmesan cheese. *Additional pine nuts can be sprinkled on pasta before serving.*

Mary Todd Tate Davis

1 June '96
Acworth, Ga

Adrian's Pasta

Serves 4-6

6 ounces medium egg noodles (especially good if homemade)
1 tablespoon vegetable oil
1 medium onion, chopped
1 pound fresh spinach, washed and chopped
1 (8 ounce) carton sour cream
1 clove garlic, minced
1½ teaspoons crumbled basil
1½ teaspoons crumbled oregano
1 cup pitted ripe olives, halved
½ pound fresh mushrooms, sliced
1 cup grated Monterey Jack cheese
1 cup grated Parmesan cheese
Salt to taste

Boil noodles according to package directions. While noodles cook, heat oil in skillet. Add onion and spinach and cook over medium-high heat for 4-5 minutes or until spinach is wilted and onion is cooked. Stir in sour cream, garlic, basil, oregano, olives, and mushrooms. Drain noodles and return to pot. Add cheeses. Heat, stirring until melted. Stir in spinach combination. Heat gently, but do not boil. Taste for salt. Turn onto warm platter and serve.

Carol Sharman Ringland

SALADS, DRESSINGS, SAUCES

Salads, Dressings, Sauces

Cold Asparagus with Pecans

Always a favorite with guests

Serves 6-8

1½ pounds fresh asparagus, as young and tender as possible or 2 (10 ounce) packages frozen asparagus
¾ cup finely chopped pecans
2 tablespoons vegetable oil
¼ cup cider vinegar
¼ cup soy sauce
¼ cup sugar
Pepper to taste

Cook asparagus in boiling water 6-7 minutes, or until tender and still bright green. Drain and rinse under cold water. Drain again. Arrange in 1 or 2 layers in oblong serving dish. Mix remaining ingredients and pour over asparagus, lifting asparagus so mixture penetrates to bottom. Sprinkle with pepper. Serve chilled. *May be marinated up to 36 hours ahead.*

Olive Gaines Arant

Cauliflower in Sour Cream

A good substitute for potatoes

Serves 6

1 large head cauliflower
½ cup sour cream
½ cup mayonnaise
1 teaspoon Worcestershire sauce
½ teaspoon salt
Pepper to taste
½ cup shredded sharp Cheddar cheese
½ cup chopped scallions

Trim cauliflower and separate into flowerets. Cook in boiling salted water for 5 mintues or until just tender. Drain and cool. Combine sour cream, mayonnaise, Worcestershire, salt and pepper. In a large bowl combine cauliflower, cheese, and scallions. Toss with sauce and refrigerate. Serve cold.

Virginia Cotten Hillhouse

Dutch Onion Rings

Serves 6

4 onions
½ cup sour cream
½ teaspoon salt
1 teaspoon celery seed
2 teaspoons lemon juice

Slice onions ¼-inch thick. Separate into rings and cover with boiling water for 2 minutes. Pour off and rinse with cold water in colander. Combine remaining ingredients. Mix with onion rings and chill. Delicious and pretty served on top of fresh sliced tomatoes and cucumbers in summer or well-drained marinated vegetables in winter. *Dressing may need to be doubled if served over other vegetables.*

Virginia Smith Shepherd

Cucumbers in Sour Cream

Serves 4

1 large cucumber, peeled and sliced
¾ teaspoon salt
Vinegar
½ cup sour cream
1 tablespoon sugar, optional
¼ teaspoon dillweed
Pepper to taste

Place cucumber slices in shallow dish and sprinkle with salt. Add enough vinegar to cover. Let stand about 30 minutes and drain well. Combine rest of ingredients and toss with cucumber. Chill several hours or overnight. *Great with sandwiches, tomato aspic or by itself.*

Tomato with Artichoke Heart Salad

Serves 5-6

Must be prepared ahead.

5 or 6 tomatoes, peeled
5 or 6 artichoke hearts, well drained
Salt
Pepper
Dill weed

Dressing

1 cup mayonnaise
½ cup sour cream
1 teaspoon curry powder
2 teaspoons lemon juice
2 spring onions, finely chopped
Dill weed for garnish

Peel tomatoes and cut out stem end. Rub tomato with salt, pepper, and dill. Drain upside down on plate for several hours in refrigerator. Place artichoke heart inside of tomato. Combine dressing ingredients a day or more ahead to blend seasonings. Serve dressing generously in and over tomato. Sprinkle dill on top. *Doubles easily for a crowd.*

Tish Preacher Long

Mushroom and Watercress Salad

Serves 4

3 bunches watercress, trimmed, washed, and dried
½ pound mushrooms, stems trimmed, washed, *dried*, and sliced

Dressing

⅔ cup vegetable or olive oil
1 clove garlic, minced
¼ cup wine vinegar
½ teaspoon dry mustard
1 teaspoon salt
½ teaspoon sugar
¼ teaspoon pepper

Combine mushrooms and watercress in bowl. Combine dressing ingredients in screw top jar or blender. Just before serving, add dressing and toss to coat lightly. *Spinach may be substituted if watercress is unavailable.*

Charlotte Bickley Maring

Marinated Curried Vegetable Salad

Prepare at least 24 hours ahead

Serves 8

1 (10 ounce) package frozen baby lima beans
1 (16 ounce) can French green beans, drained
1 (17 ounce) can Le Sueur baby English peas, drained
½ cup chopped celery
2 or 3 green onions and tops, chopped
¼ cup finely chopped green pepper
1 large pimiento, cut in thin strips (this is mainly for color—add more if desired)
1 tablespoon plus 1 teaspoon lemon juice
1 teaspoon Worcestershire sauce
⅓ cup sour cream
½ cup mayonnaise
½ teaspoon curry powder
Salt and pepper to taste
4-5 parsley sprigs
Lettuce
Cocktail tomatoes for garnish

Cook lima beans until just done and run cold water over them. Drain. Mix all ingredients together and marinate at least 24 hours before serving. Keep in refrigerator and stir occasionally. Serve on lettuce and garnish with halves of cocktail tomatoes.

Acky Jones McGriff

Marinated Vegetable Salad

Serves 20

1 bunch broccoli
1 head cauliflower
1 pound carrots
1 pound mushrooms
1-2 green peppers
2 small zucchini
4 stalks celery
Lettuce leaves

Cut all vegetables into bite-size pieces. Pour the marinade over them and chill overnight, stirring occasionally. Serve on crisp salad greens with a little marinade.

Marinade

¼ cup oil
1½ cups tarragon vinegar
2 cloves garlic, minced
1½ teaspoons prepared mustard
¼ cup olive oil
¼ cup sugar
1½ teaspoons salt
1 teaspoon tarragon leaves

Combine all ingredients and pour over vegetables. *Also good as an appetizer.*

Dee Foster King

Marinated Carrots

A delicious way to add color to your table

Serves 10

1 pound carrots, peeled and cut into matchstick pieces
½ cup cider vinegar
½ cup sugar
¼ cup salad oil
1 (2 ounce) jar diced pimientos
½ cup chopped green onions
½ cup diced green pepper

Steam carrots until tender but crunchy. Boil vinegar, sugar, and oil until sugar dissolves. Add other ingredients. Add cooked carrots to marinate and refrigerate, covered. *Will keep up to 1 week.*

Mary Phelps Mellen

Herbed Tomatoes

Serves 6

6 tomatoes, peeled and quartered
⅔ cup salad oil
¼ cup vinegar
¼ cup chopped fresh parsley or 2 tablespoons dried parsley
¼ cup chopped green onion
1 teaspoon salt
¼ teaspoon pepper
½ teaspoon marjoram
½ teaspoon thyme

Place tomatoes in a buttered 2-quart baking dish. Mix remaining ingredients and pour over tomatoes. Cover and refrigerate at least 8 hours, stirring a few times during the chilling period.

Rosemary Henning Gregory

Italian Pasta Salad

Serves 6

Take this on a picnic!

12 ounces uncooked spaghetti
1 medium zucchini, thinly sliced
¼ pound green beans, cut in ½-inch pieces
2 medium green onions, chopped
⅓ cup sliced black olives
1 cup cherry tomatoes, cut in halves
1 teaspoon salt
¼ cup grated Parmesan cheese
¼ cup white wine vinegar
⅓ cup salad oil
⅓ cup olive oil
2 tablespoons water
1 package Italian salad dressing mix

Break spaghetti in half. Cook spaghetti, drain, rinse with cold water, and toss with a small amount of vegetable oil. Cook zucchini and beans in a little water until just tender but still crisp and bright in color. Rinse in cold water to stop cooking. Drain well, and add to spaghetti along with onion, olives, tomatoes, salt and cheese. Beat together last 5 ingredients until well blended and toss lightly with spaghetti mixture. Refrigerate overnight in a sealed 2-quart container. *Beautiful served in a glass bowl.*

Sea Shell Island

Serves 6

2 cups (8 ounces) uncooked small shell macaroni
6 cups boiling water
1 teaspoon salt
1 tablespoon vegetable oil
½ cup Miracle Whip Salad Dressing
2 tablespoons sweet pickle liquid
1 tablespoon Dijon mustard
½ teaspoon prepared horseradish
½ teaspoon salt
White pepper to taste
½ cup sliced sweet gherkins
½ cup sliced celery
⅓ cup sliced radishes
3 green onions, thinly sliced
1 cucumber, cut in strips 1½ inches long
1 carrot, cut in strips 1½ inches long

Cook macaroni in boiling water with salt and oil until tender but still firm. Drain, rinse with cold water, and drain well. Cool. In large salad bowl, blend together salad dressing, pickle liquid, mustard, horseradish, salt and pepper. Add macaroni and rest of ingredients. Toss gently and chill.

Rice Salad Ceylon

May be prepared early in the day.

Serves 6

3 cups cooked rice
½ cup green pepper, cut in thin strips
1 (11 ounce) can mandarin oranges, drained
1 cup sliced celery
¼ cup seedless raisins
1 cup mayonnaise
1 teaspoon curry powder
Salt and white pepper to taste

Combine first 5 ingredients and toss lightly. Blend remaining ingredients and stir into rice mixture. Chill.

Artichoke Rice Salad

Serves 6-8

1 (6 ounce) package Uncle Ben's Chicken Vermicelli rice mix or Rice-A-Roni
2 (6 ounce) jars marinated artichoke hearts
¼-⅓ cup mayonnaise
¾ teaspoon curry powder, or less according to taste
2 green onions, chopped
½ green pepper, chopped
12 stuffed olives, sliced

Cook rice as directed. Cool. Drain artichokes, reserving liquid from 1 jar and slice in halves. Combine liquid with mayonnaise and curry powder. Mix all ingredients. Chill. Can make up to 2 days ahead.

Susie Hand Denson

Corn Salad

Serves 10-12

2 (12 ounce) cans Green Giant Shoe Peg Corn, drained
2 tomatoes, seeded, drained, and chopped but *not* peeled
1 bell pepper, seeded and chopped
1 purple onion, chopped
1 cucumber, peeled, seeded and chopped
½ cup sour cream
4 tablespoons mayonnaise
2 tablespoons white vinegar
½ teaspoon celery seed
½ teaspoon dry mustard
½ teaspoon black pepper
2 teaspoons salt

Mix all vegetables. Combine sour cream, mayonnaise, vinegar, and seasonings. Pour over vegetables. Cover and refrigerate overnight. Good with barbeque, hamburgers, or stuffed in a tomato. *Recipe can easily be doubled.* Use a box of cherry tomatoes, cut in half, in place of regular tomatoes.

Lucy Walter Burr

Salade d'Ete

Serves 4

2 cups fresh green beans, cooked until just tender
1 cup artichoke hearts, quartered
½ cup chopped green onion
1 medium cucumber, peeled, seeded, and chopped
1 medium tomato, peeled and chopped
1 teaspoon salt
½ teaspoon black pepper
4 tablespoon mayonnaise
1 teaspoon lime juice
½ teaspoon garlic salt

Combine beans, artichoke hearts, onion, cucumber, tomato, salt and pepper, and set aside. Mix mayonnaise, lime juice, and garlic salt. Toss with vegetable mixture. Chill for several hours to blend flavors. Serve on a bed of Bibb lettuce. *Recipe may be doubled and prepared up to 1 day ahead.*

Ann Abernethy Stephens

Layered Potato Salad

Serves 12-14

8 medium baking potatoes, boiled until just done
2½ cups mayonnaise
2 cups sour cream
1½ teaspoons horseradish
1 teaspoon celery seed
½ teaspoon salt
1 cup chopped fresh parsley
2 medium onions, finely chopped
Salt to taste

Peel and slice potatoes in ⅛-inch thick slices. Combine mayonnaise, sour cream, horseradish, celery seed, and salt and set aside. In another bowl, mix parsley and onion. In large serving bowl, arrange single layer of potato slices, salt *lightly*. Cover with layer of mayonnaise mixture, then layer of parsley/onion mixture. Continue layering, ending with parsley and onion. *Do not stir*. Cover and refrigerate at least 8 hours before serving. *Recipe can be doubled.*

Carole Cockrell Martin

Sour Cream Potato Salad

Serves 10-12

⅓ cup chopped chives
1 teaspoon salt
¼ teaspoon pepper
1 tablespoon chopped onion or to taste
¼ cup salad oil
¼ cup cider vinegar
7 cups warm potatoes, boiled, peeled, and sliced
½ cup chopped celery
½ cup cucumber, peeled, seeded, and diced
¾ cup sour cream
¾ cup mayonnaise

Combine chives, salt, pepper, onion, oil, and vinegar, and gently mix with warm potatoes. Chill. In another bowl mix remaining ingredients. Chill. Combine potato and sour cream mixture before serving.

Celeta Barnes Manley

Tossed Vegetable Salad

Must be prepared several hours ahead.

Serves 10

1 (10 ounce) package frozen peas, cooked until barely tender and drained
1 (10 ounce) package frozen baby lima beans, cooked until barely tender and drained
3 medium squash, sliced
½ cup thinly sliced green onion
½ cup thinly sliced celery
¼ cup chopped green pepper
1 teaspoon sugar
1 teaspoon salt
¼ teaspoon red pepper
1½ cups mayonnaise
½-1 head lettuce, shredded
Cherry tomatoes
6 slices bacon, cooked and crumbled

Mix the first 10 ingredients in a bowl. Cover and store in refrigerator for at least 4 hours, preferably overnight. Line salad bowl with lettuce. Add vegetable mixture. Garnish with cherry tomatoes and bacon crumbs. Toss before serving. This recipe is also good for individual salads, as the vegetable/mayonnaise mixture will keep well several days in the refrigerator. *If fresh squash is unavailable, 1 (10 ounce) package of frozen corn, cooked and drained, may be substituted.*

Wendy Johnson Rodde

Salade Fleurette

Better if made a day ahead; will keep several days.

Serves 6-8

1 large bunch broccoli
1 large cauliflower
1 sweet red onion, chopped

Dressing

1 cup mayonnaise
1 cup sour cream
2 tablespoons red wine vinegar
Garlic salt to taste
1 tablespoon sugar
1 teaspoon dill weed
Beau Monde seasoning to taste

Cut broccoli and cauliflower into flowerets. Use julienne blade of processor for stems. Combine dressing ingredients, onion, and processed stems with dressing. Chill overnight. *Cherry tomatoes are pretty served with this.*

Bertha Spencer Ringland

Easy Coleslaw

Serves 8-10

1 medium head cabbage, shredded
1 green pepper, chopped
1 very small onion, minced
2 tablespoons tarragon vinegar or 2 tablespoons regular vinegar plus ¼ teaspoon tarragon
2 tablespoons sugar
1 teaspoon prepared mustard
White pepper to taste
Salt to taste
1 teaspoon celery seed
½ cup mayonnaise

Stir all ingredients together and chill several hours or overnight. Taste again before serving for seasoning and mayonnaise.

Anne Hull-Ryde

Salade Nicoise

Serves 4

Vinaigrette dressing

½ cup oil
1 tablespoon minced parsley
1 teaspoon salt
1 teaspoon Dijon mustard
1 clove garlic, crushed
⅛ teaspoon pepper
3 tablespoons red wine vinegar

To prepare vinaigrette dressing, shake all ingredients together in a small jar.

Salad

6 small new potatoes, cooked and diced
1 package frozen French-style green beans, cooked and drained
1 head Boston or Bibb lettuce
1 (6½ ounce) can water packed white albacore tuna, drained
2 tomatoes, wedged
2 hard boiled eggs, quartered
Olives, if desired, green or ripe
1 small green pepper, thinly sliced in rings
1 small red onion, thinly sliced in rings
½ teaspoon salt
Fresh ground pepper

Toss potatoes with 1 tablespoon dressing; cover and chill. Arrange lettuce on large platter. Mound potatoes on platter, then arrange attractively with beans, tomatoes, eggs, olives, tuna, green pepper rings, and onion rings. Pour remaining dressing over all. Sprinkle with salt and pepper. Bring to table. Toss gently just before serving.

A whole meal! Delicious in hot weather. Serve with French bread.

Greek Layer Salad

Must be made and refrigerated at least 6 hours ahead of time.

½ large head Iceberg lettuce, cored and shredded
1 cup chopped parsley leaves
4 large eggs, hard cooked and chopped
½ teaspoon salt
Freshly ground black pepper
1 large green or red bell pepper, chopped
4 medium carrots, peeled and sliced thinly
1 (5¾ ounce) can colossal pitted olives, chopped
½ large head Iceberg lettuce, shredded
1 cup large radishes, trimmed and sliced
4 ounces Feta, chilled and crumbled
½ pound crisply cooked bacon, crumbled
2 small red onions, chopped

Layer ingredients as listed into a 2½-quart glass bowl.

Green Salad Dressing

2 cups mayonnaise
½ cup chopped parsley
1 teaspoon basil
1 teaspoon dill weed
1 tablespoon sugar, optional
½ cup sour cream

Blend all dressing ingredients and spoon half of it on top of salad and spread to seal. Top with a little reserved chopped parsley. Cover airtight with plastic wrap and refrigerate for 6 hours or more (up to 12 hours). Pass the rest of the dressing.

Allison Comer Murray

Tossed Sesame Salad

Serves 8-10

½ cup sesame seeds
1 tablespoon butter or margarine
¼ cup grated Parmesan cheese
1 (8 ounce) carton sour cream
½ cup mayonnaise
1 tablespoon red wine vinegar
1 tablespoon sugar
1 teaspoon salt
¼ teaspoon dill weed
1 clove garlic, minced
¼ cup chopped green pepper
½ cup diced cucumber
2 teaspoons minced onion
1 medium head Iceberg lettuce
1 medium head Romaine lettuce
1 medium tomato, cubed
Salt and pepper to taste

Sauté sesame seeds in butter until lightly browned. Remove from heat and add cheese, tossing lightly. In another bowl, blend sour cream, mayonnaise and vinegar until smooth. Add sugar, salt, dill weed, garlic, green pepper, cucumber, and onion and mix well. Tear lettuce into serving bowl. Add tomato. Sprinkle with salt and pepper and ¾ sesame mixture. Toss with dressing and garnish with rest of seeds.

Caesar Salad

To make at the table for a party, arrange ingredients in small bowls around the salad bowl containing lettuce. Put dressing in a small pitcher and let a guest do the honors.

Serves 6-8
Use about 1 cup greens per person

1½ cups French bread cubes (½-inch)
2 tablespoons butter
1 clove garlic, pressed
⅓ cup olive oil
2 tablespoons wine vinegar
½ teaspoon Dijon mustard
Juice of ½ lemon
Worcestershire to taste
1 egg at room temperature
1 large head Romaine lettuce
Freshly ground pepper to taste
6 anchovy fillets, chopped
¼ cup freshly grated Romano or Parmesan cheese

Sauté bread cubes in butter and garlic until nicely browned. Make dressing by combining oil, vinegar, mustard, lemon juice, and Worcestershire sauce. Drop egg into boiling water for 1 minute. Tear lettuce into salad bowl. Break the egg over the lettuce. Add dressing and rest of ingredients. Toss.

Cindy Campbell Brungart

Mung Bean Sprout Salad

For bean sprout lovers; very different, easy and delicious.

Serves 4

½ pound fresh mung bean sprouts
¼ cup scallions, chopped

Dressing

2 tablespoons soy sauce
1 tablespoon wine vinegar
1 teaspoon sugar
2 teaspoons sesame oil
2 teaspoons peanut oil

Mix dressing ingredients and set aside. Wash and drain mung bean sprouts. Plunge in boiling water for 1 minute, then immediately plunge in cold water. Chill bean sprouts in refrigerator, leaving them covered in water. When ready to serve, drain sprouts well and toss with scallions and dressing.

Salade de Champignons

Serves 4

½ pound fresh mushrooms, cleaned and sliced
2 green onions, tops and bottoms chopped
2 tablespoons lemon juice
⅓ cup salad oil or olive oil or mixture of two
¼ teaspoon salt
¼ teaspoon dry mustard
1½ teaspoons Worcestershire sauce
2 tablespoons chopped fresh parsley
Bibb or leaf lettuce, torn into bite-size pieces
5 slices bacon, fried crisply and crumbled

Lightly toss mushrooms, onions, and lemon juice. Blend the oil and spices together, add to mushrooms, and chill 4 hours or more. Tear lettuce and place on individual plates. Spoon on mushrooms and top with bacon. *Can top with chopped cashews instead of bacon.*

France-Inspired Salad

Serves 8

¾ pound fresh green beans (preferably tender young beans)
½ pound fresh mushrooms, chilled
1 (14 ounce) can hearts of palm, chilled
1 (7½ ounce) can artichoke bottoms, chilled
1 avocado, chilled
1 cup homemade olive oil mayonnaise
2 teaspoons tarragon
Salt to taste
Lettuce, optional

String the beans and French-cut in 2-inch pieces. Cook in boiling water about 6-8 minutes, as beans need to remain crisp. Chill. Wash and slice mushrooms. Wash hearts of palm and cut into bite-size pieces; remove any tough skins if necessary. Wash artichoke bottoms and cut into bite-size pieces. At serving time cut avocado into bite-size pieces. Combine all vegetables, mayonnaise, tarragon, and salt. Toss well. Serve with lettuce if desired.

Avocado Salad

2 envelopes plain gelatin
12 hard boiled eggs
2 large ripe avocados, mashed
2 tablespoons Accent
2 cups mayonnaise
4 tablespoons lemon juice
Salt to taste
4 drops Tabasco
2 tablespoons grated onion
½ cup finely chopped green pepper
½ cup chopped parsley
1 teaspoon curry powder
Red pepper to taste
2 drops green food coloring, optional

Soften gelatin in ½ cup cold water for 3 or 4 minutes then add ½ cup boiling water. Stir until dissolved and set aside. Oil a mold or Bundt pan and line the bottom with slices of egg. Chop the rest of the eggs and mix with remaining ingredients. Gently pour over eggs in mold and chill until firm. Keep covered with plastic wrap to prevent discoloration.

Crockett Radar Sellers

Zesty Congealed Asparagus

May be prepared 3 days ahead.

Serves 6-7

1 cup water
½ cup sugar
½ cup vinegar
½ teaspoon salt
Cayenne pepper to taste
Juice of 1 lemon
2 envelopes unflavored gelatin
½ cup cool water
½ cup chopped pecans
1 cup chopped celery
2 tablespoons grated onion
½ cup chopped stuffed olives
2 (14 ounce) cans asparagus, cut in 1-inch pieces
Mayonnaise
Sour cream

Combine first 6 ingredients and boil slowly for 2 minutes. Soften gelatin in cool water. Add to hot mixture and stir until dissolved. Cool slightly before adding remaining ingredients. Refrigerate until congealed. Serve on Bibb or Boston lettuce with dressing of ½ sour cream, ½ mayonnaise.

Pea Salad Toss

May be prepared 1 day ahead.

Serves 10-12

2 (10 ounce) packages frozen peas, thawed and dried
1 pound bacon, crisply fried and crumbled
6 hard boiled eggs, chopped
½ onion, chopped
2 cups mayonnaise
½-1 head lettuce, shredded, or lettuce cups
1 cup shredded Swiss cheese

Mix peas, bacon, eggs, onion, and mayonnaise. Chill. When ready to serve place on lettuce in individual salad bowls. Sprinkle with cheese. *This can also be made in a large bowl and tossed before serving, like a layered salad.*

Broccoli or Spinach Ring

Serves 8-10

2½ envelopes gelatin
½ cup cold water
2 (10 ounce) packages frozen broccoli spears or 1 (10 ounce) package frozen chopped spinach, thawed and drained
2 hard cooked eggs, chopped
1 cup mayonnaise
1 (10¾ ounce) can beef consommé, heated
3 tablespoons lemon juice
1 tablespoon Worcestershire sauce
¼ teaspoon Tabasco

Soak gelatin in cold water. Cook broccoli according to directions on package. Cool, drain, and chop finely. Add eggs and mayonnaise. Dissolve softened gelatin in heated consommé. Add seasonings and blend well. When gelatin mixture begins to set, add broccoli mixture, and pour in lightly oiled 1½-quart ring mold, or individual molds. Chill until firm. Unmold and serve with the following dressing.

Dressing

⅓ cup mayonnaise
¼ cup sour cream
1 tablespoon horseradish
1 tablespoon minced onion, optional

Mix ingredients together and serve as a dressing for the broccoli mold.

Variation: Add ½ pound bacon, cooked crisp and crumbled, to spinach ring and fill center with cherry tomatoes or marinated artichokes.

Dr. George P. Turner

Prize Winning Bloody Bullspic

This won a contest sponsored by the Birmingham News.

8-10 generous servings

2 (10½ ounce) cans Campbell's beef stock
2 bottles Mr. and Mrs. T. Bloody Mary mix
1 (17 ounce) can English peas, thoroughly drained
1 (8½ ounce) can artichoke hearts packed in water, thoroughly drained
1 cup diced green pepper
1 cup diced celery
½ cup various green herbs but NO TARRAGON (a mixture which might include any combination of chervil, thyme, onion, chives, parsley, and marjoram)
¼ cup Worcestershire sauce
Generous splash of Tabasco
Generous splash of cider vinegar
5 envelopes unflavored gelatin

Mix all ingredients together except 1 can of beef stock and gelatin. Bring remaining can of beef stock to a boil and dissolve gelatin in it, being sure that gelatin is completely dissolved. Add this to the rest of the mixture and stir carefully. Pour into a ring mold and congeal.

Garnish Sauce for Salad

1 pound leftover roast pork, beef, or veal, preferably medium rare
Sweet or dill pickle relish (your preference)
Mayonnaise
Hungarian paprika

Put meat through food chopper on coarse blade adding relish of your choice. Add enough mayonnaise to make it gooey since this is really a garnish-like sauce. Pour into center of mold and dust generously with Hungarian paprika. Serve with saltines as it needs a salty taste.

Carl Martin Hames

Hearty Congealed Gazpacho Salad

Serves 8

1½ tablespoons gelatin
¼ cup cool water
1½ cups V-8 juice
1 medium cucumber, peeled and chopped
1 green pepper, chopped
4 tomatoes, peeled and chopped
¼ cup chopped spring onions
¾ cup chopped celery
½ teaspoon Tabasco
1 teaspoon dillweed
1 teaspoon salt
Pepper to taste
1½ tablespoons lemon juice
1½ tablespoons salad vinegar
2 tablespoons olive oil for greasing mold
Mayonnaise
Sour cream
Chopped parsley for garnish

Optional additions: radishes, olives, artichoke hearts, hearts of palm, asparagus.

Soften gelatin in cool water. Heat juice in 3-quart pan; add gelatin and stir until dissolved. Cool slightly. Add chopped vegetables and seasonings and mix well. Pour olive oil in 6-cup mold and grease well. Add entire mixture and chill until molded. Serve with mixture of half mayonnaise, half sour cream, and chopped parsley.

Chicken Sour Cream Mold

Serves 8-10

2 envelopes plain gelatin
2½ cups chicken broth
2 tablespoons grated onion
1 teaspoon salt
Pepper to taste
1 (8 ounce) carton sour cream
1 cup mayonnaise
3 cups diced cooked chicken
½ cup slivered toasted almonds
½ cup sliced ripe olives

Soften gelatin in 1 cup chicken broth; stir over low heat until dissolved. Remove from heat. Stir in remaining chicken broth, onion, salt and pepper. Chill until slightly thickened. Blend sour cream and mayonnaise. Fold chicken, almonds, olives, and sour cream mixture into gelatin mixture. Put in 8-cup mold and chill until firm. To serve, unmold, and garnish with salad greens, parsley, sliced stuffed olives, or pimientos for color.

Ann McMorries Smith

Carousel Mandarin Chicken Salad

Serves 6

2-3 cups diced cooked chicken
1 cup diced celery
2 tablespoons lemon juice
1 tablespoon minced onion
1 teaspoon salt
⅓ cup mayonnaise
1 cup seedless green grapes
1 (11 ounce) can mandarin oranges, drained
½ cup slivered almonds, toasted
Leaf lettuce
Additional mandarin orange slices, optional

Combine chicken, celery, lemon juice, onion, and salt; chill well. Add mayonnaise, grapes, oranges, and almonds to chicken mixture; toss well. Taste for additional seasonings and mayonnaise. Serve on lettuce. Garnish with additional orange slices, if desired. *Cubed apples may be used if green grapes are unavailable.*

Broxie C. Stuckey
GORDO, ALABAMA

Curried Chicken Salad

Serves 6

2½ cups chicken, cooked and chopped
1 (8 ounce) can pineapple chunks, drained
¾ cup chopped celery
2 tablespoons chutney
¾ cup mayonnaise
1 teaspoon curry powder
2 small bananas, sliced
½ cup salted peanuts
½ cup flaked coconut
1 (11 ounce) can mandarin oranges, drained
Lettuce leaves

Combine first 6 ingredients. Add bananas and peanuts at last minute. Refrigerate. Garnish with oranges and coconut. Serve on lettuce leaves.

Shelly Gearheart Lindstrom

Avocado Crab Delight

Serves 8

½ stick butter
¼ cup flour
1 cup half-and-half and 1 cup milk or 2 cups milk
1 cup medium Cheddar cheese, grated
1 tablespoon grated onion
2 tablespoons dry vermouth or sauterne
1 teaspoon salt
¼ teaspoon white pepper
1 pound lump crabmeat
4 avocados, halved and sprinkled with lemon or lime juice
Buttered bread crumbs
Paprika for garnish

Preheat oven to 350°. Melt butter, add flour, stir with a wire whisk for 2 minutes over low heat. Combine cream and milk or just milk and whisk constantly until thickened. Add cheese and stir until melted. Add onion, wine, salt and pepper. Carefully toss in crabmeat to retain big chunks. Fill the 8 avocado halves with mixture. Top with bread crumbs and paprika. Bake for 15 minutes or until bubbly and slightly browned.

Joy Seals Magruder

Crabmeat Frederick

Hurricane Frederick's one good point was the abundance of crab in the lagoon, so this is dedicated to him.

Serves 4

2 cups lump crabmeat
2 eggs hard boiled and diced
⅓ cup mayonnaise
2 tablespoons Green Goddess salad dressing
Salt and pepper to taste
Juice of 1 lemon

Mix all together. May be increased to serve any number. For a variation, add chopped shrimp.

Richard J. Hydinger

Anything Goes Salad

Serves 8

1 tablespoon unflavored gelatin
½ cup cold water
½ cup boiling water
1 cup or 6 ounces any cubed meat or seafood, such as chicken, ham, turkey, shrimp, or water-packed white tuna
3 hard boiled eggs, grated
1 cup mayonnaise
Any combination of the following to make 1 cup: chopped carrots, celery, onion, green pepper, olives
2 tablespoons snipped parsley
½ teaspoon salt
1 teaspoon Worcestershire sauce
Pepper to taste
Lettuce

Soften gelatin in cold water; dissolve in boiling water. Add meat or seafood, eggs, mayonnaise, vegetables, and seasonings. Pour into 1½-quart ring mold or decorative mold. Refrigerate 6-8 hours before serving. Unmold and serve on a bed of lettuce.

Mary Elliott Woodrow

Holiday Tuna Mold

Serves 8

2 envelopes unflavored gelatin
¼ cup water
1 can cream of celery soup
1 (8 ounce) package cream cheese
¼ cup chopped onion
2 (6½ ounce) cans white tuna packed in water, drained
1 cup mayonnaise
¼ teaspoon Tabasco
Fresh parsley and pimiento for garnish

Sprinkle gelatin over ¼ cup water in a small bowl. In large saucepan, bring soup and ½ soup can of water to boil. Add gelatin and stir until completely dissolved. Remove from heat. Add cream cheese and stir until blended. Fold in onion, tuna, mayonnaise, and Tabasco. Pour into 6-cup mold. Chill for 4 hours. Garnish with parsley and pimiento. *A fish mold can be used with cucumber slices as scales.*

Debby Davis Denson

Cucumber Tuna Salad

Serves 4-6

½ cup mayonnaise
¼ cup sour cream
1 tablespoon lemon juice
½ teaspoon horseradish
1 teaspoon dried dill weed
3 tablespoons capers
⅛ teaspoon salt
1 small cucumber, peeled and cubed
2 (7 ounce) cans white tuna in springwater, drained
Lettuce

Combine first 7 ingredients. Mix in cucumber and tuna and chill several hours. Serve on bed of lettuce with sliced tomatoes or in an aspic ring. Top with a little mayonnaise and a sprinkle of paprika.

Suzanne Peavy King

Shrimp Mousse

Serves 10 as first course

1 pound cooked shrimp, minced (makes 4 cups)
1 cup minced celery
1 tablespoon minced onion
1 cup highly seasoned homemade mayonnaise
2 tablespoons lemon juice
2 packages unflavored gelatin
1 cup chicken stock
1 cup half-and-half
1 teaspoon salt or to taste
¼ teaspoon white pepper or to taste

Combine minced shrimp, celery, and onion with mayonnaise and lemon juice. Soak gelatin in ½ cup of the chicken stock for 5 minutes. Thoroughly dissolve over hot water, then add remaining stock and cream. Refrigerate gelatin until mixture thickens to the consistency of egg whites. Combine with shrimp mixture and season to taste (use plenty of salt and pepper, as the mousse will become more bland when chilled). Spoon into 5-ounce plastic cups and refrigerate. Unmold onto salad plate and surround with shredded lettuce. *Also good shaped in a large mold and served with crackers for cocktails.*

Elberta Gibbs Reid

Shrimp Melange

Serves 8

3 pounds medium shrimp
1 head cauliflower
¾ pound snow peas or 2 boxes frozen pea pods
Bibb lettuce

Shell and devein shrimp. Halve and drop in boiling water for 30 seconds. Drain and toss with ¼ cup of dressing while warm. Chill. Separate cauliflower into flowerets and cut flowerets into smaller pieces. Break off ends and remove strings from snow peas. Separately blanch cauliflower and snow peas in boiling, salted water for 1 minute. Drain and run under cold water. Toss each separately with ¼ cup of dressing and chill. Toss shrimp, cauliflower, and snow peas. Arrange on a platter of Bibb lettuce and pour on remainder of dressing.

Sherry Walnut Oil Dressing

⅓ cup sherry wine vinegar
2 tablespoons minced shallots
2 tablespoons minced parsley
Salt
Freshly ground pepper
⅔ cup walnut oil

Combine all dressing ingredients except walnut oil. Whisk walnut oil in slowly. Place in a jar and shake vigorously. Makes 1 cup.

Avocado and Shrimp Salad

May prepare a day ahead.

Serves 4

1-1½ cups cooked shrimp, chilled
1 cup ripe olives, sliced
1 cup thinly sliced mushrooms
⅓ cup minced celery
2 tablespoons minced green onion
2 avocados, halved
Alfalfa sprouts

Dressing

½ cup mayonnaise
2 tablespoons tarragon vinegar
1 tablespoon finely chopped parsley (or 1 teaspoon dried)
¼ teaspoon dill weed
¼ teaspoon salt
¼ teaspoon onion powder
1 tablespoon lemon juice
White pepper to taste

Combine shrimp, olives, mushrooms, celery, onion, and toss. Cover and refrigerate. Mix all dressing ingredients until smooth. Pour over salad and toss lightly. Cover and refrigerate several hours or overnight. Just before serving, prepare avocado, and fill each cavity with salad, mounding it high. Then sprinkle on alfalfa sprouts as desired. Serve on bed of lettuce. *Can serve in tomatoes instead of avocado, or just on crisp green lettuce leaves such as Bibb or leaf.*

Dorothy Rosamond Christian

Zippy Shrimp Salad

Prepare a day ahead.

Serves 4

2 cups mayonnaise
½ cup horseradish, cream-style or regular, drained
½ teaspoon Accent
2 teaspoons dry mustard
2 teaspoons lemon juice
½ teaspoon salt
1 pound shrimp, cooked, cleaned, and chilled
1 basket cherry tomatoes, cut in halves
1 (6 ounce) can sliced pitted black olives
1 (8 ounce) can sliced water chestnuts, coarsely chopped as desired
1-1½ cups sliced fresh mushrooms, briefly sautéed in a little butter
½ head cauliflower, cut into flowerets

Mix mayonnaise and seasonings. Add all other ingredients except cauliflower. Refrigerate at least overnight. Add cauliflower just before serving. Serve in lettuce cups or on shredded lettuce with asparagus. Adjust horseradish to taste.

Simply Sensational Shrimp Salad

All ingredients should be fresh.

Serves 6-8

1½-2 pounds fresh medium shrimp, boiled, cleaned, and cooled
1 large bunch fresh broccoli, washed
1 pound fresh mushrooms, sliced
1 large bunch green onions, sliced
1 (16 ounce) bottle Kraft Zesty Italian Dressing.
2 tablespoons wine vinegar

Cut small flowerets from broccoli stems. Place shrimp, broccoli flowerets, mushrooms, and onions in a large container with a sealed lid. May be prepared a day ahead up to this point. About an hour before serving, pour dressing and vinegar over shrimp mixture and shake well. Chill again and serve on a bed of lettuce.

Peggy Burgess Burdette

Crab Ring or Mold

Yield: 5½-cup mold

2 envelopes gelatin
½ cup cold water
1 pound lump crabmeat
1 cup chopped celery
2 tablespoons capers
2 cups mayonnaise
1 cup chopped green stuffed olives
2 tablespoons lemon juice
Pepper to taste
10 drops Tabasco
1 teaspoon finely chopped onion

Grease 5½-cup mold and set aside. Soak gelatin in ½ cup cold water for 15 minutes. Dissolve gelatin over hot water. Mix all other ingredients together. Add gelatin and place in mold. Refrigerate until mixture is well set. Unmold just before serving. *This can be made in individual molds and served for a luncheon as well.*

Laurie Candler Schobelock

Western Salad

Serves 6

1 pound ground round or chuck
1 (15 ounce) can kidney beans, drained
½ teaspoon salt
1 medium onion, chopped
2 tomatoes, chopped
1 head lettuce, chopped
1 cup shredded Cheddar cheese
1 cup Kraft Catalina dressing
Hot sauce to taste
1 (7 ounce) bag Nacho Doritos, crumbled
1 ripe avocado, sliced

Brown meat and drain well. Add beans and salt. Set aside to cool. Mix together chopped cold vegetables and cheese. Toss in dressing, hot sauce, meat mixture, and Doritos. Garnish with avocado. Serve immediately.

Henry Taliaferro

Steak Salad

2½ pounds beef tenderloin
1 (8 ounce) package mushrooms, sliced
½ cup chopped green onion
1 (8 ounce) can artichoke hearts
1 cup sliced celery
1 package Good Seasons Old Fashioned French Salad Dressing
1 teaspoon dill weed
1 pint cherry tomatoes
Green leafy and Iceberg lettuce

Cook whole tenderloin until medium rare. Let stand 1 hour or until cool, then slice into bite-sized strips. Prepare salad dressing according to package directions, adding dill weed. Marinate mushrooms, onions, artichoke hearts, and celery in dressing. Using large salad bowl, layer lettuces, tomatoes, marinated ingredients and meat; making 2 or more layers ending with meat. Pour remaining dressing over all. No need to toss just serve. *May be prepared ahead.*

Trudy Rogers Evans

Cold Beef Salad

Good use for leftover roast

Serves 6

2 tablespoons oil
1 pound mushrooms, sliced
2 tablespoons lemon juice
4 tablespoons olive oil
4 teaspoons red wine vinegar
1 medium clove of garlic, crushed
¼ teaspoon dry mustard
Pinch each of chervil, thyme, and basil
Salt and pepper to taste
1½ pounds flank steak, broiled and chilled or 3½-4 cups cooked beef cut in julienne strips
Lettuce leaves
1 tablespoon minced fresh parsley
3 tomatoes, quartered

Heat oil in large skillet. Add mushrooms, lemon juice, salt and pepper; cook just until mushrooms are tender. Set aside and cool. In large bowl beat olive oil, vinegar, garlic, mustard, herbs, salt and pepper. Add beef and mushrooms. Toss lightly to coat; arrange on bed of lettuce. Sprinkle with parsley and garnish with tomatoes.

Anna Eleanore Simmons

Fresh Fruit Bowl

Serves 6

2 peaches, sliced
1 cup blueberries
1 cup melon balls
1 cup sliced strawberries
1 cup seedless green grapes
3 tablespoons orange flavored liqueur or orange juice
⅔ cup sour cream
3 tablespoons packed brown sugar

Toss fruit with liqueur. Mix sour cream and brown sugar. Serve fruit mixture with sour cream dressing. Top with a sprinkle of additional brown sugar.

Cold Spiced Fruit Salad

Serves 15

2 unpeeled oranges, sliced in eighths and seeded
1 (20 ounce) can pineapple chunks
1 (16 ounce) can sliced peaches
1 (20 ounce) can pear chunks
1 (16 ounce) can apricot halves
1 cup sugar
½ cup plus 1 tablespoon vinegar
3 sticks cinnamon
5 whole cloves
1 (3 ounce) package cherry Jello

Cut orange slices in half. Place in saucepan and cover with water. Simmer until rind is tender. Drain and set aside. Drain canned fruit well, reserving all pineapple juice (about ¾ cup) and ½ of peach and apricot juice. Combine reserved juices, sugar, vinegar, cinnamon, cloves, and Jello. Simmer 30 minutes. Combine fruits except oranges in a 9-cup container. Pour hot juice over all. Add oranges. Refrigerate 24 hours. This does not congeal, but the Jello keeps the liquid from being too thin. Use this for brunch instead of hot fruit. Beautiful served in a large brandy snifter.

Marguerite Hanson Dunham

Frozen Cranberry Salad

This is an easy do-ahead salad to serve with turkey or chicken. It always brings compliments!

Serves 9-12

1 (16 ounce) can whole berry cranberry sauce
1 (8¼ ounce) can crushed unsweetened pineapple, drained
1 (8 ounce) carton sour cream
¼ cup confectioner's sugar, sifted

Mix all ingredients together and freeze in 8″ x 8″ pan. To serve, let stand about 15 minutes and cut into squares. Serve on a bed of lettuce.

Millymac Jenkins Shackelford

Mandarin Orange Salad

Serves 4

3¾ ounces slivered almonds
2 tablespoons sugar
1 (11 ounce) can mandarin oranges, drained
1 head Romaine lettuce, rinsed and well drained
½ cup chopped green onions, include tops
½ cup chopped celery

Dressing

¼ cup wine vinegar
1 tablespoon sugar
½ cup salad oil
2-3 drops Tabasco sauce
Salt and pepper to taste

To candy almonds: Place almonds in skillet, add sugar, and stir over moderate heat until sugar melts and coats almonds. This burns easily, so watch carefully. Cool. Mix together all dressing ingredients and chill. Combine all salad ingredients and toss with dressing just before serving.

Marti Knight
HOUSTON, TEXAS

Holiday Spirit Salad

Yield: 2 10-inch ring molds

2 (3 ounce) packages Jello; 2 raspberry, or 1 raspberry and 1 lemon or apricot
1 (20 ounce) Cross & Blackwell Mincemeat with Rum and Brandy
1 can whole berry cranberry sauce
1 can plain cranberry sauce
1 tablespoon lemon juice
1 cup pecans, optional
2 (11 ounce) cans mandarin oranges, drained
1 (8 ounce) package cream cheese, cut in wedges
Mayonnaise
Sour cream

Dissolve gelatin in 1½ cups boiling water. Stir in mincemeat, cranberry sauces, lemon juice, and nuts if desired. Slightly cool to thicken. When thickened, press mandarin orange wedges and wedges of cream cheese onto outside of mold to decorate. Congeal. Top with mixture of half mayonnaise and half sour cream.

Jean Rountree Cox

Lemon Cheese Mold

Yield: 1-quart mold

1 package unflavored gelatin
¼ cup cold water
½ boiling water
3 tablespoons sugar
6 ounces cream cheese
1 cup milk
1 (6 ounce) can frozen lemonade, thawed
1 quart fresh strawberries

Soften gelatin in cold water. Add boiling water and stir until dissolved. Cream sugar into cream cheese and slowly add milk. Add gelatin and lemonade to cream cheese mixture. Pour into 1-quart ring mold and refrigerate. Unmold and fill center with strawberries.

Red Cherry Salad

May be prepared 5 days ahead.

Serves 10

1 (16 ounce) can pitted tart red cherries
1 (20 ounce) can crushed pineapple in syrup
1 tablespoon lemon juice
¼ cup orange juice
¾ cup sugar
Salt to taste
1 (3 ounce) package raspberry Jello
1 package unflavored gelatin, softened in 2 teaspoons of water
1 cup chopped pecans
Mayonnaise
Sour cream

Drain cherries and pineapple, reserving the juice. Mix all juices with sugar and salt in a medium saucepan. Bring mixture to a boil over medium heat, stirring constantly to prevent sticking. Remove from heat and add Jello plus softened gelatin, stirring until dissolved. Fold in cherries, pineapple, and nuts. Pour into a 13″ x 9″ x 2″ pyrex dish or lightly oiled ring mold and chill. Garnish with a mixture of mayonnaise and sour cream.

Marjorie Tindall Clark

Naturally Good Congealed Fresh Fruit

Serves 10-12

1 pint strawberries, hulled
½ cup apple juice
1 teaspoon gelatin
1 package plus 1 teaspoon gelatin
2 cups unsweetened pineapple juice
4 cups other fruit:
2 or 3 oranges, sectioned and well drained
1 grapefruit, sectioned and well drained
2 (15 ounce) cans unsweetened pineapple chunks, well drained
¼ cup broken pecans

Arrange strawberries hull-side up in the bottom of a 6-cup ring mold. Soften 1 teaspoon gelatin in apple juice. Let stand 5 minutes. Dissolve over hot water. Pour around strawberries and refrigerate until set. Sprinkle remaining gelatin over ½ cup of the pineapple juice. Allow to stand 5-10 minutes. Dissolve over hot water, then mix into remaining pineapple juice. Mix fruit and nuts and arrange over fully congealed apple juice and strawberries in the mold. Pour the pineapple juice over this until mold is full. Refrigerate several hours or overnight until set. Serve with poppy seed dressing.

Elberta Gibbs Reid

Gourmet Blender Dressing

This is a very good, spicy dressing.

Yield: 3 cups

1⅓ cups oil
4 green onions with tops
½ cup tarragon vinegar
2 tablespoons minced garlic
½ teaspoon salt
2 teaspoons pepper
3 tablespoons parsley
1 teaspoon basil
1 teaspoon oregano
1 tablespoon plus 1 teaspoon anchovy paste
⅓ cup olives with pimientos
1 tablespoon capers
¼ cup Parmesan cheese
1 tablespoon plus 1 teaspoon lemon juice
1 teaspoon sugar

Mix all ingredients in blender. Use for tossed salads—a little goes a long way.

Roquefort Dressing

Yield: 3 cups

½ pound Roquefort cheese
2 hard boiled eggs, grated
1 medium onion, grated
2 cups mayonnaise (homemade is better)
3 tablespoons bourbon
Pepper to taste
NO SALT!

Crumble cheese and mix well with other ingredients. If the mixture appears too thick, thin with milk. Chill until ready to serve. *This is great on green salads, aspic, or mixed raw vegetable salads.*

Lucinda Leeth Grissom

Tomato French Dressing

Good on fresh fruit

Yield: 1½ pints

1 (10¾ ounce) can tomato soup
1 cup cooking oil
½ cup cider vinegar
2 tablespoons Worcestershire sauce
2 teaspoons dry mustard
2 tablespoons sugar
½ teaspoon salt
2 teaspoons black pepper
2 garlic cloves, whole

Mix all ingredients in a quart jar by shaking well. Refrigerate at least 6 hours before using. *Can be doubled.*

Millie Elmore Hulsey

Macadamia Nut Dressing for Fruit Salad

This is a cooked dressing.

Yield: 2½ cups

1 cup sugar
¾ cup light corn syrup
½ cup hot water
1 tablespoon grated orange peel
2 egg whites
¼ teaspoon vanilla
Salt to taste
¼ cup mayonnaise
½ cup Macadamia nuts, chopped (3.5 ounce jar)

Cook sugar, syrup, water, and orange peel until firm (248° on jelly thermometer). Beat egg whites slightly. Add sugar syrup in a thin stream while continuing to beat egg whites. Add vanilla and salt. Cool. Fold in mayonnaise and nuts.

Joy Seale Magruder

Fruit Salad Dressing

A cooked dressing that is different from poppy seed.

Yield: 2½ cups

½ cup sugar
1 teaspoon salt
3 tablespoons flour
½ teaspoon powdered ginger
2 eggs
¼ cup vinegar
1 cup pineapple juice
½ cup orange juice

Place all dry ingredients in saucepan. Add eggs and mix thoroughly. Add vinegar and fruit juices. Cook over low heat until thick and smooth, stirring constantly. Chill.

Dana Blair Davis

Delicious Spinach Salad Dressing

The longer it sits the better it gets.

Yield: 1½ cups

½ cup grated green onion
¼ cup vinegar
¼ cup sugar
1 tablespoon Worcestershire sauce
½ cup catsup
1 teaspoon salt
¼ teaspoon pepper
½ cup salad oil

Mix all ingredients. Pour in jar and refrigerate. Shake well before using. Serve with spinach, bean sprouts, water chestnuts, eggs, and bacon.

Jeanne Edwards Rogers

Poppy Seed Dressing

Yield: 4½ cups

1½ cups sugar
2 teaspoons dry mustard
1½ teaspoons salt
⅔ cup red wine vinegar
3 tablespoons onion juice
2 cups salad oil
1 tablespoon poppy seeds

Mix first 5 ingredients. Gradually add oil, beating constantly until thick. Add poppy seeds. Store in covered container in refrigerator.

Seasoned Mayonnaise

Good on smoked turkey sandwiches with slices of avocado.
Yield: 9 cups

1 quart mayonnaise
1 teaspoon salt
2 teaspoons pepper
2 tablespoons prepared mustard
4 tablespoons chopped parsley
4 tablespoons chopped celery tops
4 tablespoons chopped onion

Blend all ingredients in a blender or food processor until thoroughly mixed.

Marion Wainwright Kauffman

Sauce Louis

Yield: 3½ cups

1½ cups mayonnaise
½ cup whipping cream
2 tablespoons chives
½ cup chili sauce
2 tablespoons horseradish
4 teaspoons lemon juice
½-1 teaspoon salt
¼ teaspoon pepper
¾ teaspoon Worcestershire sauce
½ cup scallions
2 tablespoons chopped capers

In mixer, slowly add cream to mayonnaise until blended and smooth. Add all ingredients except scallions and capers. Mix remaining ingredients into sauce by hand.
Salad Suggestions: Lettuce, tomato, and hard boiled eggs; shrimp or crabmeat salad stuffed in tomato or avocado—make shrimp salad by mixing shrimp, onion, celery, and hard boiled eggs with sauce.

Delicious Tartar Sauce

Yield: 2 cups

1½ cups Hellman's or homemade mayonnaise
1 medium onion, finely chopped
1 large dill pickle, finely chopped
1 tablespoon dill pickle juice
2 tablespoons capers
1 tablespoon caper juice
6 stuffed olives, sliced and chopped, optional
Salt and pepper to taste

Mix all ingredients and serve with fish, fried shrimp, or scallops.

Acky Jones McGriff

Remoulade Sauce

Should be prepared 2-3 days ahead.

Yield: 2½ cups

½ cup finely chopped green or purple onions
½ cup finely chopped celery hearts
1 cup finely chopped fresh parsley
4 tablespoons creole mustard
½ teaspoon black pepper
½ teaspoon salt
3 tablespoons paprika
¼ teaspoon cayenne pepper
⅓ cup red wine vinegar
¾ cup good virgin olive oil

Place all ingredients in quart jar and shake well. Refrigerate. Shake well and serve on shrimp, salad greens, or avocados.

Ginger Heacock Stewart

White Cocktail Sauce for Shrimp

Also delicious on roast beef sandwiches

Yield: 1½ cups

1 cup mayonnaise
1 (5 ounce) jar Kraft's Cream Style Horseradish
¼ medium onion, grated
1 teaspoon lemon juice
1 garlic bud, finely chopped
Salt to taste

Mix all ingredients and refrigerate for several hours before using. *A delightful white cocktail sauce.*

Tish Preacher Long

Shrimp Cocktail Sauce

Yield: 1 cup

⅓ cup chili sauce
⅓ cup catsup
⅓ cup mayonnaise
2 tablespoons lemon juice
1 teaspoon dehydrated onion flakes
1 teaspoon celery seed
Tabasco to taste
1 teaspoon salt

Mix all ingredients with a spoon. Make a day or 2 ahead to allow flavors to blend. *Variation:* Add Worcestershire sauce or horseradish to taste.

Beverly Bradley Finch

Mexican Hot Sauce

Yield: 2 cups

1 (14½ ounce) can whole, peeled tomatoes
¼ cup chopped onion
1 jalapeño pepper, chopped
½ teaspoon garlic salt
½ teaspoon fresh chili powder
½ teaspoon Tabasco

Blend ingredients in blender or processor for 30 seconds. Use sparingly on tacos and tostadas. *This sauce is also good to spice up chili.*

Lou Bell Lanier

Marchand de Vin Sauce

A delicious sauce for beef or chicken

Yield: 2 cups

4 tablespoons clarified butter
⅓ cup minced mushrooms
⅓ cup minced shallots
½ cup minced onions
1 clove garlic, minced
½ cup minced ham
2 tablespoons flour
½ teaspoon salt
⅛ teaspoon pepper
Dash cayenne pepper
1 cup beef stock
½ cup red wine
½ stick butter

Clarify butter by heating until it foams, then skimming off foam. Pour the clear, yellow portion into a 9-inch skillet (it burns less easily) and sauté the minced ingredients. When onion is golden brown, add the flour, salt, pepper, and cayenne pepper. Brown flour well, stirring constantly over moderately low heat about 7-10 minutes. Bring stock and wine to a boil and add to flour mixture. Return to heat and stir until sauce simmers. Simmer over low heat, partially covered, for 30 minutes. Correct seasonings. *May be made ahead and refrigerated.* If too thick, add more stock. Gradually add an additional 4 tablespoons butter at serving time.

Elberta Gibbs Reid

Gail's Plum Sauce

1 medium onion, chopped
½ stick butter or margarine
1 (11 ounce) can pitted purple plums
1 (6 ounce) can frozen lemonade concentrate
⅓ cup chili sauce
1 teaspoon Worcestershire sauce
¼ cup soy sauce
1 teaspoon ginger
2 teaspoons prepared mustard

Sauté onion in butter, then put in blender with remaining ingredients. Blend until smooth. Put in skillet and simmer 20-30 minutes. Serve warm. Refrigerate if not used immediately. *Fantastic with duck!*

Marsha Gear Oliver

Butterfly Lamb Marinade

Serves 8

6-pound leg of lamb, boned and butterflied
⅓ cup ginger
⅓ cup olive oil
⅓ cup lemon juice
¼ onion, minced
1½ tablespoons honey
1 tablespoon coriander
1½ teaspoons garlic
1½ teaspoons salt
1 teaspoon cumin seed
⅛ teaspoon pepper
⅛ teaspoon red pepper

Blend all ingredients in blender 2 minutes. Marinate meat 10-12 hours. Cook on charcoal grill 17 minutes 1 side and 15 minutes on other side.

Jane Hill Head
PAST PRESIDENT

Big Rick's Barbeque Sauce

Yield: 5½ cups

1 (24 ounce) bottle catsup
½ cup butter
2 cups apple cider vinegar
Juice of 2 lemons
1 teaspoon salt
1 teaspoon black pepper
1 teaspoon sugar
1 teaspoon red pepper
1 teaspoon baking soda

In a saucepan, mix catsup, butter, vinegar, and lemon juice. Heat until butter is melted. Add remaining ingredients. *Delicious on ribs, chicken, or pork chops.*

Henry Taliaferro

White Barbeque Sauce for Chicken

Try this for a change from tomato barbeque sauce!

Yield: 1⅔ cups

¾ cup mayonnaise
⅓ cup lemon juice
⅓ cup vinegar
¼ cup sugar
2 teaspoons salt

Mix all ingredients well, but it is not necessary to get the sauce completely smooth. Use this sauce for chicken cooked in the oven as well as on the grill.

Helen Weber Smith

Mustard Sauce

Yield: 2 cups

½ cup brown sugar
½ cup mild vinegar (cider or wine)
¼ cup dry mustard
½ cup butter
3 egg yolks

Put all ingredients in top of double boiler and stir over medium heat until thickened. May be served hot with cocktail sausages or cold with ham or roast pork. *Keeps about 10 days.*

Kathryn Hallman Sweeney

ENTRÉES

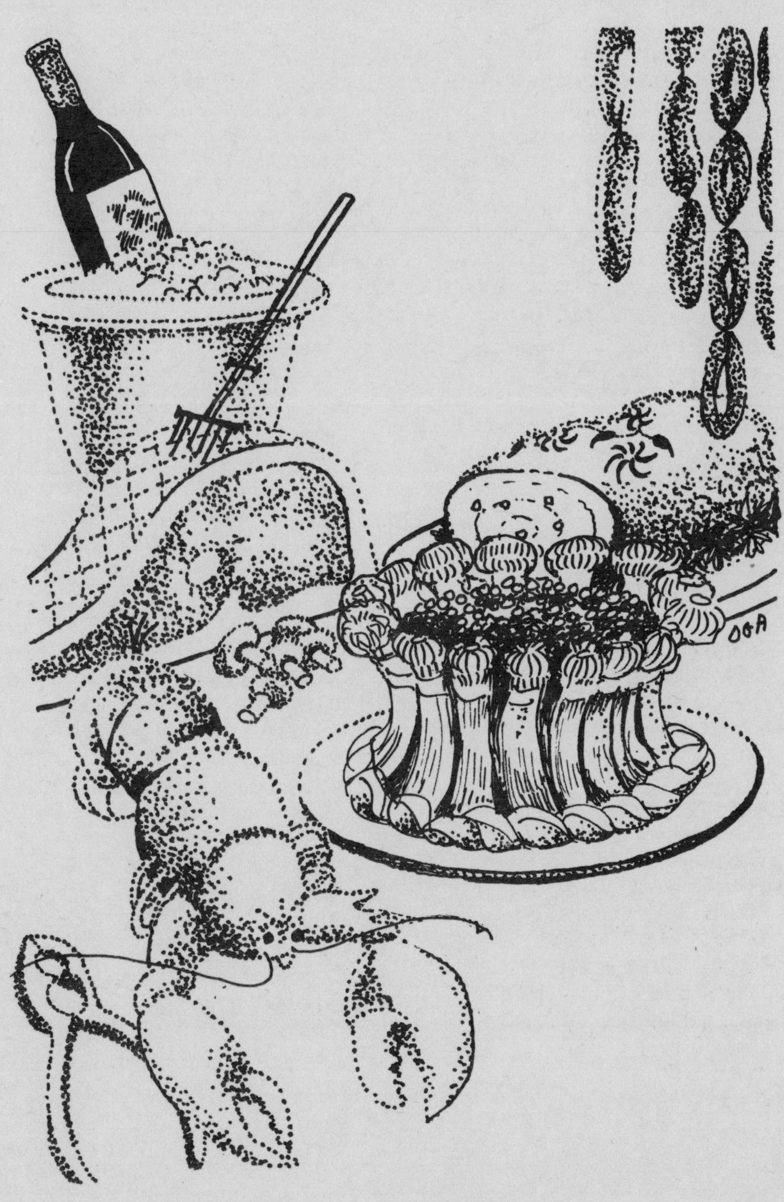

Entrées

Steak Capuchina

Serves 4

4 filet steaks (8 ounces each)
Garlic salt
Pepper
¼ cup brandy
4 teaspoons butter
4 (12 inch) squares aluminum foil
½ cup sliced natural almonds, toasted

Liver Sauce Almondine

1 medium onion
1 medium green pepper
1 clove garlic
½ cup olive oil
Tabasco to taste
Thyme to taste
1 bay leaf
2 tablespoons chopped parsley
¼ cup finely chopped almonds
½ cup Burgundy wine
1 teaspoon Kitchen Bouquet
¼ cup water
6 chicken livers

Preheat oven to 450°. Arrange steaks on platter. Sprinkle with seasonings. Pour brandy over steaks and marinate at room temperature. Meanwhile prepare Liver Sauce Almondine. Wipe steaks dry, reserving marinade. Sear steaks quickly in very hot, lightly greased skillet. Place 1 teaspoon butter in center of each square of foil. Place steaks on butter. Spoon ⅔ cup Liver Sauce Almondine over each steak. Top with 2 tablespoons sliced almonds. Wrap steaks tightly in foil, sealing edges well. Place on baking sheet. Bake to desired doneness: 8-10 minutes, medium; 20-25 minutes, well done. **Liver Sauce Almondine:** Finely chop onion, green pepper, garlic and half the olive oil in food processor. Sauté processed ingredients in remaining olive oil about 20 minutes, or until golden. Add Tabasco, thyme, bay leaf, parsley, and chopped almonds. Simmer about 10 minutes, stirring occasionally. Add wine, Kitchen Bouquet, water, and chicken livers. Simmer 20 minutes. Remove livers from sauce. Cool. Chop finely and return to sauce. Add brandy marinade. Simmer 5 minutes longer. Remove bay leaf.

Rose Anne Ferrante Waters

Steak au Poivre

Serves 2

1 teaspoon whole peppercorns
Steak for 2
1 tablespoon vegetable oil
1 tablespoon butter
Salt to taste

Put peppercorns between 2 clean pieces of cloth, crush with the bottom of a glass. Salt steak with 2 pinches of salt for each side. Push crushed peppercorns into the steak with the back of a spoon. On medium heat, melt butter and oil until it sizzles, put steak in the pan. Cook 3 minutes on each side. Remove steak and put on a platter.

Sauce

1 teaspoon cognac
1 tablespoon butter
2 tablespoons sour cream
Salt to taste

In saucepan add cognac, 1 tablespoon butter, sour cream, and salt to taste. Stir over medium heat for 1 minute. Pour over steak.

Cooking Instructions

Very rare steak—*3 minutes first side, 2 minutes second side*

Well done steak—*7 minutes each side*

Medium rare steak—*5 minutes each side*

Charlotte Blackwell Coleman

Steak Diane

Serves 6-8

6-8 steaks, individual filets, rib eyes, or sirloin steak cut into individual serving pieces
¼ cup oil
½ stick butter
1 cup chopped onions
3 tablespoons chili sauce
2 teaspoons mustard
½ teaspoon freshly ground pepper
6 tablespoons lemon juice
2 tablespoons Worcestershire sauce
½ cup brandy
Minced parsley for garnish

Heat oil in heavy skillet. Sauté steaks in oil over high heat until cooked to desired doneness. For medium rare, it will take 4-5 minutes. Remove to a warm platter. Add butter to pan and sauté onions in juices until limp. Add remaining ingredients except brandy and parsley. Return steaks to sauce. Coat in sauce and reheat. Warm brandy. Pour over steaks. Ignite and let flame burn off alcohol. When flame subsides, serve and garnish with parsley.

Cindy Campbell Brungart

Beef or Venison Tenderloin

2 tablespoons soy sauce
6 tablespoons olive oil
1 tablespoon seasoned salt
¼ teaspoon pepper
⅛ teaspoon garlic salt
4-6 slices bacon (more for large roast)
Beef or venison tenderloin, all fat and membrane removed

Combine first 5 ingredients and marinate meat at least 12 hours. Wrap tenderloin in bacon, securing with toothpicks, making sure meat is completely covered.
Bring meat to room temperature. Cook on grill over searing heat about 20 minutes or until still pink inside.

James William Gewin

Stuffed Rib Roast

Serves 8

½ cup long grain rice
¾ cup water
⅓ cup dry sherry
1 beef bouillon cube, crumbled
1 tablespoon curry powder
2 tablespoons snipped parsley
1 tablespoon water
1 clove garlic
½ teaspoon turmeric
⅛ teaspoon pepper
5-6 pound rolled beef rib roast

Preheat oven to 325°. Combine rice, ¾ cup water, sherry, and crumbled bouillon cube in a saucepan and bring to a boil. Reduce heat and simmer until rice is tender, about 15 minutes. Meanwhile, make a paste of curry powder, parsley, water, garlic, turmeric, and pepper. Cut strings on roast and carefully unroll. Rub meat with curry paste and spread rice mixture over it. Reroll and tie securely. Season with salt and pepper and insert a meat thermometer. Cook on rack in an open pan for 20-25 minutes per pound for medium rare or until meat thermometer reads 150°. Let stand 15 minutes before serving.

Caroline McCall Graves

Stuffed Flank Steak Florentine

May prepare ahead except for final cooking.

Serves 8

2 (1 pound each) pieces beef flank steak
1 egg, slightly beaten
1 (10 ounce) package frozen chopped spinach, cooked and drained
½ cup shredded sharp Cheddar cheese
½ teaspoon ground sage
Salt and pepper to taste
¾ cup soft bread crumbs (1 slice)
2 tablespoons cooking oil
1 (8 ounce) can tomato sauce
½ cup dry red wine
½ cup chopped onion
1 clove garlic, minced
2 tablespoons flour
¼ cup cold water

Preheat oven to 350°. Pound each steak with meat mallet to ¼-inch thick; set aside. Combine egg, spinach, cheese, sage, salt and pepper; stir in bread crumbs. Spread mixture over steaks. Starting from narrow side, roll up jelly-roll fashion and tie with string. In large skillet, brown steak rolls on all sides in oil. Place rolls in baking dish. Mix tomato sauce, wine, onion, and garlic: pour around rolls. Cover with foil; bake for 1½ hours or until meat is tender. Remove meat to platter and keep warm. Measure pan juices and add enough water to juices to equal 1¾ cups liquid. Pour into a 1-quart saucepan. Combine flour and ¼ cup cold water. Stir into pan juices; cook and stir over medium heat until thickened and bubbly. To serve meat, remove string, slice, and garnish with parsley. Pass sauce with meat roll.

Freida Walls Gammill

Steak/Bacon/Spinach Tournedos

Serves 4

1-1½ pounds flank steak
Instant non-seasoned meat tenderizer
½ pound bacon
1-2 (10 ounce) packages frozen spinach
1 teaspoon garlic salt
½ teaspoon freshly ground pepper
2 tablespoons snipped parsley
2 cups Hollandaise sauce
¼ teaspoon dried tarragon, crushed

Pound flank steak to even thickness, about ½-inch. Use meat tenderizer according to directions. Cook bacon until almost done, but not crisp. Cook spinach according to package directions and drain thoroughly. Sprinkle steak with garlic salt, pepper, and score steak diagonally, making diamond shaped cuts. Sprinkle with parsley and place bacon lengthwise on steak. Spread spinach on top of bacon as generously as desired. Roll up the steak starting at the narrow end. Skewer with toothpicks about 1 inch apart and cut in 1-inch slices with a sharp knife. Grill over medium coals about 15 minutes or cook in oven for about 30 minutes at 375° (depending on degree of doneness desired). Add tarragon to Hollandaise sauce and serve with steaks.

Mena Hazzard Mitchell
TAMPA, FLORIDA

Marinated Grilled Flank Steak

Serves 4-6

Juice of 1 lemon
½ cup soy sauce
¼ cup (or more) dry red wine
3 tablespoons vegetable oil
2 tablespoons Worcestershire sauce
1 large clove garlic, sliced
Pepper to taste
Chopped green onion or chives, optional
Chopped dill weed, optional
Celery seed, optional
1½-pound flank steak, trimmed

Mix all ingredients and marinate flank steak, turning occasionally, for 2-12 hours in refrigerator. Broil meat over hot coals for 5 minutes per side for rare meat. Slice meat on diagonal across the grain and serve.

Kay Blount Miles

Beef Stroganoff

Great use for leftover beef of any kind!

Serves 6-8

2 tablespoons olive oil
2 tablespoons butter
1 cup thinly sliced onions
1½ cups sliced, fresh mushrooms
4 cups cooked beef, sliced into strips
1 cup beef stock or consommé
1½ tablespoons flour
1 teaspoon salt
½ teaspoon carraway seeds, optional
2 cups sour cream

Heat oil and butter in skillet. Add onions and mushrooms and sauté until soft. Add beef and cook 2 minutes. Add consommé and cook 15 minutes. Mix flour, salt, and carraway seeds into sour cream. Add this to meat mixture in skillet. Cook slowly until thickened, *do not boil.* Serve over buttered egg noodles.

Genie Brooks Wilson

Beef Bourguignonne

Serves 6

1½ pounds round steak, cut into 3-4 inch strips
2 tablespoons cooking oil
2 tablespoons flour
1 (5 ounce) package brown and wild rice
1 (10½ ounce) can beef bouillon
2 tablespoons brandy
½ pound small white onions
½ pound fresh mushrooms, sliced
½ teaspoon salt

Brown beef strips well in oil, drain and leave in skillet. Sprinkle with flour and contents of rice seasoning packet; stir well. Stir in bouillon, brandy, and onions. Cover skillet and cook over low heat for 50 minutes or until meat is almost tender. Add mushrooms, cook 10 minutes longer. Meanwhile, cook rice according to directions, omitting seasoning packet and adding salt. Serve beef over rice.

Maude McDaniel McNiel
ATLANTA, GEORGIA

Hawaiian Strip Steak

Serves 6-8

½ teaspoon ginger
1 clove garlic, minced
2 tablespoons salad oil
1½-2 pounds round or sirloin steak, cut into narrow strips
1 package frozen French-style beans
1 onion, sliced in rings
½ cup julienne sliced carrots
2 small turnips, julienne sliced
2-4 tablespoons soy sauce
1 teaspoon salt

Combine ginger, garlic, and salad oil and sauté steak until red color is gone. Add green beans, onions, carrots, and turnips. Cover and let simmer for 10-12 minutes. Add soy sauce and salt. Serve over hot rice. *May substitute water chestnuts for the turnips, but you'll be sorry. Turnips add a nice flavor.*

Ann Cammack McCabe
MONTGOMERY, ALABAMA

Oriental Beef and Peppers

Serves 4

- **1 tablespoon cornstarch**
- **2 tablespoons soy sauce**
- **2 tablespoons oil**
- **1 clove garlic, crushed**
- **1 pound round steak, cut in thin strips**
- **1 teaspoon salt**
- **Pepper to taste**
- **1 cup soup stock or beef bouillon**
- **½ teaspoon finely chopped fresh ginger root**
- **1 cup green pepper sliced lengthwise**
- **2 cups cooked rice**

Mix cornstarch and soy sauce. Heat skillet and add oil and garlic. When garlic turns brown, remove. Add round steak and brown. Season with salt and pepper. Add soup stock and continue to cook one minute. Add cornstarch mixture, then add ginger and green peppers. Heat thoroughly and serve hot over rice. *Noodles may be substituted for rice.*

Babs Davies Quinn

Beef with Cauliflower and Snowpeas

- **2 tablespoons oil**
- **1 clove garlic**
- **1 pound beef, cut in small thin slices**
- **4 tablespoons chopped onion**
- **2 teaspoons salt**
- **½-1 cup bouillon**
- **1 medium cauliflower, broken in small pieces**
- **1 pound snowpeas**
- **2 tablespoons cornstarch**
- **1 teaspoon soy sauce**
- **¼-½ cup water**

Brown garlic in oil and remove. Add beef slices and sauté briefly. Add onions and salt. Remove. Add cauliflower to oil and toss for 1 minute. Add snowpeas and toss. Add bouillon and cook for 3-4 minutes, or until vegetables are tender yet crisp. Add mixture of cornstarch, soy sauce and water and stir constantly until thickened. *Your choice of brown bean sauce, Hoisin sauce, oyster sauce or fermented black beans may be added as well.*

Zucchini Lasagna

Serves 10

Meat sause

2 medium onions, chopped
1 green pepper, chopped
1 pound lean ground chuck
½ pound sausage
1 clove garlic, pressed
4 fresh tomatoes, chopped or 2 (16 ounce) cans, drained
1 (15 ounce) can tomato sauce
1 (6 ounce) can tomato paste
1 bay leaf
½ teaspoon thyme
1 teaspoon each oregano and basil
Salt and pepper

Sauté meat, sausage, onions, green pepper, and garlic until meat is browned and onion is clear. Drain thoroughly. Add all remaining ingredients and simmer 10 minutes, stirring occasionally.

Filling

6 medium zucchini
12 ounces Ricotta cheese
12 ounces cottage cheese
¼ cup parsley, chopped
½ cup Parmesan cheese
2 eggs beaten
12 ounces sliced Mozzarella cheese

Slice zucchini lengthwise ¼-inch thick. Arrange half the slices in baking dish. Combine Ricotta cheese, cottage cheese, parsley, Parmesan, eggs, and spread half of this mixture over the zucchini. Then spread on half the meat sauce and 6 of the Mozzarella slices. Repeat layers: zucchini, cheese mixture, meat sauce, and finally top with Mozzarella. If desired, sprinkle top with more Parmesan. Bake uncovered 40 minutes at 350°. To bake in microwave, cook about 15 minutes on a medium-high setting.

Debby Hull-Ryde Tanner

Italian Meatball and Sausage Sauce

Serves 10-12

3 garlic cloves, diced
2 tablespoons oil
2 pounds ground chuck
4 slices bread, blended into crumbs
2 cloves garlic, minced
2 teaspoons salt
2 teaspoons oregano
2 teaspoons dried basil
1 cup grated Romano cheese
2 eggs, lightly beaten
1 pound Italian sausage, sliced
2 (15-16 ounce) cans tomato sauce
2 (6 ounce) cans tomato paste
½ teaspoon salt
¼ teaspoon pepper
2 teaspoons dried basil
3 teaspoons oregano
¼ teaspoon garlic powder
⅛ teaspoon cayenne pepper
3 cups water
¼ teaspoon soda

Brown diced garlic in oil. Remove garlic. Mix the next 8 ingredients and form into balls. Brown meat balls in oil. Remove meat balls. Brown sausage and remove. Drain off some of the grease. Add the rest of the ingredients except the soda. Stir well. Add soda and stir. Simmer for 1 hour and then add sausage. Simmer 1 more hour and add meatballs. Simmer third hour and serve over your favorite pasta.

Connie Strickland Frazier

Bologneseauce for Spaghetti

Serves 4-6

3 tablespoons butter
4 slices bacon, chopped
1 large onion, finely chopped
1 medium carrot, finely chopped
1 stalk celery, finely chopped
2 tablespoons olive oil
⅓ pound ground beef
⅓ pound ground pork
⅓ pound ground veal
½ cup white wine
2 cups beef stock
3 tablespoons tomato paste
1 teaspoon oregano
Dash grated nutmeg
Salt and pepper to taste
1 cup whipping cream, optional
Grated Parmesan cheese

Melt butter in frying pan; sauté bacon, onion, carrot, and celery. Cook uncovered, stirring often for about 10 minutes. Set aside. Heat oil in another skillet and brown the meats, until mixture is crumbly. Pour off fat. Stir in wine over medium-high heat, letting most of it evaporate. Stir in beef stock, tomato paste, oregano, nutmeg, salt and pepper. Add reserved vegetables and bacon. Simmer mixture partially covered, until it has reduced to a thick sauce, about 40-60 minutes. Add all or some of the cream, but do not boil again. Serve sauce over pasta, topped with grated cheese.

Rose Anne Ferrante Waters

Bavarian Pot Roast

Serves 6

5 pounds boneless chuck roast
2 tablespoons bacon grease or shortening
2 cups water
1½ cups beer
1 cup tomato sauce
1 tablespoon vinegar
⅔ cup chopped onion
2 tablespoons sugar
2 teaspoons salt
1 teaspoon cinnamon
½ teaspoon ginger
½-2 cloves garlic
1 large bay leaf

In heavy kettle, brown meat on all sides in hot bacon grease. Combine remaining ingredients. Pour over meat. Simmer covered, about 3½ hours until tender. Thicken broth as desired.

Melanie Drake Parker

Stuffed Hamburgers

Serves 4

1 pound ground chuck
4 tablespoons sliced mushrooms
4 tablespoons chopped onion
Worcestershire sauce to taste
Salt and pepper to taste
8 slices bacon
¼ cup lemon juice
¼ cup Worcestershire sauce
½ cup soy sauce
¼ teaspoon coarsely ground black pepper

Divide ground chuck into 8 patties. Make a cavity in middle of 4 patties. Fill each with 1 tablespoon mushrooms and 1 tablespoon onions, dash of Worcestershire, salt and pepper. Cover with second patty. Pinch sides together and wrap with bacon. Secure with toothpicks. Marinate patties in remaining ingredients. Cook on hot grill 3 minutes on each side for rare.

Elsie Lupton Conzelman
PAST PRESIDENT

Firehouse Chili

Yield: 6-8 servings

2 tablespoons oil
1½ pounds ground chuck or very lean ground beef
1 large onion, chopped
1 clove garlic, crushed
1½ teaspoons salt or to taste
¼ teaspoon cayenne pepper
¼ teaspoon cumin
¼ teaspoon oregano
1½-2 tablespoons chili powder
2 (10 ounce) cans Rotel tomatoes, undrained
1 (8 ounce) can tomato sauce
2 (16 ounce) cans red kidney beans, undrained

Heat oil in large skillet. Add meat, stirring to break up, and cook until brown. Add onion, garlic, and cook until onion is limp. Drain grease and place in Dutch oven. Add salt, cayenne pepper, cumin, oregano, and chili powder. Break up tomatoes and add along with tomato sauce and kidney beans. Mix well and bring to simmer. Taste for seasonings and correct if necessary. Simmer ½ hour uncovered and 1½ hours covered. If mixture becomes too thick, add a little tomato juice. *This is a very hot chili so adjust seasonings to your taste.*

James Bailey Knight, Jr.

Anticuchos *(Peruvian Shish Kabobs)*

Must marinate overnight

Serves 8

2 pounds boneless sirloin, cut 1½-inch thick
1 cup tarragon vinegar
1½ teaspoons saffron
1 canned green chili pepper, drained and mashed
1 (28 ounce) jar ready-to-use mincemeat
3 cloves minced garlic
1 teaspoon salt
½ teaspoon pepper
½ cup water
2 large green peppers, cut into large chunks
2 large onions, cut into chunks
Cherry tomatoes
Oil for brushing

Cut steak into 1-inch cubes. In medium bowl, mix vinegar, saffron, chili pepper, mincemeat, garlic, salt, pepper, and water to make a marinade. Add meat, cover and refrigerate overnight. Stir occasionally. Next day, drain meat, reserving marinade. Alternate meat, chunks of green pepper, onions, and tomatoes onto skewers. Brush with oil. Broil 3 minutes on 1 side (can be cooked on grill outside). Baste with reserved marinade; turn skewers and baste again. Broil another 3 minutes, or until meat is of desired doneness.

Cynda Mathis Screws

Escalopes de Veau á la Normande

Serves 6

12 veal scallops
2 tablespoons butter
1 tablespoon oil
3 tablespoons shallots or green onions, minced
⅓ cup dry vermouth
⅔ cup brown stock or canned beef bouillon
1½ cups whipping cream
½ tablespoon cornstarch blended with 1 tablespoon water
Salt and pepper to taste
2 tablespoons butter and 1 tablespoon oil
½ pound sliced mushrooms
Parsley sprigs

Dry meat on paper towels. Sauté veal on both sides in butter and oil. Remove veal. Using the same pan, sauté onions slowly for 1 minute (do not brown). Deglaze pan with vermouth and bouillon. Boil liquid down rapidly to ½ cup. Add cream and cornstarch mixture to skillet and boil for 3-4 minutes until cream has reduced and thickened slightly. Take off heat and season with salt and pepper. In another skillet sauté mushrooms in oil and butter for 4-5 minutes and brown lightly. Salt and pepper mushrooms and veal and add to cream sauce. Baste scallops with sauce. You may prepare dish ahead to this point and leave partially covered. Just before serving, cover the skillet and bring to a simmer for 4-5 minutes. Just warm the veal, don't overcook it.

Susan Hill

Sautéed Veal Chops

Serves 6

6 thick veal chops, or 6 boneless chicken breasts
6 slices Mozzarella or Swiss cheese
Salt and pepper to taste
2 eggs, slightly beaten
1 stick butter
Flour
½ pound mushrooms, sliced and sautéed

Cut chops lengthwise but do not remove from the bone. Pound each side out until it is ¼ inch thick. Place 1 slice of cheese between the sides (in the "butterfly"), bring the sides together and seal them by pounding the edges. This closes the cheese inside the chop. Salt and pepper each side. Dip into the egg and dredge it in flour, then sauté over moderate heat until golden brown. This should not take over 10 minutes. *Do not overcook.* Add mushrooms and serve.

Lucy Chappell Tutwiler

Scallopini al Limone

Serves 4

8 thin slices of veal
1 teaspoon salt
Lemon pepper to taste
Worcestershire sauce to taste
1 cup fresh cracker crumbs, finely crushed
½ stick butter
4 thin lemon slices
Chopped parsley
¼ cup dry vermouth

Pound veal that has been salted, peppered, and lightly sprinkled with Worcestershire sauce. Pat cracker crumbs into meat. Melt butter in nonstick skillet and add lemon slices. Gently sauté veal slices, 4 or 5 minutes on each side. Remove to warm platter and garnish with fresh parsley. Add vermouth to skillet. Simmer until reduced by half and pour over veal.

Veal Stroganoff

Serves 4

1½ pounds boneless veal
1 tablespoon butter
1 tablespoon oil
1 small onion
½ pound mushrooms, sliced
1 tablespoon flour
⅓ cup chicken stock
¾ cup sour cream
½ teaspoon salt
⅛ teaspoon pepper

Preheat oven to 300°. Cut veal into cubes and brown it in oil and butter. Place meat in an ovenproof dish and sauté onion and mushrooms in remaining butter and oil. Remove from heat and stir in the flour, stock, sour cream, salt and pepper. Pour sauce over meat, cover and bake for 1 hour.

Betty Clark Brower

Marinated Lamb Chops

Serves 8

8 lamb rib chops, 1-inch thick
1 teaspoon grated lemon rind
⅓ cup lemon juice
3 tablespoons olive oil
¼ cup minced parsley
¾ teaspoon salt
1 teaspoon tarragon leaves
1 clove garlic, crushed

Trim fat from chops. In small bowl combine lemon rind, lemon juice, 2 tablespoons olive oil, parsley, salt, tarragon, and garlic. Pour over chops and marinate for at least 1 hour in tightly sealed bowl. Shake or turn container occasionally. Drain chops. Dry with paper towels. Pan-fry chops using remaining oil about 3-4 minutes each side or until done. Can heat remaining marinade and serve over chops. *Also may charcoal broil the chops.*

Susan Nabers Haskell

Barbequed Leg of Lamb

Serves 8

6-pound leg of lamb, boned and butterflied
½ teaspoon ground pepper
½ cup red wine vinegar
3 tablespoons olive oil
2 cloves garlic, minced
1 teaspoon rosemary
½ teaspoon salt
½ cup Dijon mustard
2 bay leaves, crumbled
½ teaspoon ginger
2 tablespoons soy sauce

Combine all ingredients and marinate lamb overnight, covered and refrigerated. Turn occasionally. Remove 1 hour before cooking. Put on grill fat side up. Cook 40-45 minutes. Turn and baste with marinade every 5 minutes (use medium-heat setting on gas grill).

Oven method: Preheat broiler and broil fat side up 6 inches from heat for 25 minutes on one side and 25 minutes on the other. Test for doneness. This will be rare.

Charlotte McCauley King
FLORENCE, ALABAMA

Grilled Marinated Leg of Lamb

Serves 8

Leg of lamb, boned and rolled
1 (10 ounce) jar Crosse and Blackwell Mint Sauce
Garlic buds sliced, to taste
Salt, pepper, dry mustard to taste
1 stick butter
1 clove garlic, crushed
1 tablespoon grated onion

Place garlic buds in folds of meat. Rub with salt, pepper, and dry mustard. Marinate lamb at least 4 hours (or overnight) in mint sauce. Heat together butter, garlic, and onion. Place on grill and baste often with warm sauce. Pink lamb will take about 35-45 minutes.

Helene Elkus

Crown Roast of Lamb with Sausage Stuffing

Serves 6-8

Crown Roast

6-7 pound crown roast
Salt
2 strips bacon
½ cup red wine
24 mushroom caps
2-3 tablespoons butter
1 teaspoon Dijon mustard
2 cups chicken stock, divided
1 tablespoon butter
Currant jelly
Fresh mint leaves, minced
Parsley

Have butcher prepare crown roast, cutting through the bones completely. Rub roast inside and out with salt. Lay bacon strips around lower sides. Cover the top inch of each bone with foil to prevent burning. Place on a roasting rack and fill center with stuffing. Cover stuffing with foil. Insert meat thermometer into thickest part of meat for most accurate roasting. Cook in a preheated 375° oven 1 hour and 20-25 minutes or until desired doneness, basting every 15 minutes with wine. Let stand 10-15 minutes before serving. Briefly sauté mushroom caps in butter. Season with salt, pepper and 1 tablespoon wine. Combine 1 tablespoon stock with mustard. Add remaining stock and wine, and reduce over high heat to 1½ cups. Remove fat from pan juices and add to sauce. Correct seasonings, adding 1 tablespoon butter just before serving. Serve the thin sauce and pass currant jelly mixed with fresh mint leaves. Garnish platter with mushrooms and parsley.

Sausage Stuffing

¾ cup chopped onions
1 clove garlic, mashed
½ cup chopped parsley
¼ cup chopped celery
2 cups bread crumbs (4-5 slices bread)
6 tablespoons butter
Large pinch of each:
Nutmeg
Summer savory
Thyme
¼ teaspoon sage
1 pound mild sausage
⅓ cup vermouth
Salt and pepper to taste

Process vegetables and bread in a food processor. Sauté vegetables lightly in butter. Add crumbs, seasonings, and sausage. Moisten with vermouth or dry white wine and cook over low heat about 10 minutes while stirring, scraping, and breaking sausage into small pieces with a spoon. Season with salt and pepper. This may be prepared a day or 2 in advance and kept refrigerated.

Elberta Gibbs Reid

Bahama Lamb Chops

Lamb chops
⅓ part Worcestershire sauce
⅓ part lemon juice
⅓ part gin

Make a marinade of all ingredients except lamb chops. Using hypodermic needle, inject lamb chops with the marinade and let sit in remaining marinade for 2-3 hours. Broil to desired doneness.

Gayle Whitney Chapman

John's Red Beans and Rice

Begin this dish the night before serving.

Serves 8-10

1 pound dried red beans
2 (12 ounce) packages Italian sausage, sliced thin
1 large onion, coarsely chopped
2 stalks celery, coarsely chopped
2 cloves garlic, minced
1 teaspoon pepper
2 bay leaves
½ teaspoon cumin
6 dashes Tabasco
Ham hock, optional
Salt to taste
Cooked rice

Wash beans in colander, culling out bad ones. Place beans in cooking pot. Add water to cover by 2 inches and let stand overnight. In the morning, add additional water to cover by 2 inches again. Brown sausage and add to beans. Sauté onion, celery, and garlic in sausage drippings. Add to beans. Add bay leaves, cumin, pepper, and Tabasco. Cook slowly for 8 hours, stirring from time to time to prevent sticking to bottom. Midway through cooking, taste for salt and pepper. *Ham hock may be added at this time if used.* Serve over rice.

John Weeks
BATON ROUGE, LOUISIANA

Layered Red Beans and Rice

Serves 6

2 medium onions, peeled and thinly sliced
2 medium green peppers, chopped
3 tablespoons butter
1 clove garlic, minced
2 (16 ounce) cans red kidney beans
1 cup burgundy
1 bay leaf
2 tablespoons tomato paste
¾ pound smoked sausage, thinly sliced
Salt and pepper to taste

Sauté onions and green pepper in butter for about 5 minutes. Stir in garlic and add beans. In another pan bring the wine and bay leaf to a boil. Add the tomato paste to hot wine and stir until dissolved. Arrange beans and sliced sausage in layers in a 9"x 13" casserole. Salt and pepper each layer. Remove bay leaf from the wine mixture and pour this over top of beans and sausage. Bake at 350° for 40-50 minutes. Serve over rice. *Amanda Neel Perry*

Barbequed Pork Roast

Serves 8-10

8-pound pork loin roast
Salt to taste
Pepper to taste

Barbeque Sauce

1½ cups catsup
¼ cup vinegar
1 cup brown sugar
¼ cup Worcestershire sauce
3 drops liquid smoke
½ teaspoon curry powder
6 drops Tabasco sauce
½ cup water
1 teaspoon onion salt
⅛ teaspoon black pepper
1 lemon, juice and rind

Preheat oven to 325°. Salt and pepper the roast and place it in small amount of water in a roasting pan. Cover and bake until it falls off the bone (3-4 hours). Cool and tear into shreds. Place in 9"x 12" pan. Cover with sauce and broil until it bubbles.

Barbeque Sauce

Mix all ingredients. Bring to a boil over medium heat, stirring frequently. Cook 20 minutes. Pour over roasted pork or chicken.

Carol Hollis Baumgartner

Don's Barbequed Ham

Serves 4

½ cup pineapple juice
¼ cup garlic vinegar
½ cup brown sugar
1 tablespoon dry mustard
2 ham steaks, ½-¾ inches thick

Combine pineapple juice, vinegar, brown sugar, and mustard. Marinate ham steaks for several hours. Grill over fire for about 10-15 minutes, turning and basting several times.

Jody Hamre

Barbeque Spareribs

Allow 1 pound spareribs per person. Mop sauce makes enough for 5-6 pounds of ribs.

Mop Sauce

1 teaspoon salt
1 teaspoon dry mustard
¾ teaspoon garlic powder
½ bay leaf
¾ teaspoon chili powder
½ teaspoon paprika
¼ teaspoon hot pepper sauce
½ cup Worcestershire sauce
¼ cup vinegar
2 cups beef stock or bouillon
¼ cup salad oil

Combine "mop" ingredients and let stand overnight. Combine dry seasonings and sprinkle on spareribs before cooking. Do not skimp. Cook spareribs as far from fire as possible, basting frequently. Should take ribs 1-1½ hours over gray ash fire. Dry seasonings keep indefinitely in airtight container. *"Mop" sauce can be frozen indefinitely.*

Dry Seasoning

3 tablespoons salt
3 tablespoons sugar
1½ teaspoons unsweetened lemonade powder
1¼ tablespoons pepper
1½ teaspoons paprika

L. B. J.'s White House Recipe

Superb Spareribs

For 3 pounds spareribs

Must be prepared ahead.

1 teaspoon salt
¼ teaspoon sugar
⅛ teaspoon each: turmeric, paprika, celery salt, and pepper

Combine ingredients and sprinkle over ribs.

Marinade

1 cup catsup
¾ cup water
½ cup chopped green pepper
½ cup minced onion
⅓ cup cider vinegar
¼ cup packed dark brown sugar
1 tablespoon Worcestershire sauce
1½ teaspoons minced garlic
1 teaspoon dry mustard
½ teaspoon Tabasco
½ teaspoon salt
¼ teaspoon basil
¼ teaspoon pepper

Combine ingredients and spoon over ribs and marinate overnight. Smoke about 4-6 hours.

Jane Hill Head
Past President

Roast Loin of Pork in Beer

Serves 8-10

5 pounds boneless pork loin roast, well tied
5 tablespoons shortening
8-10 large onions, chopped coarsely
Salt and pepper to taste
8 tablespoons bread crumbs
2 (12 ounce) cans beer
Bouquet garni thyme, bay leaf, parsley in cheese cloth

Preheat oven to 300°. Heat shortening in a skillet and brown meat on all sides. Remove roast. In same skillet, sauté onions until golden, stirring frequently. Line bottom of roasting pan or casserole with half of the onions. Insert meat thermometer and place meat over onions. Add rest of onions, sprinkle with salt, pepper, and bread crumbs. Pour in beer and add bouquet garni. Cover and bake 2-3 hours. Reduce heat if liquid starts to bubble hard. Use thermometer to tell when meat is done. Transfer to platter and slice thinly. Decorate with parsley. Serve juice with meat and put onions in a separate dish. Can half this recipe, using 3-pound roast, 1 can of beer, and 8 onions.

Tandy Sweeney Graves

Pork Roast with Sauterne Sauce

Serves 6

5-6 pound pork roast
1 teaspoon salt
¼ teaspoon pepper
1 cup sauterne
1 (12 ounce) jar red currant jelly
1 (10¾ ounce) can beef consommé

Preheat oven to 325°. Wipe roast with damp cloth. Trim excess fat. Season with salt and pepper and place in open roasting pan. Roast for 35-40 minutes per pound. About an hour and a half before meat is done, remove from oven and pour off fat. Heat sauterne and jelly in saucepan until blended and pour over meat. Continue cooking and baste frequently. Skim excess fat from sauce, stir in consommé, and serve gravy with roast.

Creagh McCollum Richardson

Chicken With Red Wine

Must be prepared 24 hours ahead.

Serves 4-6

1 cup red wine
¼ cup soy sauce
¼ cup salad oil
2 tablespoons water
1 clove garlic, minced
1 teaspoon ginger
¼ teaspoon oregano
1 tablespoon brown sugar
6 chicken breast halves

Mix all ingredients and marinate chicken for 24 hours in a baking dish covered with aluminum foil. Cook for 1-1½ hours in a 350° oven, uncovering for the last 15 minutes to brown. *Pan juices may be used for gravy.*

Patricia Patton Day

Sesame-Baked Chicken

Serves 8-10

3½-4 pounds chicken breasts
2 cups buttermilk
2 sticks butter, melted
½ teaspoon tarragon
3 tablespoons lemon juice
2 cups white bread crumbs
¼ cup parsley, minced
1 cup sesame seeds
3 teaspoons seasoned salt

Wash and dry chicken and place in a shallow dish. Pour buttermilk over chicken, cover tightly and refrigerate overnight. Next day, pour off buttermilk and dry chicken with paper towels. Melt the butter, add tarragon and lemon juice and place in a bowl. Combine bread crumbs, parsley, sesame seeds, and seasoned salt in another bowl. Dip chicken first in butter mixture and then in crumbs and arrange in baking dish. Spoon any remaining butter over the pieces. Cover tightly and refrigerate at least 1½ hours before baking. Bake uncovered at 350° for 45 minutes for boneless breasts or 1-1¼ hours for breasts with bones. Baste occasionally with pan drippings while cooking.

Harriet Hicks Gee

Chicken Dijon

Serves 6

6 chicken breasts, boned and skinned
1 (16 ounce) jar Dijon mustard
1 (16 ounce) carton sour cream
Seasoned bread crumbs
1 stick butter

Preheat oven to 400°. Rinse chicken and pat dry. Spread both sides liberally with mustard, dip in sour cream, and roll heavily in bread crumbs. Line baking dish with foil. Place chicken on top and dot with butter. Cover chicken with foil and bake for 30 minutes. Take off top layer of foil and bake at 450° for 15 minutes to brown.

Lucinda Leeth Grissom

Chicken Breasts and Hearts of Palm

Serves 6

6 boneless chicken breasts, skinned
6 hearts of palm
Seasoned salt to taste
Pepper to taste
Butter
Hollandaise sauce

Preheat oven to 400°. Wrap each chicken breast around a heart of palm. Sprinkle with seasoned salt and pepper and fasten with toothpicks. Place seam side down in buttered pyrex dish. Dot with butter. Bake for 25 minutes. Serve with Hollandaise sauce.

Beverly White Dunn
PAST PRESIDENT

Baked Chicken Supreme

Serves 8

4 chicken breasts, split and boned
½ cup flour
1 teaspoon salt
¼ teaspoon pepper
1 stick butter, divided
¼ cup minced green onions
¼ cup chicken broth
¾ cup dry white wine
½ pound fresh mushrooms, sliced
2 cups seedless grapes

Preheat oven to 350°. Coat chicken breast with flour seasoned with salt and pepper; brown in 5 tablespoons butter and remove. Arrange breasts close together in shallow pan. Add onions to pan drippings; cook until tender. Stir in chicken broth and wine; bring to boil and pour over chicken. Cover and bake for 1 hour or more until chicken is tender. Cook mushrooms in remaining 3 tablespoons of butter. Add to chicken along with grapes. Cover and continue to bake for 10 minutes or until grapes are just heated.

Patti Rajala Waxweiler

Fried Chicken

Serves 12

2 fryers, cut up or 24 legs and 12 thighs
3 eggs
3 cups milk
3 cups flour
2 teaspoons thyme
3 teaspoons basil
1¼ teaspoons garlic salt
1⅓ teaspoons oregano
1½ teaspcons onion salt
2 teaspoons sage
3 teaspoons Lawry's seasoned salt
⅛ teaspoon pepper
Oil for frying

Wash chicken, pat dry and soak in mixture of eggs and milk for 30 minutes. It will be necessary to put the chicken in 2 *large* containers in order for them to be fully covered with milk mixture. Combine dry ingredients, and pat onto chicken, 1 piece at a time, making sure chicken is well coated. Fry floured chicken. When it starts to brown, gently turn and cook until golden, about 30 minutes. Drain and serve.

Adele Williamson Scielzo

Lemon Chicken

Serves 6-8

6 boneless chicken breasts
1 stick butter
Salt and pepper to taste
2 tablespoons cooking sherry
2 tablespoons grated lemon rind
2 tablespoons lemon juice
1 cup whipping cream
¼ cup Parmesan cheese

Sauté chicken breasts in butter until light brown. Salt and pepper chicken to taste. Place in baking dish. Add sherry, lemon juice, and rind to butter. Cook over low heat and stir for 3-4 minutes, slowly blend cream into sauce, stirring constantly. Remove from heat and pour over chicken. Sprinkle cheese over chicken. Bake uncovered at 350° for 20-30 minutes.

Eleanor Bridges Griffin

Chicken in Currant Orange Sauce

Serves 6

½ cup currant jelly
¼ cup frozen orange juice concentrate, undiluted
2 teaspoons cornstarch
1 teaspoon dry mustard
Dash hot pepper sauce
½ cup flour
1 teaspoon salt
1 fryer (2½-3 pounds, cut up) or 5-6 breasts
Cooking oil

Combine jelly, orange juice, and ⅓ cup water. Cook and stir until smooth. Blend next 3 ingredients with 1 tablespoon cold water. Stir into jelly mixture and cook until thickened. Combine flour and salt in paper bag. Shake chicken pieces in bag and brown in hot oil. Drain off excess oil. Add sauce. Cover and simmer 45 minutes. Turn chicken occasionally. Serve with rice.

Jane Clark Wilson
JACKSON, MISSISSIPPI
Wife of General Louis H. Wilson, retired Commandant of the Marine Corps and the 1980 recipient of Birmingham's annual Distinguished National Veteran Award

Chicken Kiev

Serves 8

2 sticks butter
2 tablespoons chopped chives
2 tablespoons chopped parsley
1 clove garlic, minced
½ teaspoon salt
¼ teaspoon white pepper
8 chicken breast halves, skinned, boned, and flattened
Flour
1 egg, beaten
Saltine cracker crumbs

Mix butter, chives, parsley, garlic, salt and pepper. Form into 8 balls. Freeze. Place 1 butter ball in center of each chicken breast and roll so that butter is completely enclosed. Secure with toothpick. Dust with flour; brush with egg. Roll in cracker crumbs. Fry until golden in deep fat, about 10-15 minutes. *Good with long grain and wild rice.*

Company Favorite Chicken

May prepare 1 or 2 days ahead.

Serves 4

8 chicken breasts, skinned and boned
1 (8 ounce) package cream cheese
½ cup finely chopped green onion (onions and green stems)
Salt to taste
16 strips bacon

Cover chicken breasts with wax paper and pound thin. Divide cream cheese into 1-ounce balls and roll in chopped onion. Salt chicken and place onion-covered cream cheese ball in center of each piece. Wrap chicken around cheese and then wrap chicken in 2 strips bacon (1 strip at a time), so that cheese is completely sealed inside. Place on broiler pan. Place in oven so that chicken is 4 inches from broiler. Cook 8-10 minutes on each side. Serve immediately.

Becky Weeks Miller
ATLANTA, GEORGIA

Chicken Rhodo

Serves 8

8 chicken breasts

Marinade

Salt to taste
Freshly ground pepper to taste
4 sprigs chopped parsley or 1 tablespoon parsley flakes
2 teaspoons garlic salt or to taste
2 teaspoons lemon pepper
1 teaspoon oregano
Juice of 1 medium lemon
2 tablespoons Worcestershire sauce
½ cup Italian dressing

Place chicken in shallow dish. Combine marinade ingredients and pour over top. Let sit in refrigerator for 2 hours. Cook on outside grill and smoke for 30 minutes. Move chicken over coals and continue cooking until chicken is done, approximately 25-30 minutes more.

Warren St. John

Florentine Chicken

Serves 4

1 pound fresh spinach or 1 (10 ounce) package frozen spinach
3 tablespoons butter, divided
3 tablespoons flour
1 teaspoon Accent
1 teaspoon salt
Cayenne pepper to taste
1½ cups milk
½ cup shredded Swiss cheese
½ cup half-and-half
2 cups diced cooked chicken
⅓ cup dry bread crumbs

Cook spinach and drain well, finely chop and place in a 1½-quart casserole dish. Preheat broiler. Melt 2 tablespoons butter in a saucepan. Stir in flour, Accent, salt and pepper. Gradually add milk. Cook, stirring constantly, until mixture thickens and comes to a boil. Add cheese and cream and cook over low heat until cheese is melted. Remove from heat. Add chicken and pour mixture over spinach. Sprinkle with bread crumbs and dot with remaining butter. Place under broiler until lightly browned.

Jan Skinner Noojin

Glazed Chicken on the Grill

Serves 4

1 (8 ounce) can tomato sauce with onions
1 teaspoon garlic salt
½ cup orange juice
½ cup olive oil
¼ teaspoon coarsely ground black pepper
1½ teaspoons oregano
1 whole fryer, cut up or 8 pieces of chicken

Glaze

½ teaspoon dry hot mustard
¼ cup honey

Combine all ingredients except glaze and mix thoroughly. Marinate chicken at least 3 hours at room temperature. Turn every ½ hour. Remove chicken, reserving marinade. Cook chicken on grill until done, approximately 1 hour. While cooking, baste with marinade every 15 minutes, turning at same time. When chicken is done, brush with glaze and serve.

James E. Wilson

Stir-Fried Chicken

Serves 4

4 large chicken breasts, skinned and boned
1 tablespoon cornstarch
1 tablespoon sherry
1 tablespoon soy sauce
1 green pepper
¼ cup cashews
12 water chestnuts, sliced
¼ pound fresh mushrooms, chopped
½ teaspoon salt
4 tablespoons vegetable oil
2 tablespoons hoisin sauce, from the Chinese grocery store, optional

Slice chicken into pieces ½-inch wide. Toss chicken with cornstarch. Mix sherry and soy sauce and toss with chicken. Let stand ½ hour. Cut green pepper into squares. Roast cashews in oven until just golden brown. Stir-fry green pepper, water chestnuts, mushrooms, and salt in 1 tablespoon oil for 3 minutes. Remove from skillet. Add 3 tablespoons oil and stir-fry chicken for 3 minutes. Add hoisin sauce, vegetables, and cook 1 minute. Add cashews and stir to heat. Serve at once over rice or crisp Chinese noodles.

Catherine Caldwell Cabaniss

Oriental Chicken

Serves 6

6 chicken breasts, skinned, boned, and cut into strips
¼ cup soy sauce
1 onion, sliced
2 celery stalks, sliced diagonally
2 carrots, chopped
6 mushrooms, sliced
1 cup fresh snow pea pods (or 1 10 ounce package frozen)
3 tablespoons margarine
¾ cup chicken broth
2 tablespoons soy sauce
1 tablespoon cornstarch
Salt, pepper, MSG to taste
½ cup alfalfa sprouts

Marinate chicken in soy sauce for 1 hour and drain. Sauté first 5 vegetables in margarine for 2 minutes. They *must* stay crisp. Remove from skillet. Add chicken strips to skillet and cook until chicken turns white. Return vegetables to skillet and stir in remaining ingredients and heat thoroughly, about 3 minutes.

Emily Chenoweth Major

Additional vegetable suggestions:

Cabbage, celery, onion, mushrooms; bamboo shoots, celery, onion; green pepper, carrots, celery, bean sprouts; mushrooms, green peas; cauliflower, green peas; bamboo shoots, snow peas; potatoes, spinach.

Stuffed Chicken

Serves 8

4 fryers (3 pounds each), cut into quarters with backbones removed
8 ounces fresh mushrooms, sliced
1 green pepper, chopped
1 large white onion, chopped
2 tablespoons margarine
2 cups Uncle Ben's long grain and wild rice, cooked
½ cup pecans, toasted with butter and chopped
⅛ teaspoon sage
⅛ teaspoon garlic powder
1 teaspoon Worcestershire sauce
Salt and pepper to taste
1 stick butter, melted
¼ cup dry white wine
⅛ teaspoon thyme
⅛ teaspoon rosemary
⅛ teaspoon celery seed
1 teaspoon dried green onions

Wash and dry chicken and place in baking dish. Sauté mushrooms, pepper, and onion, in margarine and stir in rice. Add next 5 ingredients and season with salt and pepper. Carefully stuff this mixture under the skin of each chicken quarter, being careful not to pierce the skin. You may use toothpicks to seal the edges but remove them during cooking. Combine butter and wine. Using a pastry brush, baste chicken with wine butter mixture and sprinkle with herbs. Bake at 325° for 1½ hours, or until tender and brown on top, basting every 15 minutes. Any extra rice may be reheated and served as a side dish. This dish may be prepared the day before and reheated in 350° oven. Use pan juices to baste chicken while reheating.

Debby Hull-Ryde Tanner

Dilled Chicken

Delicious for summer entertaining

Serves 8

8 chicken breast halves
2 celery stalks, quartered
1 onion, quartered
Bay leaf
1 teaspoon salt
2 (8 ounce) packages cream cheese, softened
4 tablespoons mayonnaise
1 tablespoon lemon juice
Rind of ½ lemon
2 teaspoons dill weed
Slivered almonds

Simmer chicken in water seasoned with celery, onion, bay leaf, and salt. When tender, let cool in broth. Remove skin and bones carefully, keeping breasts intact. Blend cream cheese, mayonnaise, lemon juice, and rind in blender until it is well mixed and rind is finely chopped. Add dill weed. Mix gently. Cover breasts with sauce (not more than 1 or 2 hours before serving). Sprinkle with almonds and serve cold. May prepare chicken day or two ahead; do not prepare sauce until ready to serve.

Chicken Breasts with Artichoke Hearts

Serves 6

3 pounds chicken breasts, boned
1 teaspoon salt
½ teaspoon white pepper
½ teaspoon paprika
6 tablespoons butter, divided
1 (14 ounce) can artichoke hearts
½ pound sliced mushrooms
2 tablespoons flour
⅔ cup chicken broth
¼ teaspoon dried rosemary
3 tablespoons sherry

Sprinkle chicken breasts with salt, pepper, and paprika. Brown in 4 tablespoons butter. Remove to ovenproof casserole, arrange artichoke hearts between chicken pieces. Add remaining 2 tablespoons butter to drippings and sauté mushrooms. Sprinkle flour over mushrooms and cook, stirring, a few minutes. Stir in chicken broth, rosemary, and sherry. Cook a few minutes and then pour over the chicken and artichoke hearts. Bake in 375° oven for 40 minutes or until breasts are tender. Serve over brown and wild rice mixture.

Bettie Gray Cox

Cannelloni

Serves 8

2 cups finely chopped chicken

1 cup finely chopped ham

1½ cups freshly grated Parmesan cheese

⅓ cup plus 1 tablespoon butter

¼ pound mushrooms, finely chopped

¾ teaspoon salt

¼ teaspoon freshly ground black pepper

¼ teaspoon ground nutmeg

⅓ cup flour

3 cups milk

1 cup whipping cream

12 manicotti noodles or 25 cannelloni noodles

Mix chicken, ham, and 1 cup grated cheese. Melt 1 tablespoon butter in skillet. Add mushrooms and sauté for 1 minute, stirring constantly. Mix mushrooms, salt, pepper, and nutmeg into meat mixture. Melt remaining butter over low heat in large saucepan. Remove from heat and stir in flour. Add ½ cup milk, return pan to heat and gradually add remaining milk, stirring for 10 minutes or until sauce is very thick and smooth. Add cream, mix well and remove from heat. Combine ⅔ cup sauce with meat mixture. Cook cannelloni or manicotti noodles until tender. Stuff noodles with meat mixture. Arrange in a greased casserole dish. Top with sauce and sprinkle with remaining grated cheese. Bake at 350° for 30 minutes, or until bubbling and golden. *Freezes well.*

Judy Robinson Feagin

Al's Barbequed Duck

Serves 4

4 wild ducks (Mallards preferred)
4 cups V-8 juice
½ cup honey
¼ cup Worcestershire sauce
1 clove garlic, minced, or 1 medium onion, chopped
¼ teaspoon hot sauce
¼ teaspoon salt
¼ cup soy sauce

Start preparing sauce when you start the charcoal for the grill. Combine all ingredients except ducks in saucepan. Bring to boil and let simmer for 30 minutes. As you place ducks on grill, completely immerse the duck in sauce. Let ducks cook slowly for at least 1 hour, basting frequently with the sauce.

Note: These ducks are best served with either wild rice or garlic grits and fresh spinach salad.

Alan J. Dreher

Wild Duck in Orange Sauce

Serves 2

1 package brown gravy mix
¼ cup flour
1½ teaspoons salt
1 cup hot water
2 tablespoons orange marmalade
1 (6 ounce) can frozen orange juice, thawed
1 Brown-in-bag
1 large wild duck
Orange slices for garnish

Preheat oven to 350°. Place all ingredients except duck in bowl and mix well. Put mixture in oven bag with duck and close bag. Place bag in roasting pan and slit the top of the bag. Bake for 2 hours. Gravy can be used over wild rice. Serve garnished with orange slices.

Note: Duck is better if soaked overnight in salt water to remove game taste.

Phoebe Donald Robinson

Duck with Cherries and Brandy

Serves 4

5-6 pound duck
¼ teaspoon freshly ground pepper
2 teaspoons salt
¾ cup sliced carrots
1 medium onion, sliced
1 teaspoon thyme
3 tablespoons butter
1½ cups cherry brandy
2 tablespoons arrowroot or cornstarch
1 cup chicken broth
3 tablespoons vinegar
4 tablespoons sugar
½ cup cherry liqueur
1 (17 ounce) can pitted black cherries, drained

Preheat oven to 400°. Wash and dry duck. Rub with salt and pepper inside and out. Place duck in roasting pan, dot with butter. Add carrots and onions to pan with thyme. Roast 30 minutes and reduce heat to 350° and roast 1½ hours longer or until tender, basting occasionally. Transfer duck to heated platter. Discard vegetables and skim the fat. Add cherry brandy to pan, scraping the bottom for brown particles, and then pour sauce in saucepan. Mix arrowroot with the chicken broth, then stir into saucepan. Cook over low heat, stirring constantly, until thickened. Cook the vinegar and sugar until caramel colored. Stir a little of the brandy sauce into the sugar mixture. Then return all to saucepan. Add ½ cup cherry liqueur. Add cherries and heat for 2-3 minutes. Taste for seasonings. Arrange the cherries around the carved duck and pour sauce over all.

Caroline McCall Graves

Roast Duck and Wild Rice

Serves 2-4

5-6 pounds dressed duck
½ cup brandy or red wine, divided
1 teaspoon salt
¼ teaspoon pepper
Flour
1 apple, chopped
1 stalk celery, chopped
1 small yellow onion, chopped
½ stick butter, melted
1 (7 ounce) box wild rice
1 teaspoon salt
½ cup toasted pecan pieces
2 tablespoons butter or margarine

Wash and dry duck. Rinse cavity with ¼ cup brandy or wine. Sprinkle with salt, pepper, and flour. Fill cavity with apple, celery, and onion. Brush generously with butter. Place on large piece of heavy foil and pour ¼ cup wine over it. Wrap closely. Bake in oblong pyrex dish for 3-4 hours at 325°. Meanwhile, cook rice according to package directions. Add pecans and butter right before serving.

Laura Dee Wood

Dove on the Grill

Dove (allow at least 2 per person)
Salt, pepper, and Worcestershire sauce to taste
Bacon (½ slice per bird)

Sprinkle dove with salt, pepper, and Worcestershire. Wrap each dove in bacon. Secure with toothpick if necessary. Cook over a medium fire until done, about 20-30 minutes. Turn occasionally.

Variation: Wrap half a strip of bacon around a water chestnut and boneless dove breast. Season lemon butter with Worcestershire sauce and baste frequently. Cook on grill or broil until bacon is done.

Michael Goodrich

Doves in Red Wine Sauce

Serves 4

4 tablespoons butter
1 onion, chopped
16 dove breasts
1 teaspoon salt
1 teaspoon pepper
2 teaspoons parsley
2 teaspoons Worcestershire sauce
¼ teaspoon thyme
½ cup red wine
1 cup beef bouillon
2 tablespoons flour
2 tablespoons softened butter

Melt butter and sauté onions. Salt and pepper dove breasts and brown both sides. Add parsley, Worcestershire, and thyme. Reduce heat to simmer. Arrange breasts so meat side is up. Add wine and reduce to half. Add bouillon. Cover and cook 45 minutes or until tender. Remove dove from skillet. Mix flour and softened butter to form a roux. Add to sauce in skillet to thicken. Arrange breasts on platter and pour sauce over them.

Geny Davis Duffey

Dove Dinner

Serves 6

18 dove breasts, cleaned
Salt and pepper to taste
¾ stick butter
1½ cups dry white wine
½ cup chopped celery
1 (12 ounce) can mushrooms
½ cup sour cream

Salt and pepper birds. Brown in butter. Add wine, celery, and mushrooms (not drained). Cover and simmer until tender, approximately 2 hours. When birds are done, remove from skillet and set aside. Add sour cream to gravy in pan. Serve over game on brown rice.

Kathy Bushnell Miller

Quail á la Ben and Toots

Serves 4-5

10 quail (cleaned and washed thoroughly)
Salt and pepper to taste
Meat tenderizer to taste
1½ sticks butter
Paprika
8 tablespoons flour
¼ teaspoon cayenne pepper
2 (10¾ ounce) cans chicken broth
1½ cups sauterne

Preheat oven to 400°. Place birds breast side up in greased baking dish. Salt and pepper to taste. Sprinkle with meat tenderizer. Dot with ½ stick butter. Sprinkle with paprika. Place in oven and bake until brown. Place flour and 1 stick butter in Dutch oven and heat without browning. Add cayenne pepper and chicken broth. Blend well. Remove from heat. Add sauterne. Place browned birds in Dutch oven with sauce. Simmer for 35-40 minutes.

Patty Strain Ringland

Heavenly Sole

Serves 6-8

2 pounds sole or other skinless fillets
2 tablespoons lemon juice
½ cup grated Parmesan cheese
½ stick butter, softened
½-⅔ cup mayonnaise
3 tablespoons chopped green onion
¼ teaspoon salt
Tabasco to taste, optional
Parsley, optional
Garlic salt, optional

Place fish in single layer in flat baking dish. Brush with lemon juice and let stand 10 minutes. Combine remaining ingredients. Broil fish about 4 inches from heat for 6-8 minutes, until fish flakes easily. If desired, may pour off lemon juice. Remove from heat and spread cheese mixture over fish. Broil for 2-3 minutes.

Marti Knight
HOUSTON, TEXAS

Poached Sole with Mushroom Sauce

Serves 6

Sauce

1 chicken bouillon cube
½ cup fish stock
3 tablespoons butter or margarine
3 tablespoons flour
½ cup milk
2 tablespoons sherry
½ teaspoon salt
¼ teaspoon pepper
½ cup fresh mushrooms, sautéed or 4 ounces canned mushrooms drained
6 fresh cooked shrimp, chopped
3 artichoke hearts, chopped
Parsley sprigs for garnish
Paprika

Dissolve bouillon in the fish stock. Melt butter in medium saucepan. Add flour, mix thoroughly, until smooth and bubbly. Remove from heat. Add milk and fish stock mixture. Stir constantly over medium heat until sauce thickens and then boils 1 minute. Add sherry, salt, pepper, mushrooms, artichokes, and shrimp. Heat through.

Sole

6 sole fillets
1 slice onion
3 lemon slices
1 bay leaf
3 sprigs parsley (or 1 teaspoon dried chopped)
3 or 4 turns of fresh ground black pepper
1 teaspoon salt

Preheat oven to 350°. Fold sole fillets in half and place in a 2-quart casserole. Place all other ingredients on top. Fill casserole with 1½ inches water or enough to cover fish. Cover with aluminum foil and bake 10 minutes. Remove from oven and pour off ½ cup of fish stock for sauce. Cover and return to oven for no more than 10 more minutes. Remove from the oven. The fish is better if not overcooked. To serve, remove sole from casserole with a spatula and place on a warm platter. Spoon sauce over all. Add parsley sprigs and small amount of paprika. *Can be doubled easily.*

Patricia Jenkins Noble

Cashiers Valley Stuffed Trout

Serves 4

4 trout, cleaned, 10 ounces or 10-12 inches

Stuffing

2 tablespoons butter
1½ tablespoons flour
½-¾ cup white wine
¼ cup chopped green onions
¼ cup chopped mushrooms
¼ teaspoon thyme
¼ teaspoon basil
¼ teaspoon dill
⅛ teaspoon crushed bay leaf
Salt and pepper to taste

Make a roux with butter, flour, and wine. Should be quite thick. Then add all other ingredients and stuff each trout cavity. Place each trout individually on a piece of greased, heavy-duty aluminum foil. Fold foil together at the top, leaving a lot of space inside around trout. Place foil packets on charcoal grill, filled with grey coals. Cover grill partially and cook about 20 minutes. Check 1 package at that time. *Trout meat should be white.*

Sara Jennings Eason
CASHIERS, NORTH CAROLINA

Snapper Fillets

Serves 6

2-4 pounds snapper fillets
1 (10¾ ounce) can cream of shrimp soup
3 tablespoons sherry
¼ teaspoon salt
¼ teaspoon white pepper
¼ teaspoon basil
1 cup Parmesan cheese

Place fish fillets in bottom of greased baking dish in one layer. Mix soup with sherry, salt, pepper, and basil. Spread this over fish fillets. Sprinkle Parmesan cheese over top. Bake at 350° for 20-30 minutes until fish flakes. Garnish with lemon wedges and parsley.

Libby Forman Norwood
ROCKVILLE, MARYLAND

Red Snapper Vera Cruz

This spicy sauce is also for chicken.

Serves 4-5

2 pounds red snapper or other fish fillets
¼ cup lime juice
2 onions, chopped
2 cloves garlic, minced
2-3 tablespoons oil
2 pimientos, sliced lengthwise
2 chilies or jalapeños, or 1 green pepper, sliced
1 tablespoon capers
12 pitted green olives
1½ tablespoons dry sherry
¼ cup wine vinegar
½ teaspoon chili powder
½ teaspoon oregano
1 piece cinnamon bark or ⅛ teaspoon ground cinnamon
⅛ teaspoon cloves
2 sprigs parsley
2 cups tomato purée

Preheat oven to 350° Pour lime juice over fish and let stand while you make the sauce. Sauté the onions and garlic in the oil. Then, add remaining ingredients except fish. Cook 15 minutes to thicken. Place fish in casserole and pour sauce over it. Cook covered for 20-30 minutes. Check to see that it does not stick or burn. Garnish with additional limes.
Menu Suggestion: start with a cup of consommé, then serve fish with Mexican fried or brown rice, crusty rolls or tortillas and red wine. Wonderful flavor. Don't let the number of ingredients scare you—it's easy!

Gail Andrews Trechsel

Beer Batter for Fish

1 cup Bisquick
½ teaspoon salt
1 egg
½ cup beer
2-3 tablespoons Bisquick
Fish fillets or shrimp

Combine batter ingredients. Wash and pat dry fish or shrimp. Sprinkle with 2-3 tablespoons Bisquick. Dip into batter. Drop into deep fat. Brown quickly. Drain on paper towels. Serve immediately. *Deliciously crisp and not greasy!*

Dorothy Jarrell Estes

Fish Quenelles with Nantua Sauce

Quenelles are fish dumplings made in France usually with pike, a fish that is almost unobtainable, and they are served in a delicious sauce called Sauce Nantua. This simplified Quenelle would be an insult to Alexandre Dumaine at the Hotel Cote D'Or where I first ate them in the early 60's, but this methodology I worked out makes them possible.

Serves 6

Quenelle Paste

1 pound pike or white fish ***(skin, clean, and bone—save head for stock)***
1 cup hot milk
1 cup white bread crumbs
1 teaspoon salt
⅛ teaspoon white pepper
1/16 teaspoon ground nutmeg
2 sticks butter
4 eggs

Cut the fish into pieces. Heat the milk and combine with the remaining ingredients in a food processor. Process until smooth and allow the mixture to stand for at least 2 hours but no more than overnight.

Stock

1 fish head (reserved)
1 carrot
1 stalk celery
1 onion
½ cup dry vermouth
1 cup water

Combine stock ingredients and bring to a boil. Simmer 10 minutes and strain, discarding all but the liquid.

Cooking: Shape the quenelle mixture into small balls and place them in a Teflon or buttered skillet. Pour the hot stock into the pan and simmer for 10 minutes. Remove the quenelle to a warm serving dish with a slotted spoon reserving stock. You may prepare these ahead to this point. If the quenelles are prepared ahead, cook them only 10 minutes in the poaching liquid, then cover them and refrigerate. To reheat, simmer them first a few minutes in the reserved liquid or in hot water. Garnish the quenelles with fresh boiled shrimp and top with Nantua Sauce. Sprinkle parsley on top.

Nantua Sauce

6 tablespoons butter
4 tablespoons flour
Reserved poaching stock plus milk to make 1½ cups
½ cup whipping cream
1 teaspoon salt
½ teaspoon white pepper
¼ cup lobster or crabmeat, minced
⅛ teaspoon cayenne pepper

Melt 4 tablespoons butter in a 1-quart saucepan and stir in the flour. Cook and stir until it begins to bubble (approximately 1 minute). Slowly stir in the milk and stock mixture and cook over medium heat, stirring until thickened. When the first bubble appears, mince the lobster or crab with 2 tablespoons butter and cayenne, and stir into sauce with seasonings and cream. Cook 30 seconds more. Pour over the quenelles, garnish and serve!

Carl Martin Hames

Sautéed Fresh Water Fish Fillets

Fish may be prepared for cooking hours ahead, but should be sautéed just before serving.

Fresh lemon juice to taste
Fish fillets (Bass, bream, crappie), lightly rinsed and drained
Salt to taste
Lemon pepper to taste
Fresh cracker crumbs, Saltines or Ritz
2 tablespoons butter per fish fillet (no substitute)
Thyme to taste
Lemon slices
Fresh parsley, chopped
¼ cup vermouth

Squeeze fresh lemon juice on both sides of fish fillets and sprinkle with salt and lemon pepper. Coat fish with crumbs, pressing firmly with hands. Heat butter in non-stick skillet until very hot but not burned. Add thyme and a few thin slices of lemon. Sauté fillets carefully until just golden brown on both sides. Add butter as needed Remove fish to heated platter. Sprinkle with parsley. Add vermouth to skillet and reduce liquid slightly. Pour over fish.

Note: Red snapper, redfish, flounder, scamp, etc., may be prepared the same way and baked (instead of pan frying) with lemon slices and butter and parsley on top.

Joy Seals Magruder

Salmon Roll

Serves 8

Roll

- **1 (15½ ounce) can red salmon**
- **1 cup sharp Cheddar cheese, shredded**
- **1 tablespoon fresh parsley, minced**
- **1 cup mayonnaise**
- **1 tablespoon Worcestershire sauce**
- **1 puff pastry crust**

Preheat oven to 375°.

Mince salmon and mix with Cheddar cheese, parsley, mayonnaise, and Worcestershire sauce. Spread mixture on pastry; close ends, fold over and seal. Place seam side down on baking dish. Brush with margarine and prick with fork. Bake for 30-40 minutes. Let stand for 10 minutes before slicing.

Sauce

- **2 tablespoons margarine**
- **2 tablespoons flour**
- **¼ teaspoon salt**
- **1 cup milk**
- **½ cup chopped celery**
- **½ cup chopped onions**
- **2 tablespoons butter**
- **1 (4½ ounce) can English peas**
- **2 hard boiled eggs, chopped**
- **1 small jar pimiento**
- **2 tablespoons Cheese Whiz**

Melt margarine in saucepan over low heat. Blend in flour and salt. Add milk all at once. Cook quickly, stirring constantly, until mixture thickens and bubbles. Remove sauce from heat. In separate pan, sauté onions, and celery in butter. Add to above white sauce. Then fold in peas, eggs, pimiento, and Cheese Whiz. Serve hot over Salmon Roll that has been sliced.

Ann Dawkins Holloway

Oysters Rockefeller

Excellent!

Serves 4

1½ sticks butter
1 cup chopped celery
1 cup chopped green onion
1 cup chopped fresh parsley
1 cup chopped fresh spinach or frozen, drained
1½ cups croutons
Juice of 1 lemon
1 teaspoon garlic salt
Dash thyme, tarragon, oregano, and cayenne. (A dash of Pernod can be added if desired).
1 (12 ounce) can fresh select oysters

Preheat oven to 450°. Melt butter and sauté vegetables for 2-3 minutes until liquid is absorbed. Add croutons and mix well. Add lemon juice and other seasonings. Mix well. Place oysters on shells or in ramekins. Top oysters with generous helping of above mixture. Bake oysters for 10-15 minutes.

Henry Taliaferro

Escalloped Oysters

Serves 8-10

1 cup bread crumbs
½ cup Ritz cracker crumbs
1 stick butter, melted
3 (12 ounce) cans fresh oysters, drained, reserving 4 tablespoons liquid
2 tablespoons half-and-half
6 eggs, whipped
Salt and pepper to taste

Preheat oven to 350°. Grease 3-quart casserole. Combine bread and cracker crumbs with melted butter. Mix oyster liquor, half-and-half, and eggs together. Arrange layers in casserole beginning with half of the crumbs, then half of the oysters, and salt and pepper. Pour half of liquor, egg and milk mixture over oysters, then repeat layers. Heat for 30 minutes or until liquid is set and not runny.

Mary Moren Sellers Crommelin

Oysters Mosca

Serves 4

1 stick butter
½ cup olive oil
2-4 cloves garlic, crushed
2 cups Italian bread crumbs
1 cup grated Parmesan cheese
Juice of 2 lemons
¼ teaspoon red pepper
4 tablespoons chopped parsley
1½ pints oysters, drained (2 12-ounce cans)

In heavy saucepan melt butter over low heat. Mix in olive oil and heat a few minutes longer. Add all other ingredients except oysters and mix well, then remove pan from heat. Barely cover the bottom of a shallow pan with the crumb mixture. Place well-drained oysters on top and cover with the remainder of the crumb mixture. Bake in preheated 450° oven until topping is well browned, about 18 minutes.

Laide Long Karpeles

Betty Clyde's Baked Oysters

Serves 4

4 tablespoons butter
2½ tablespoons chopped green onions
1 garlic clove, minced
2 tablespoons chopped fresh parsley
½ teaspoon celery seed
¼ teaspoon oregano
¼ teaspoon Lawry's seasoned salt
Pepper to taste
¾ cup bread crumbs
1 (12 ounce) jar fresh oysters, drained
1 tablespoon lemon juice
4 slices bacon, halved

Preheat oven to 425°. Melt butter and add onion and garlic. Cook until tender. Add seasonings and bread crumbs. Mix well. Place oysters in 4 shell ramekins and add lemon juice. Sprinkle dressing mix on top of oysters and mix. Add bacon on top of each ramekin. Bake until bacon is crisp, about 15 minutes. May be prepared in small casserole dish.

Jan Hardy Hobson

Deviled Crab

Serves 4

1 pound lump crabmeat
¼ pound fresh mushrooms, sliced
2 tablespoons melted butter
2 tablespoons flour
1½ teaspoons salt
⅛ teaspoon pepper
1 cup milk
1 tablespoon minced onion
1 tablespoon minced parsley
⅛ teaspoon cayenne pepper
½ teaspoon dry mustard
1 tablespoon horseradish
2 tablespoons sherry
¾-1 cup buttered bread crumbs

Preheat oven to 450°. Remove bits of shell from crabmeat. Sauté mushrooms in butter. Blend in flour, salt, and pepper, stirring to form a smooth paste. Gradually add milk stirring constantly over low heat and add other ingredients except crumbs. Fill individual ramekins or casserole and cover with crumbs. Bake about 20 minutes or until brown.

Joan Gerbec Ellis

Crab Casserole

Serves 6

2 medium zucchini, sliced ¼-inch thick
1 medium onion, chopped
1 stick butter
2 cloves garlic, crushed
1 pound crabmeat, picked
1½ cups Swiss cheese, cut in strips
3 tomatoes, chopped
1 teaspoon dried basil
Salt and pepper to taste
1 cup Italian bread crumbs

Preheat oven to 375°. Sauté zucchini and onion in butter, covered; add garlic and crabmeat. Mix lightly; add 1 cup cheese, tomatoes, basil, salt, pepper, and ⅔ bread crumbs. Place mixture in greased 3-quart casserole; cover with remaining cheese and crumbs. Bake for 30-40 minutes.

Beth Miller Major

Sautéed Shrimp with Mushrooms

Serves 4

4 dozen shrimp, raw
1 stick butter or margarine
16 medium mushroom caps
1 tablespoon freeze-dried chives
1 tablespoon minced parsley
Juice of medium lemon
1 tablespoon minced green pepper
½ teaspoon salt or to taste
¼ teaspoon pepper or to taste
¼ cup white wine

Peel and clean shrimp. Melt butter. Slice mushroom caps. Sauté mushrooms in butter then remove from butter. Sauté shrimp, turning until pink all over and firm. Add chives, parsley, lemon juice, green pepper, mushrooms, salt and pepper. Mix well. Add wine and simmer 5-7 minutes. Serve over toast or hard French bread. Garnish with parsley sprigs. Can be increased counting on 12 shrimp per person.

Mary Jane Inge Tingle

Baked Shrimp and Artichokes

May be assembled in advance.

Serves 6

3 cloves garlic, minced
¼ cup lemon juice
½ teaspoon salt
2 pounds jumbo shrimp, peeled and deveined
1 (9 ounce) box frozen artichokes, thawed
3 tablespoons chopped parsley
1 stick butter

Preheat oven to 400°. Mince garlic into lemon juice, add salt and stir. Place half of shrimp in bottom of casserole and pour ⅓ lemon juice mixture over shrimp. Sprinkle with 1 tablespoon parsley. Layer artichokes and then rest of shrimp, following each layer with ⅓ lemon juice mixture and 1 tablespoon parsley. Slice butter over top. Bake for 20 minutes.

Susan Walter Rediker

Quick Shrimp Casserole

Serves 6-8

½ stick butter
1 (16 ounce) carton sour cream
Cavender's or seasoned salt to taste
½ teaspoon mace
1 pound cooked shrimp, shelled and deveined
2 (14 ounce) cans artichoke hearts, heated, drained and kept warm
4 (10 ounce) packages frozen chopped spinach, cooked, squeezed dry and kept warm
Paprika
Parsley for garnish

Melt butter in double boiler. Fold in sour cream and gently heat until warm. Season with Cavender's or seasoned salt and mace. Add shrimp. Arrange artichoke hearts in casserole. Top with spinach and pour sour cream/shrimp mixture over this. Sprinkle with paprika and garnish with parsley flakes. Serve immediately. *Do not try to reheat before serving.*

Margaret Gresham Livingston

Cameron Todd's Shrimp

Serves 2-4

1½ pounds raw shrimp, peeled and deveined
6 tablespoons butter
1 teaspoon lemon peel
½ cup sour cream
¼ cup dry white wine
Orange liqueur to taste

Sauté shrimp in butter with lemon peel for several minutes. Combine sour cream, wine, and orange liqueur and stir into shrimp. Cook over low heat until warmed through. *Do not boil.*

Virginia McWhite

Broiled Shrimp with Herbed Wine Sauce

Serves 4

2 pounds raw shrimp, peeled and deveined
⅓ cup melted butter
1 tablespoon lemon juice
Onion salt to taste
Seasoned salt to taste
Thyme to taste
Pepper to taste
Parsley, fresh chopped or flakes
⅓ cup dry white wine

Preheat broiler. Dry shrimp *thoroughly* on paper towels. Place shrimp in greased baking dish in *1 layer*. Combine butter and lemon juice and pour over shrimp. Season to taste with onion salt, seasoned salt, thyme, and pepper. Sprinkle with parsley. Place shrimp in oven about 4 inches from heat and broil for 8 minutes. Add wine and cook an additional 2 minutes. Serve in individual ramekins.

June March Wilson

Aunt Glenn's Shrimp

Serves 6

1 egg
1 teaspoon salt
2 tablespoons oil
1 cup *ICE* water
1 cup flour
8 dozen peeled raw shrimp
Hot oil

Beat egg well, add salt and oil. Beat again and add ice water all at once. Blend well and add flour all at once. Beat well, add shrimp, and coat with batter. Deep fry, serve immediately. *Batter may be prepared a few hours ahead, but beat again prior to use.* Serve with Delicious Tartar Sauce on page 140.

Ginger March Waters

Curried Shrimp With Grapes

Serves 6

1 medium onion, chopped finely
½ stick butter or margarine
1 (10¾ ounce) can mushroom soup, undiluted
1 teaspoon curry powder
1 tablespoon lemon juice
Salt and pepper to taste
2 pounds shrimp, cooked and shelled
1 cup green seedless grapes, cut in half
1 (8 ounce) carton sour cream

Sauté onion in margarine in Dutch oven until clear. Add mushroom soup, curry powder, lemon juice, salt and pepper, and heat. Add shrimp and grapes. Add sour cream right before serving. Do not let sour cream boil. Serve over rice.

Frog Legs á la Percy

Serves 4

8 frog legs
½ cup white wine
Salt and pepper to taste
½ cup flour
1 stick butter
2 cloves garlic
¼ cup chopped shallots
Juice of ½ lemon
1 cup minced parsley
¼ cup brandy
1½ cups sliced fresh mushrooms

Marinate frog legs in white wine overnight. Salt and pepper frog legs. Dredge in flour and sauté in butter until brown. Add garlic and continue to brown 3 minutes. Remove garlic. Add remaining ingredients and cook 5 more minutes.

Shelley Percy Weathers

Paella

Serves 8

2½-3 pound chicken, cut up
¼ cup olive oil
1 cup water
1 (16 ounce) can tomatoes
3 teaspoons instant chicken bouillon
½ teaspoon garlic powder
1½ tablespoons salt
1 tablespoon paprika
½ teaspoon pepper
⅛ teaspoon cayenne pepper
⅛ teaspoon saffron
2 (9 ounce) packages frozen lobster tails, optional
1½ cups rice
1½ pounds (about 2 cups) raw shrimp
1 (24 ounce) can steamed clams in shell, drained, optional
1 (10 ounce) package frozen green peas, thawed
1 (15 ounce) can artichoke hearts, drained
1 (2 ounce) jar sliced pimiento, drained

Wash chicken and pat dry. Brown oil in large pan. Add water, heat to boiling. Reduce heat, cover and simmer 20 minutes. Drain, reserving liquid. Cool chicken, cover and refrigerate. In large bowl, combine reserved liquid plus enough water to measure 3 cups, the tomatoes, bouillon, and seasonings. Cover and refrigerate. Cook lobster as directed on package. Cut away undershell and loosen meat, leaving attached just at the tip of shell. Put lobster in bowl. Cover and refrigerate. May be prepared a day ahead up to this point. About 40 minutes before serving, stir rice and tomato mixture in Dutch oven or large pot. Heat to boiling, stirring twice. Add chicken, reduce heat. Cover and simmer 20 minutes. Carefully stir in shrimp and clams, cover and simmer 5 minutes. Add lobster, peas, and artichoke hearts. Cover and heat through, about 5 minutes. Serve in large, shallow dish. Garnish with pimiento.

Lee McLaughlin Gewin

Ramekins of Seafood in Sour Cream

Serves 8

½ pound fresh shrimp, shelled
½ pound crabmeat, picked
½ pound or 2 cups oysters, rinsed
½ pound scallops, rinsed
5 green onions
1 stick butter
2 cups sour cream
Lawry's seasoned salt
Jane's Krazy Mixed-Up Salt to taste
3 tablespoons soy sauce
Paprika to tint
½ cup grated Parmesan cheese

Steam seafood except crabmeat. Sauté onions in butter for about 3 minutes. Heat sour cream to boiling point, but do not boil; season to taste with salts and soy sauce. Add just enough paprika for a rich pink tint. Add the seasoned sour cream to the seafood mixture, blend well, and cook over low heat until sauce is thickened and smooth. Divide seafood and sauce among 8 buttered individual ramekins or a large buttered casserole. Sprinkle with Parmesan cheese and glaze under broiler until slightly browned.

Mallie Moughan Ireland

Coquilles Saint Jacques

Serves 3-4

1 pound scallops, cut in bite-size pieces
3 slices bacon
2 tablespoons butter or margarine
2 shallots, finely chopped
Salt and pepper to taste
Flour for dusting
¼ teaspoon curry powder
⅓ cup dry white wine
2 teaspoons chopped parsley
½ cup bread crumbs

Wash scallops, drain, and cut into proper size if necessary. Blanch bacon, dry, then sauté in butter until crisp. Remove, drain, and crumble onto warm platter. Add shallots to butter and sauté for approximately 2 minutes. Remove to warm platter. Sauté scallops which have been seasoned with salt and pepper and lightly dusted with flour. Cook 5 minutes. Remove to warm platter. Add curry powder to pan and stir well. Add wine. Scrape pan well and cook 2 minutes. Return scallops, shallots, and bacon to pan and add parsley. Blend well. Put mixture into shells or ramekins. Pour sauce over and sprinkle with bread crumbs. Bake at 400° for 5 minutes. Serve immediately.

Lenore Picard

Seafood Élégante

Must be prepared ahead.

Serves 10

1 tablespoon sugar
½ cup flour
2½ teaspoons salt
1 teaspoon ginger
3 sticks butter, divided
1 cup minced onions
1½-2 cups peeled and grated green apples
1 cup chicken broth
2½ cups milk
3 pounds peeled raw shrimp
2 cups uncooked lobster meat
3 tablespoons lemon juice
1 teaspoon paprika

Day before serving, mix together sugar, flour, salt, and ginger. In a large skillet melt 1½ sticks butter. Sauté onions and apples until tender. Remove from heat and blend in flour mixture. Return to heat and stir 2-3 minutes. Slowly add chicken broth and milk. Stir carefully until sauce is smooth and quite thick. In another skillet melt remaining butter. Add seafood. Cook and stir over medium-high heat about 5 minutes. In saucepan combine sauce, lemon juice, and paprika to seafood mixture being careful to stir liquid in slowly. Let cool and refrigerate overnight, as flavor improves with time. To serve, heat in oven. Serve over rice or in patty shells. *May substitute shrimp or scallops for lobster.*

Lucy Trabue Watson

VEGETABLES

Vegetables

Purée of Artichokes

A good side dish with filet of beef

Serves 4-6

2 (7½ ounce) cans artichoke bottoms
⅓ cup whipping cream
1 stick unsalted butter, cut in pieces
1 teaspoon salt
½ teaspoon freshly ground black pepper

Drain artichokes bottoms and rinse with cold water. Chop artichokes and place in food processor with remaining ingredients. Process for 1-2 minutes, occasionally scraping down sides of bowl, until purée is smooth. Adjust seasonings to taste. Transfer mixture to saucepan and heat.

Trent Douglass Caddis

Simple Artichoke-Spinach Soufflé

Serves 6

2 (12 ounce) packages frozen spinach soufflé, partially thawed
1 (14 ounce) can artichoke hearts, drained and sliced
1 (8 ounce) package cream cheese, softened

Preheat oven to 350°. Place soufflé and artichokes in a buttered 2-quart baking dish. Add cream cheese which has been cut into small cubes. Place in oven for about 5 minutes or until ingredients have melted enough to be combined. Stir until cheese is well incorporated and return to oven for 50-60 minutes.

Katherine Meadow McTyeire
PAST PRESIDENT

Asparagus and Tomato Slices

An easy, colorful dish for luncheons or buffet dinners.

Serves 6-8

- **4 medium, firm, ripe tomatoes**
- **1 (15 ounce) can asparagus spears, drained**
- **½ cup mayonnaise**
- **2 cups grated sharp cheese**
- **Tabasco sauce to taste**
- **½ teaspoon Worcestershire sauce**
- **3 tablespoons grated onion**

Preheat oven to 350°. Cut stem ends off tomatoes and slice each into 3 thick slices. Cut asparagus spears in half and arrange on top of tomato slices in a buttered, shallow baking dish. Combine remaining ingredients and spoon over asparagus. Bake for 10-15 minutes or until cheese is melted. Do not overbake. *Tomatoes may be prepared early in the day and refrigerated before baking.*

Browning Piper Rochefort

Green Beans and Tomatoes

Serves 8-10

- **4 (16 ounce) cans whole green beans**
- **3 medium onions, sliced**
- **2 (16 ounce) cans tomatoes and juice**
- **1 green pepper, chopped**
- **5 slices bacon, preferably thick sliced**
- **1 teaspoon Italian seasoning**

Preheat oven to 375°. Boil beans in their liquid for 5 minutes; drain. In a buttered 3-quart baking dish, layer beans, onions, tomatoes and juice, and green pepper. Cut bacon slices in half and place on top. Sprinkle with Italian seasoning. Bake covered for 45 minutes. Remove cover and bake an additional 15 minutes.

Lilian Culp Stiles
PAST PRESIDENT

French String Bean Casserole

Serves 6-8

2 (10 ounce) packages frozen French-style green beans, cooked and drained
1 (16 ounce) can bean sprouts, drained
1 (8 ounce) can water chestnuts, drained and sliced
½ cup grated Parmesan cheese
½ stick butter
2 tablespoons flour
1¼ teaspoons salt
¼ teaspoon pepper
Cayenne pepper to taste
¼ teaspoon Worcestershire sauce
1 pint whipping cream
½ cup slivered almonds

Preheat oven to 425°. In a buttered 2-quart baking dish, layer beans, bean sprouts, and water chestnuts; sprinkle with cheese. Repeat layers. Melt butter, add flour and seasonings. Gradually add cream and cook until thick, stirring constantly. Pour sauce over beans. Sprinkle with almonds. Bake 20-30 minutes or until bubbly. *Casserole may be prepared a day ahead and refrigerated before baking.*

Ginger Stockham Ladd

Spicy Baked Beans

Serves 8

1½ pounds ground beef
2 (3 pound, 5 ounce) cans pork and beans, drained
1 cup hot barbecue sauce
1 cup regular barbecue sauce
1 (4 ounce) can chopped green chilies
1 tablespoon lemon juice
2 onions, chopped

Brown beef in heavy skillet or Dutch oven. Drain off fat. Add all other ingredients. Cover and simmer for 20-30 minutes, removing cover occasionally to let steam escape.

Mrs. A. W. Stevens

Buttered Spiced Beets

Serves 6

2 small bunches unpeeled beets (4 or 5 beets per bunch)
2-3 tablespoons vinegar
½ cup water
½ cup sugar
¼ teaspoon cloves
2 tablespoons butter

Boil beets covered over low heat for 3 hours. Drain beets and rinse with cold water. Peel and slice. Place beets in saucepan and add remaining ingredients. Heat until syrup is boiling. Serve hot.

Helen McWane Allison

Broccoli Soufflé

Serves 4

1½ cups cooked fresh broccoli or 1 (10 ounce) package frozen chopped broccoli, cooked
½ cup sour cream
¼ cup grated Parmesan cheese
1 stick butter, melted and cooled
4 egg yolks, beaten
1 tablespoon grated onion
½ teaspoon salt
¼ teaspoon pepper
1 clove garlic, crushed
1 tablespoon lemon juice
4 egg whites, stiffly beaten

Preheat oven to 375°. Drain broccoli, pressing out as much moisture as possible. Place all ingredients except egg whites in blender or processor fitted with the steel blade. Purée until all ingredients are combined. Stir in ¼ of the egg whites to lighten the mixture; gently fold in remaining whites. Pour into a buttered 6-cup soufflé dish. Reduce oven temperature to 350°. Bake for 40 minutes or until firm. Soufflé can be assembled early in the day; add egg whites just before baking. To double use a larger dish or two 6-cup dishes.

Barbara Chenoweth Shelton

Broccoli Mold

Serves 6-8

2 (10 ounce) packages frozen chopped broccoli, thawed and drained
Juice of ½ lemon
3 tablespoons butter
3 tablespoons flour
¼ cup chicken broth
1 8 ounce carton sour cream
¼ cup sliced green onions
3 eggs
⅓ cup grated Swiss cheese
1 (2 ounce) package slivered almonds, toasted
1 teaspoon salt
½ teaspoon pepper
½ teaspoon ground nutmeg

Preheat oven to 350°. Finely chop broccoli by hand or in processor. Add lemon juice. Melt butter and blend in flour. Add broth, sour cream, and green onions. Cook, stirring constantly, over very low heat until thick and well blended. Beat eggs lightly and stir into hot mixture. Cook 1 minute. Remove from heat and stir in cheese until melted. Add broccoli, almonds, and seasonings. Pour into a buttered 1-quart ring mold or Bundt pan. Place mold in a pan of hot water and bake about 50 minutes or until knife inserted into broccoli comes out clean.

Variation: Fill ring with sautéed mushrooms and cauliflower.

Trent Douglass Caddis

Brussels Sprouts Almondine

Serves 6-8

2 (10 ounce) packages frozen Brussels sprouts
2 teaspoons instant chicken bouillon granules
1 (10¾ ounce) can cream of chicken soup
1 (2 ounce) jar diced pimiento, undrained
⅛ teaspoon thyme leaves
⅛ teaspoon pepper
1 tablespoon butter
½ cup almonds

Preheat oven to 350°. Cook Brussels sprouts in 1 cup water with chicken bouillon granules until tender; drain. Combine soup; pimiento and juice, thyme and pepper. In a buttered 1½-quart baking dish, mix Brussels sprouts and sauce. Melt butter and sauté almonds for 3 minutes. Spoon over Brussels sprouts. Bake for 20 minutes or until hot and bubbly.

Marjorie Webster Ellington
GREENWOOD, MISSISSIPPI

Governor's Mansion Cabbage

Served as a favorite vegetable in the Alabama Governor's Mansion many years ago.

Serves 8

1 medium head cabbage, about 1½ pounds
1 stick butter, melted
3 tablespoons butter
3 tablespoons flour
2 cups milk
1 teaspoon Worcestershire sauce
2 hard boiled eggs, sliced
1 cup grated sharp Cheddar cheese
Toasted slivered almonds

Preheat oven to 350°. Coarsely shred or chop cabbage. Sauté in 1 stick butter until just limp. Melt remaining butter in separate saucepan. Add flour until well combined; gradually add milk. Cook over medium heat, stirring constantly, until thickened. Add Worcestershire. Combine white sauce, cabbage, and eggs in buttered 2-quart baking dish. Top with cheese and almonds. Bake, uncovered, for 30 minutes or until bubbly. *May be prepared early in the day before baking or reheated after baking.*

Nan Manly Adams

Carrot Soufflé

Serves 6

3 tablespoons butter, melted
3 tablespoons flour
1 cup hot milk
¼ teaspoon salt
3 eggs, slightly beaten
2 cups cooked carrots, mashed
1 teaspoon vanilla
1 tablespoon sugar
½ teaspoon nutmeg

Preheat oven to 350°. In mixing bowl blend butter and flour. Add milk and stir until smooth. Add remaining ingredients. Pour mixture into a buttered 2-quart baking dish. Bake for 40 minutes.

Edith Tynes Quarles
PAST PRESIDENT

Healthy Carrots

Serves 6

8-10 carrots
Cooking oil
Salt
Lettuce leaves
Lemon juice, optional
Butter, optional
Lemon-pepper marinade, optional

Peel carrots and cut in ½-inch slices. Heat thin layer of oil in skillet. Add carrots and salt. Cover with very wet lettuce leaves and a tight lid. Cook 10-15 minutes over medium heat until barely tender. Discard lettuce. Add butter, lemon juice, or marinade if desired.
Variation: 2 (10 ounce) packages frozen green peas may be added to or used in place of carrots.

Mike Casey Vann

Sautéed Cauliflower and Zucchini

Serves 6

1 head cauliflower, separated into flowerets
1 stick butter
1½ teaspoons salt
¼ teaspoon pepper
1 teaspoon lemon juice
1 teaspoon basil
1 teaspoon oregano
1 tablespoon grated onion
3 medium zucchini, sliced ½-inch thick
½ cup grated Parmesan cheese

In large skillet cook cauliflower in boiling salted water about 5 minutes or until just tender. Pour off water and remove cauliflower. Melt butter in skillet; stir in salt, pepper, lemon juice, basil, oregano, and onion. Add zucchini and cauliflower. Cover and cook over low heat for 10-15 minutes or until zucchini is tender. Remove from heat and toss with cheese. *Variation:* Yellow squash may be substituted for zucchini.

Kate Johnson Nielsen

Cheese-Topped Cauliflower

Serves 4-6

1 large head cauliflower
1 cup mayonnaise
2 teaspoons prepared regular or Dijon mustard
1¼ cups shredded sharp Cheddar cheese
Paprika

Preheat oven to 350°. Remove leaves and stem end from cauliflower. Soak in salted water to cover for 15-20 minutes. Drain well. Steam cauliflower in a small amount of boiling salted water for 10-15 minutes, being careful not to overcook. Drain thoroughly. Place cauliflower in shallow 2-quart buttered casserole. Combine mayonnaise and mustard and spread over cauliflower. Sprinkle with cheese and paprika and bake for 10 minutes or until cheese melts.

Virginia Henking Lowry

Bean Sprouts and Celery

Serves 4

1 scallion, cut in strips
1 small piece ginger, minced
3 tablespoons peanut oil
1 pound bean sprouts
1 stalk celery, sliced on the diagonal in 1-inch strips
2 tablespoons soy sauce
1 teaspoon sugar
1 teaspoon salt
½ teaspoon MSG
½ cup chicken broth
1 teaspoon cornstarch

Heat oil over medium high heat. Fry scallion and ginger until golden brown. Add vegetables and quick fry for 2 minutes. Combine remaining ingredients and add to skillet, quick frying for 2 minutes.

Fresh Creamed Corn

Serves 4

6 ears fresh corn
1 tablespoon whipping cream
2 tablespoons butter
Salt and pepper to taste
1 teaspoon sugar
Nutmeg

Cut kernels from corn, scraping corn to include the milk for added flavor. Place corn in saucepan; add cream and butter and cook over low heat for 5-10 minutes or until corn is tender. Add salt, pepper, and sugar. Grate nutmeg lightly over corn and serve immediately.

Jeanne Vigeant Marks

Corn and Tomato Casserole

Serves 6-8

Great with barbecue

3 strips bacon
½ cup minced onion
3 tablespoons chopped green pepper
1 (16 ounce) can tomatoes
2 tablespoons brown sugar
1 teaspoon salt
⅛ teaspoon pepper
1 (12 ounce) can whole kernel white corn, drained
⅔ cup bread crumbs, divided
⅔ cup grated sharp Cheddar cheese, divided

Cook bacon and set aside, reserving 1 tablespoon drippings. Sauté onion and pepper in drippings until tender. Add tomatoes and juice, brown sugar, salt and pepper, and simmer for 15 minutes. Stir in corn, crumbled bacon, half of bread crumbs, and half of cheese. Mix well and simmer for 10 minutes. Preheat broiler. Pour vegetable mixture into buttered 2-quart casserole, top with remaining bread crumbs and cheese, and run under broiler until cheese melts. *This may be prepared a day or 2 ahead and reheated before serving.*

Tish Preacher Long

Corn Pudding

Serves 6

½ stick butter
¼ cup flour
2 teaspoons salt
1½ tablespoons sugar
1¾ cups milk
3 cups fresh corn, cut from the cob, or 1 (17 ounce) can cream style corn
3 eggs, beaten

Preheat oven to 325°. Melt butter in saucepan. Blend in flour, salt, and sugar. Gradually add milk and cook over medium heat, stirring constantly, until thickened and smooth. Stir in corn. Gradually add hot mixture a little at a time to eggs. Pour into buttered 2-quart baking dish. Place dish in large pan and pour water into pan until about ¼ up the sides of casserole dish. Bake for 1½ hours. *If using canned corn, decrease amount of salt.*

Carolyn Young Carter

Eggplant Soufflé

Serves 6

1 medium eggplant, peeled and chopped
2 tablespoons butter
2 tablespoons flour
1 cup milk
½ cup grated Cheddar cheese
¾ cup bread crumbs
2 tablespoons grated onion
1 tablespoon catsup
1 teaspoon salt
2 egg yolks, beaten
2 egg whites, stiffly beaten

Preheat oven to 350°. Cook eggplant in boiling, salted water 5-10 minutes or until tender. Drain and mash. Melt butter and blend in flour. Gradually add milk and stir over medium heat until thickened. Combine sauce, eggplant, cheese, bread crumbs, onion, catsup, salt, and egg yolks. Fold in egg whites. Place in a buttered 2-quart soufflé dish and bake for 45 minutes.

Cathy Criss Adams

Gratin of Eggplant and Tomatoes

Serves 6-8

3 tablespoons butter
½ small onion, finely chopped
Salt and pepper to taste
2 pounds ripe tomatoes, peeled, seeded, and diced
¼ cup whipping cream
3 tablespoons butter
2 eggplants, peeled and cut in thin slices
Flour
1 stick butter, melted
½ cup grated Parmesan cheese
1 cup shredded Mozzarella cheese

Preheat oven to 425°. Melt 3 tablespoons butter in saucepan. Add onion and sauté until golden. Add salt, pepper, and diced tomatoes and cook until tomatoes are soft. Stir in cream and 3 tablespoons butter; remove from heat. Season eggplant slices with salt and pepper, dip in flour, and sauté in remaining butter until soft. In a gratin dish or shallow buttered 2-quart baking dish, arrange a layer of eggplant, cover with some of the tomato mixture and sprinkle with cheeses. Continue in this manner until all ingredients are used, ending with Mozzarella. Bake 15-20 minutes or until sauce bubbles and cheese is melted.

Gray Evans
GREENWOOD, MISSISSIPPI

Eggplant and Tomato Pie

Serves 4-6

1 small eggplant, peeled and sliced
½ medium onion, sliced
1 stick butter
9-inch pie shell, unbaked
2 tablespoons grated Parmesan cheese
2 medium tomatoes, sliced
½ green pepper, sliced
½ teaspoon crushed garlic
Salt and pepper to taste
4 tablespoons grated Parmesan cheese

Preheat oven to 350°. Sauté eggplant and onion slices in butter until tender. Sprinkle pie shell with 2 tablespoons cheese. Top with layers of eggplant, onion, tomatoes, and green pepper. Sprinkle with seasonings and cheese and bake for 45 minutes.

Susie Owings Rather

Dilled Mushrooms

Serves 6

1 pound fresh mushrooms or 2 (6 or 8 ounce) jars sliced mushrooms
3 tablespoons butter or margarine
2 tablespoons finely chopped onion
¼ teaspoon salt
White pepper to taste
1 tablespoon flour
¼ cup grated Parmesan or Romano cheese
1-2 teaspoons dill weed
1 cup whipping cream
2 egg yolks, beaten
3 tablespoons bread crumbs

Preheat oven to 425°. Rinse, pat dry, and slice fresh mushrooms, or drain commercially prepared mushrooms. Melt butter in skillet. Add mushrooms, onion, salt and pepper. Cover and simmer 1 minute. Stir in flour and cheese. Cook about 3 minutes. Turn into buttered 8-inch ovenproof dish or individual ramekins. Sprinkle with dill weed. Mix cream and egg yolks. Pour over mushrooms. Sprinkle with bread crumbs. Bake for 12-15 minutes or until set and golden brown on top.

Louise Bradford Clayton

Mushroom Puff

Serves 6-8

½-1 pound fresh mushrooms, sliced
2-3 tablespoons butter
6 slices bread
3-4 tablespoons butter, melted
½ cup chopped onion
½ cup chopped green pepper
½ cup chopped celery
½ cup mayonnaise
¾ teaspoon salt
¼ teaspoon pepper
2 eggs, slightly beaten
1½ cups milk
1 cup grated sharp Cheddar cheese

Sauté mushrooms in butter until they begin to brown. Place in buttered 2-quart casserole. Brush 4 bread slices with melted butter. Trim crusts and cut bread into 1-inch cubes. Top mushrooms with half of bread cubes. Combine onions, peppers, celery, mayonnaise, salt and pepper, and spread over bread. Top with other bread cubes. Combine eggs and milk. Pour over bread. Refrigerate overnight. Preheat oven to 325°. Brush other 2 bread slices with butter, cube, and sprinkle over casserole. Bake uncovered for 45 minutes. Top with cheese and return to oven for 10-15 minutes or until cheese melts.

Ardis Parrott Albany

Baked Mushrooms

An elegant alternative to sautéed mushrooms

Serves 4

½ pound fresh mushrooms
Salt and pepper to taste
1 stick butter
1 tablespoon whipping cream

Preheat oven to 350°. Place mushrooms in flat baking dish; salt and pepper generously. Dot with butter and add cream. Cover and bake 20 minutes.

Mallie Moughan Ireland

Sesame Mushroom Tart

Serves 6

Pastry

1 cup white flour
1 cup whole wheat flour
1 teaspoon salt
1 teaspoon Fines Herbes
⅔ cup shortening
1 egg, separated
6-8 tablespoons water

Combine flours, salt, and Fines Herbes. Cut in shortening until crumbly. Stir in egg yolk (reserving egg white) and add 2 tablespoons of water. Add enough additional water to form a dough. Divide dough in half. Roll each half into a 9-inch circle. Grease 9-inch quiche pan. Line pan with 1 rolled circle. Trim edge to ½ inch.

Filling

1 medium onion, chopped
1 clove garlic, chopped
2 tablespoons butter
1 (10 ounce) package frozen chopped spinach, cooked and drained
1½ cups grated Cheddar cheese
2 tablespoons tomato paste
1½ teaspoons Fines Herbes
½ teaspoon salt
2 cups sliced fresh mushrooms
1½ teaspoons sesame seeds

Sauté onion and garlic in butter until soft. Combine sautéed vegetables, spinach, cheese, tomato paste, Fines Herbes, and salt. Spoon into prepared pastry shell. Arrange mushrooms evenly over top of spinach mixture. Place second pie crust on top. Trim edge to ½ inch and flute. Make 4 slits in crust. Brush with reserved egg white. Sprinkle with sesame seeds. Bake 350° for 30-35 minutes. Cool 10 minutes. Serve hot or at room temperature.

Sallie Sherrod Sherrill

Okra and Tomatoes

Serves 4-6

1 medium onion, chopped or sliced in rings
1 green pepper, chopped or sliced in rings
1 tablespoon butter
2 (16 ounce) cans tomatoes, reserve juice
1 (10 ounce) package frozen cut okra, thawed
2 teaspoons sugar
½ teaspoon Tabasco sauce
Salt and pepper to taste
Parsley flakes and basil leaves to taste
2 tablespoons cornstarch, dissolved in 2 tablespoons tomato juice
Butter
1 cup seasoned stuffing mix
Grated Cheddar or Parmesan cheese, optional

Preheat oven to 350°. Sauté onion and green pepper in butter until tender. In a buttered 2-quart baking dish combine onion, green pepper, tomatoes and juice, okra, sugar, Tabasco, salt, pepper, parsley flakes, and basil. Blend in cornstarch. Dot with butter. Bake covered about 30 minutes or until liquid is thickened. Uncover and top with stuffing mix and cheese. Return to oven for 5 minutes or until crumbs have browned slightly.

Doris D. Urquhart
MOBILE, ALABAMA

Amber Onions

Serves 8

4 large white onions
1½ tablespoons butter, melted
3 tablespoons tomato juice
3 tablespoons strained honey
1½ tablespoons lemon juice
1½ teaspoons salt
½ teaspoon paprika

Preheat oven to 350°. Peel onions and cut crosswise in halves. Place onions in buttered shallow 2-quart baking dish. Combine remaining ingredients and pour over onions. Bake covered for 1 hour. *Onions may be served on strips of hot buttered toast.*

Jane Hill Head
PAST PRESIDENT

Herbed Onion Slices

Especially good with steak

Serves 6

3 tablespoons butter or margarine
1 tablespoon brown sugar
½ teaspoon salt
Dash of pepper
2 large onions, cut in ½-inch slices
¼ teaspoon oregano, optional
2 tablespoons parsley flakes

Melt butter in a large skillet. Add brown sugar, salt, and pepper. Place onion slices in a single layer in butter mixture. Cover and cook over low heat for 10 minutes. Turn slices; sprinkle with oregano and parsley. Cook uncovered for 10 minutes longer.

Patricia Shaefer Miree

Dijon Peas

Serves 4

1 (17 ounce) can English peas, drained
1 teaspoon Dijon mustard
1 garlic clove, pressed
½ cup mushrooms, sliced
1 teaspoon salt
1 tablespoon water

Combine all ingredients in a small saucepan. Cover tightly. Cook over medium heat for 10 minutes, shaking pan occasionally.

Ann Abernethy Stephens

Chinese Green Peas

Serves 4

1 (10 ounce) package frozen green peas, cooked and drained
2 cups shredded lettuce
¼ cup chopped onion
2 tablespoons butter, melted
¼ teaspoon salt
¼ teaspoon pepper
¼ teaspoon tarragon or basil

Sauté the green peas, lettuce, and onion in melted butter. Add seasonings. Serve at once.

Margot Kessler Marx

Sautéed Green Peppers

Serve on a grilled steak.

Serves 4

1 cup sliced onion
1 tablespoon salad oil
3 large green peppers, sliced in rings
½ pound fresh mushrooms, sliced
1 teaspoon salt
⅛ teaspoon cayenne pepper
⅛ teaspoon oregano

In a large skillet sauté onion in oil until golden. Add remaining ingredients, stirring to mix. Cover and cook over medium heat about 5 minutes or until green peppers are tender.

Marcia Howay Scott

Oven-Fried Potatoes

Great with steak as an alternative to baked potatoes

Serves 12

6-8 medium baking potatoes, unpeeled
½ cup oil
2 tablespoons grated Parmesan cheese
1 teaspoon salt
¼ teaspoon pepper
½ teaspoon garlic powder (or more to taste)
Paprika

Preheat oven to 375°. Cut each potato in half lengthwise. Repeat lengthwise cuts to form long thick strips. Arrange potato strips, peel side down, in pie pans. Combine remaining ingredients except paprika and brush over potatoes. Sprinkle with paprika. Bake, uncovered, for 45 minutes, basting several times.

Vivian Yielding Mattison

Mushroom Potatoes

Serves 6-8

4-5 medium potatoes, peeled and thinly sliced
¼ teaspoon salt
¼ teaspoon pepper
1 clove garlic, thinly sliced
1 stick butter
1½ pounds mushrooms, sliced
1 cup grated Swiss or Cheddar cheese
Small bunch parsley, chopped
1 small onion, finely chopped
1 pint whipping cream
2 tablespoons butter

Preheat oven to 375°. Season potatoes with salt and pepper. Rub a 2-quart baking dish with garlic, then butter. Alternate layers of potatoes and mushrooms in baking dish, sprinkling each layer with cheese, parsley, and onion. Repeat layers until all ingredients are used, ending with potatoes and reserving some cheese. Pour cream over potatoes. Sprinkle with remaining cheese and dot with butter. Bake for 45 minutes.

Cathy Connelley Wells
ATLANTA, GEORGIA

Potatoes Gruyère

Serves 8

6 large baking potatoes
1 stick butter
1½ teaspoons salt
½ teaspoon white pepper
1 cup whipping cream
½ cup shredded Gruyère cheese
½ cup grated Parmesan cheese

Preheat oven to 400°. Bake the potatoes for about 1 hour or until crisp on the outside and soft inside. Reduce oven temperature to 375°. Split potatoes and remove pulp. With electric mixer, blend hot potato pulp, butter, salt and pepper until well blended. Place in shallow buttered 2-quart baking dish. Pour cream over potatoes and sprinkle with cheeses. Bake for 15 minutes.

Katherine Baier Nelson
CLINTON, MISSISSIPPI

Coconut Sweet Potatoes

Serves 6

1 (1 pound 13 ounce) can sweet potatoes, drained
¼ cup sugar
½ cup canned evaporated milk
½ teaspoon nutmeg
½ teaspoon cinnamon
1 teaspoon vanilla
½ stick butter, melted

Topping

½ cup coconut
½ cup chopped nuts
½ cup brown sugar
½ stick butter, melted

Preheat oven to 350°. With electric mixer at high speed, combine sweet potatoes, sugar, milk, nutmeg, cinnamon, vanilla, and butter until light and fluffy. Place in buttered 2-quart baking dish. Combine topping ingredients and sprinkle over sweet potatoes. Bake for 20-25 minutes.

Mrs. Verl L. Cameron

Spinach Soufflé

Serves 4

1 (10 ounce) package frozen chopped spinach
6 slices bread, crusts trimmed
6 ounces sharp Cheddar cheese, grated
3 eggs, separated
2 cups half-and-half or milk
¼ teaspoon salt
⅛ teaspoon paprika
¼ teaspoon dry mustard
Nutmeg

Cook and drain spinach well. Make crumbs from bread in blender or processor. Mix cheese, crumbs, and spinach. In mixing bowl, beat egg yolks; add half-and-half and seasonings. Pour over spinach mixture in a buttered 1½-quart ovenproof dish. Let stand 1 hour. May be done ahead to this point. Preheat oven to 350°. Beat egg whites until stiff and fold into mixture. Bake 1 hour 10 minutes and serve hot. Recipe can be doubled. *This may be frozen after baking.* Thaw and reheat 30 minutes at 350°.

Spinach and Artichokes

Serves 6-8

2 (10 ounce) packages frozen chopped spinach
½ cup finely chopped onion
2 tablespoons butter
1 (14 ounce) can artichoke hearts, well drained
1 pint sour cream
Salt and pepper to taste
¾ cup grated Parmesan cheese, divided

Preheat oven to 350°. Cook spinach according to package directions and drain well. Sauté onion in butter. Combine spinach, onion, artichoke hearts, sour cream, salt and pepper, and ½ cup grated Parmesan. Place in buttered 1½-2 quart casserole dish and top with remaining cheese. Bake for 20-30 minutes. *May be prepared early in the day and refrigerated before baking.*

Joan White Starnes

Acorn Squash with Applesauce

Delicious with pork or turkey

Serves 4

1 cup applesauce
4 teaspoons brown sugar
2 acorn squash
4 teaspoons rum, optional
Cinnamon

Preheat oven to 400°. Combine applesauce and brown sugar and set aside. Cut squash in half lengthwise and scoop out seeds and pulp. Place squash halves cut side down in shallow baking pan. Place water in pan to a depth of ¼ inch. Bake for 45 minutes or until squash are fork tender. Cooking time is determined by the size of the squash. Turn squash over and fill each cavity with ¼ of the applesauce/sugar mixture. If desired, sprinkle each squash half with 1 teaspoon rum. Sprinkle with cinnamon. Return to oven for about 15 minutes or until applesauce is bubbly. *The squash may be prepared early in the day and reheated before serving.*

Karen Valentine Sanders

Squash Croquettes

Serves 6-8

1½ pounds yellow squash, sliced
1 medium onion, minced
1 tablespoon butter
1⅓ cups light bread crumbs
1 egg
2 teaspoons salt
1 teaspoon pepper
⅔ cup cornmeal

Cook squash in small amount of water until tender. Drain well. Sauté onion in butter until tender. Mash squash and add all ingredients except cornmeal. It is helpful to chill mixture at this point so that it will hold together when making croquettes. Form into oblong croquettes and roll in corn meal. Fry in deep fat until light golden brown.

Squash Florentine with Almonds

Serves 8-10

8 medium yellow squash
½ pound fresh mushrooms, sliced
1½ tablespoons butter
1 (10 ounce) package frozen chopped spinach, cooked and drained
1 (4 ounce) package garlic and herb semi-soft cheese
1 egg, beaten
½ teaspoon salt
1 (3 ounce) package slivered almonds

Preheat oven to 350°. Boil whole squash for 5 minutes and rinse under cold water. Halve and remove centers. Sauté mushrooms in butter until just tender. With mixer thoroughly combine spinach, cheese, egg, and salt. Fold in mushrooms. Stuff squash halves with spinach mixture and sprinkle with almonds. Place in shallow buttered 3-quart baking dish and bake for 20 minutes. *May be prepared a day before baking.*

Susan Walter Rediker

Squash Soufflé

Serves 6

1½ pounds yellow squash
1 medium onion, chopped
1 tablespoon butter
1 cup finely chopped almonds
2 tablespoons sugar
⅛ teaspoon nutmeg
4 tablespoons butter
4 tablespoons flour
1½ cups milk
1 teaspoon salt
⅛ teaspoon cayenne
1 teaspoon Worcestershire sauce
Tabasco sauce to taste
½ pound extra sharp Cheddar cheese, grated
4 egg yolks
5 egg whites
1 teaspoon cream of tartar
Bread or cracker crumbs

Dice squash and cook in slightly salted water until tender. Drain and mash. Sauté onion in butter and add to squash. Add almonds, sugar, and nutmeg and mix well. In a large saucepan melt butter, add flour and stir until well blended. Add milk and stir with a wire whisk until mixture is smooth and thickened. Stir in salt, pepper, Worcestershire, Tabasco, and mix well. Remove from heat and let it cool slightly. Stir in grated cheese until melted. Add egg yolks, 1 at a time, beating well with the whisk after each addition. Return mixture to heat and beat for 1 minute. Remove and add squash mixture. Let cool briefly. May be prepared ahead to this point. Preheat oven to 375°. Beat egg whites with cream of tartar until they are stiff, but not dry. Fold into squash mixture and pour into baking dish that has been greased and sprinkled with fine crumbs. Bake on the bottom shelf of the oven for 50 minutes.

William F. Adams
TUSCALOOSA, ALABAMA

Curried Green Tomatoes

Serves 10-12

8 medium green tomatoes, peeled and sliced
3 large onions, chopped
Salt and pepper to taste
1 teaspoon curry powder
1½ cups sour cream
½ cup buttered bread crumbs
3 slices bacon, cooked and crumbled, optional
¼ cup grated Parmesan cheese

Preheat oven to 350°. In a heavy skillet over low heat, cook tomatoes and onions until soft. Remove from heat, stir in seasonings, and let cool. Add sour cream and place in a buttered 2-quart baking dish. Top with bread crumbs, bacon, and cheese. Bake for 10-15 minutes or until bubbly and browned.

Agnes Payne Perry

Zucchini and Tomato Casserole

Serves 8

1½-2 pounds zucchini squash, sliced
2 medium onions, sliced
3 large tomatoes, sliced
Salt and pepper to taste
½ teaspoon oregano, optional
½ cup shredded Cheddar cheese or ¼ cup grated Parmesan cheese
4-5 strips of bacon, uncooked

Preheat oven to 350°. In a shallow buttered 3-quart baking dish layer the squash, onions, and tomatoes, sprinkling each layer with seasonings. Top with cheese and cover with bacon slices. Bake for 1 hour. It may be necessary to cover the casserole during the last 30 minutes if vegetables seem to be drying out.

Frances Blackwell Robinson
PAST PRESIDENT

Baked Cheddar Tomatoes

Serves 6

1½ pounds tomatoes, peeled and thinly sliced
2 tablespoons dry sherry
Salt and pepper
¾ cup whipping cream
2¼ cups grated Cheddar cheese
Minced parsley

Preheat oven to 300°. Divide tomato slices among 6 buttered 4-inch gratin dishes and add 1 teaspoon dry sherry to each dish. Sprinkle the tomatoes with salt and pepper and bake for 30 minutes. Add to each dish 2 tablespoons cream and 3 tablespoons grated Cheddar cheese. Bake for 15 minutes more and garnish with minced parsley.

Tomato Parmesan Pie

A marvelous brunch dish

Serves 6

9-inch pie shell, baked
3 medium tomatoes, peeled and sliced
⅛ teaspoon pepper
2 teaspoons flour
1 cup mayonnaise
1 cup grated Parmesan cheese

Preheat oven to 350°-400°. Top pie shell with tomato slices. Sprinkle with pepper and flour. Combine mayonnaise and cheese; spread over tomatoes and bake for 15 minutes or until tinged with brown.

Mrs. Charles S. Jones
ATLANTA, GEORGIA

World's Best Turnip Greens

Serves 4

5 or 6 strips bacon
1 small onion, chopped
2 tablespoons chopped green pepper
1 teaspoon sugar
1 teaspoon salt
1 tablespoon vinegar
Dash of Tabasco
3 pounds turnip greens, well washed
1 hard boiled egg, chopped

Cut bacon into small pieces and cook in a large Dutch oven until crisp. Remove. Sauté onion and pepper in bacon drippings until soft. Add sugar, salt, vinegar, Tabasco, and greens. Cook over medium heat for 15 minutes until greens are wilted. Reduce heat and continue cooking 30 minutes or until tender. Garnish with reserved bacon and egg.

Lynette Angell McCary

East Indian Curried Apples

Serves 8-10

½ cup sugar
1 tablespoon curry powder
2 tablespoons finely chopped onion
¾ teaspoon salt
Juice of 1 lemon
1 cup water
15 tart cooking apples, peeled and quartered

Preheat oven to 350°. Combine all ingredients except apples in a saucepan. Bring to a boil; cook and stir until sugar is dissolved. Place apples in a buttered 2-quart shallow baking dish. Pour hot syrup over apples and bake 30 minutes. *Variation:* Add raisins, nutmeg, or cinnamon to taste.

Helen Benedict Byrd

Brandied Peaches

Great with chicken, turkey or roast pork

Serves 6-8

1 (24 ounce) can peach halves
1 (12 ounce) box mincemeat
4 tablespoons brandy

Preheat oven to 350°. Drain peaches, reserving ¾ cup syrup. Crumble mincemeat in a saucepan and add syrup. Boil, stirring for 3-4 minutes or until thickened. Add brandy and boil 1 minute longer. Place peach halves in a buttered shallow 1½-quart baking dish. Spoon mincemeat mixture over peaches. Bake 15 minutes.

Murray Spencer South

Pineapple Casserole

Especially good with pork

Serves 4

1 (20 ounce) can pineapple chunks
½ cup sugar
3 tablespoons flour
1 cup shredded Cheddar cheese
½-1 stick butter
1 cup cracker crumbs

Preheat oven to 350°. Drain pineapple, reserving 3 tablespoons juice. Combine sugar and flour and stir in juice. Add cheese and pineapple chunks, mixing well. Spoon into buttered 1½-quart casserole. Combine butter and cracker crumbs and sprinkle over pineapple. Bake uncovered for 20-30 minutes or until crumbs are lightly browned.

Lillian Lochrane Coleman

BREADS

Bread

Helpful hints for beginning bread bakers: Allow any refrigerated ingredients to reach room temperature. Yeast stops growing when chilled and is killed when overheated. Use 2-3 cups unbleached white flour and remainder whole wheat to insure successful first results. As you become proficient, use all whole wheat flour if desired; 2-3 cups whole wheat pastry flour, and remaining whole wheat will give excellent results.

Angel Biscuits

Yield: 4 dozen

5 cups flour
¼ cup sugar
3 teaspoons baking soda
1 teaspoon salt
1 cup Crisco
1 package yeast dissolved in 2 tablespoons warm water
2 cups buttermilk, room temperature

Sift flour with dry ingredients. Cut in shortening. Add yeast to buttermilk. Stir buttermilk mixture into flour mixture until well moistened. Roll out, cut into desired shape and place on cookie sheet. Freeze and place in plastic bag when hard. When ready to bake, remove number desired, let thaw and rise. Bake in preheated 450° oven for 10-15 minutes or until brown.

Louise Goodwin Strickland

Bernice's Biscuits

Yield: 3 dozen

5 cups flour
6 teaspoons baking powder
1 teaspoon salt
1 teaspoon soda
1½ cups shortening
2½ cups buttermilk

Preheat oven to 400°. Stir flour, baking powder, soda, and salt together. Blend in shortening. Add buttermilk making a soft dough. Cover top with flour. Knead only until smooth. Roll out ½-inch thick, cut with 2-inch cutter. Place on greased cookie sheet. Bake 15 minutes or until desired degree of brownness is reached.

Bernice Reeves
JASPER, ALABAMA

Crunchy Biscuits

This dry mixture can be prepared ahead and kept in jar for use any time. It is a good idea to double the recipe and keep some on hand. Can make any number of biscuits depending on how many cans of biscuits are used.

Yield: 40 biscuits

1 tablespoon Lawry's seasoned salt
1 tablespoon sesame seeds
1 tablespoon caraway seeds
2 cups Rice Krispies, finely crushed
2 cans biscuits (Hungry Jack Buttermilk suggested)
1 stick margarine, melted

Preheat oven to 400°. Mix Lawry's salt, sesame seeds, caraway seeds, and Rice Krispies to form dry mixture. Cut biscuits in half. Dip in melted margarine and then in dry mixture. Bake for 6-8 minutes. *These are really easy and different. Any leftover biscuits can be kept and reheated.*

Mary McKenzie Williamson

Buttery Biscuit Rolls

Delicious and simple to prepare

Yield: 2 dozen

2 sticks butter (no substitute)
1 (8 ounce) carton sour cream
2 cups self-rising flour, unsifted

Preheat oven to 350°. Melt butter in large saucepan. Add sour cream and flour to butter and mix. Drop batter into miniature, ungreased muffin tins. Fill to top. Bake for 25 minutes. Makes 24 small biscuit rolls. *May be prepared ahead and frozen.*

Carol King Nolen

Food Processor Butter Rolls

Yield: 18 rolls

1 package dry yeast
¼ cup warm water
2½-3 cups flour
¼ cup sugar
1 teaspoon salt
1 egg
¼ cup milk, scalded and returned to room temperature
½ stick butter, at room temperature and cut into 1 tablespoon pieces
1 egg, beaten
1 tablespoon water

Sprinkle yeast over warm water (100-110°) and stir; set aside. Using steel blade of processor, place 2 cups flour in processor bowl with the sugar and salt, turning on and off to combine. Add dissolved yeast, egg, and milk, then butter. Process until combined. Gradually add remaining flour until dough is kneaded and no longer sticky but smooth and shiny. Take out of bowl and knead by hand for a short time. Place dough in a greased bowl and cover. Allow it to rise until doubled in bulk. Punch down. This dough may be kept unshaped and well covered up to 3 days in refrigerator.

To shape rolls:

Pinch off enough dough for one roll. Roll each piece on a lightly floured surface. With the palms of your hands, roll dough into a narrow roll about 8 inches long. Twist into a knot (like a pretzel) and place on buttered pan 1 inch apart. Allow to rise in pan about 1 hour. Brush with a mixture of beaten egg and water. Bake 20 minutes at 375°.

Deedee Tomkins Cowin

Never-Fail Ice Box Rolls

Yield: 3 dozen

⅓ cup sugar
½ cup shortening
1 egg
1 teaspoon salt
1 package dry yeast
1 cup lukewarm water
3¼ cups flour, sifted

Cream sugar and shortening well. Add egg and salt. Cream well again. Dissolve the yeast in lukewarm water. Add flour and yeast water alternately to creamed mixture. Cover and store in refrigerator. The dough will keep 2 weeks. About 3 hours before you plan to use, knead the dough and roll out on floured surface. Cut and shape into Parker House rolls and place on pan with rolls touching. Put in warm place and allow to rise. Bake at 425° for 10 minutes. *Anne Griffin Thompson*

No-Knead Rolls

Yield: 7 dozen

2 packages yeast
½ cup lukewarm water
¾ cup shortening
1 cup boiling water
2 eggs, beaten
¾ cup sugar
2 teaspoons salt
½ cup cold water
7½ cups flour

Dissolve yeast in lukewarm water. Mix shortening and boiling water until shortening is melted. Set aside. Mix eggs, sugar, salt, and cold water. Combine yeast, shortening, and egg mixture. Add flour, mixing well. Cover tightly and refrigerate overnight or at least 8 hours. Shape into rolls. Let rise at room temperature 1-1½ hours. Bake in preheated 400° oven about 12 minutes. *Broxie C. Stuckey*
GORDO, ALABAMA

Bernice's Muffins

Yield: 12 muffins

2 cups cornmeal (stone ground)
½ teaspoon salt
½ teaspoon baking soda
2 cups buttermilk
1 egg, beaten
¼ cup salad oil

Preheat oven to 400°. Combine all ingredients. Spoon into greased muffin pan. Bake 25-30 minutes. May be baked in a skillet.

Bernice Reeves
JASPER, ALABAMA

Cocktail Cheese Muffins

Good for picnic baskets

Yield: 5 dozen

2 sticks butter
8 ounces sharp Cheddar cheese, grated
2 tablespoons frozen chives, defrosted
1 cup sour cream
2 cups self-rising flour

Preheat oven to 375°. In saucepan melt butter over medium heat. Remove from heat and add cheese. Stir well and let cool 2 minutes. Add chives and sour cream, stirring after each addition. Add flour, blending thoroughly. Fill ungreased small-size muffin tins ⅔ full. Bake for 10-12 minutes or until golden. To serve, defrost if frozen and reheat. *May be prepared in larger muffin tins to serve with soup or salad.*

Refrigerator Bran Muffins

Yield: 4 quarts

5 cups All-Bran cereal
1 (15 ounce) box seedless raisins
2 cups boiling water
1 cup sugar
1 cup corn oil
2 cups molasses
4 eggs, well beaten
1 quart buttermilk
5 cups flour
5 teaspoons baking soda
1 teaspoon salt

Preheat oven to 400°. Put 2 cups bran and raisins in a bowl. Pour boiling water over it and set aside to cool. Put sugar in large bowl and add the oil, molasses, eggs, buttermilk, and remaining bran, stirring completely after each addition. Put flour, soda, and salt in a bowl and stir until well mixed. Add to bran/milk mixture. Finally, stir in the cooled bran/raisin mixture. Fill greased muffin pans ⅔ full. Bake exactly 20 minutes. Allow to cool slightly in pan on rack. *Refrigerated batter keeps up to 2 months.*

Evelyn Britton Stutts

Highlands Beer Muffins

Good with soups

Serves 18

4 cups Bisquick
¼ cup melted butter
4 tablespoons sugar
1 (12 ounce) can beer (regular or Lite)

Preheat oven to 400°. Mix all ingredients. Place in greased and floured muffin pan. Bake for 15-20 minutes or until golden brown.

Alpha Johnson Goings

Mexican Cornbread

Serves 12

1 cup yellow cornmeal
½ teaspoon soda
½ teaspoon salt
1 (8 ounce) carton sour cream
2 eggs
½ cup cooking oil
1 onion, chopped
1 clove garlic, chopped
1 (17 ounce) can yellow creamed corn
1 cup grated sharp Cheddar cheese
Jalapeño peppers, chopped (4 or 5 if you like it hot, 2 or 3 if you want it milder)

Preheat oven to 400°. Grease a 9″ x 13″ pyrex dish. Mix all ingredients well and pour into the dish. Bake for 20-30 minutes. *This can also be baked in a jelly roll pan and cut into small squares for appetizers.*

Lessley Oliver Whittington
JACKSON, MISSISSIPPI

Southern Spoonbread

Serves 6-8

1 cup cornmeal
1 teaspoon salt
1 cup water
2 cups hot milk
2 eggs, beaten
3 tablespoons margarine, melted

Preheat oven to 375°. Combine cornmeal and salt in a pan. Stir in water and gradually add milk. Place over low heat and stir until thick and smooth. Spoon small amount of hot mixture into eggs and mix well. Add egg mixture to remaining hot mixture, stirring constantly. Stir in margarine. Pour mixture into a 1½ quart greased baking dish (a flat dish makes more crust!) and bake for 40-50 minutes, or until desired brownness.

Martha Smith Vandervoort

Popovers

Yield: 8

Margarine, used for greasing
4 eggs
1¼ cups milk
½ stick margarine, melted
1¼ cups flour, sifted
½ teaspoon salt

Preheat oven to 400°. Grease 8 custard cups thoroughly with margarine. Beat eggs in a mixing bowl with a beater or blend in a food processor. Beat in, or process milk and melted margarine. Add the flour and salt and mix until smooth. Pour into prepared custard cups and place on cookie sheet. Bake for 50 minutes. Serve immediately. *Batter may be prepared ahead and stored in refrigerator.*

Marjorie Harris Johnston

Thin and Crisp Waffles or Pancakes

Serves 8

¾ cup vegetable oil
2 eggs
1 cup whole wheat flour
1 cup corn meal
2 cups milk
4 tablespoons baking powder

Put oil and eggs in blender and blend well. Add flour and 1 cup milk and blend again. Add meal and 1 cup milk and blend. Add baking powder, scrape sides of blender, and blend until batter is thin and smooth. Cook on hot griddle or waffle iron until brown and serve with hot syrup.

Beverly Hart Smith

French Bread

Yield: 2 loaves

1 package yeast
1 tablespoon sugar
1 cup warm water
2½ cups unbleached flour
1 teaspoon salt

Glaze

1 egg
1 tablespoon water

Dissolve yeast and sugar in warm water and set aside. In a large ceramic bowl or in a food processor bowl combine flour and salt. Add the sugar/yeast mixture and mix until the dough forms a ball. Remove dough and let rise in an oiled bowl, covered until doubled in bulk. Punch down, shape into 2 loaves in a French bread pan, and let rise again. Preheat oven to 350°. Brush the loaf tops with a mixture of 1 whole egg and 1 tablespoon water for a shiny glaze. Bake for 25-30 minutes. Before removing from oven to a cooling rack, turn the oven on broil until the tops brown evenly.

Sam Franks

French Pizza

Yield: 2 pizzas

Pastry

4 cups flour
1 teaspoon salt
2 sticks unsalted butter, softened
¾ cup cold water

Combine flour with salt. Work butter into flour with hands. Slowly add water to flour. Mix, roll into dough ball, wrap in wax paper and chill. Roll out chilled dough and line 2 pie plates or pizza pans. Partially bake crust at 350° for 10 minutes. Let crust cool. *Crust may also be used for quiche.*

Pizza

Thin slices of tomato
Sliced olives
Anchovies
Ham
Salami
Grated mozzarella and Parmesan cheese
Sliced mushrooms
Sliced onions
Sliced green pepper
Olive oil

Place on crust any combination of ingredients. Bake at 350° for 1 hour. When removed from oven, sprinkle pies with a few drops of olive oil. *Wonderful first course or light lunch.*

Dominique Lathrop

Pizza

Yield: 2 10-inch pizzas

Dough

1 package yeast
1 cup warm water
1 teaspoon sugar
1 teaspoon salt
2 tablespoons oil
2½ cups flour

Dissolve yeast in water. Add remaining ingredients. Beat 20 strokes. Let rest while preparing sauce.

Sauce (*or use canned*)

½ cup chopped onion
1 (8 ounce) can tomato sauce
¼ teaspoon garlic, minced
Salt to taste
⅛ teaspoon pepper

Mix sauce ingredients, set aside. Divide dough in half and pat each half onto greased baking sheets in 2 thin 10-inch circles, making raised rim around edges. Spread sauce on dough.

Topping

¼ cup grated Parmesan cheese
2 teaspoons oregano
1 cup (4 ounces) Pepperoni slices or Italian sausage or other desired toppings
2 cups (8 ounces) shredded mozzarella cheese

Sprinkle with Parmesan and oregano. Arrange Pepperoni (and other desired toppings) on top and sprinkle with mozzarella cheese.
Bake 20-25 minutes at 425° until hot and bubbly.

Lucie Mason Bynum

Polly's Basic Whole Wheat Bread

Yield: 2-3 loaves

1-2 tablespoons dry yeast
1 cup lukewarm water
2 tablespoons raw honey
3 cups warmed milk
1 tablespoon salt
2 tablespoons safflower oil
7-9 cups stone ground whole wheat flour, unsifted

Substitutions for stone ground whole wheat flour: 3 cups unbleached flour, 3 cups whole wheat, and 3 cups rye; or 3 cups unbleached, 1 cup raw wheat germ, 1 cup bran, and 2-4 cups whole wheat.

Mix dry yeast and water; add honey and let stand in a warm place until dissolved. Add warmed milk, salt, and oil. Add 5 cups unsifted flour. Beat 7 minutes with electric mixer at low speed. If dough is not beaten sufficiently, the bread will be heavy. Add 2-3 cups whole wheat flour or enough to make a stiff dough, cleaning the bowl. Sprinkle approximately 1 cup flour over bread board and turn dough on to it. Knead 10 minutes until dough is smooth and elastic. Use more flour if necessary to prevent sticking. It is essential to knead thoroughly. The elastin in whole wheat flour dough takes longer to develop than with white flour. Put into oiled bowl, smooth side down, and turn greased side up, cover with clean cloth and set in a warm place (85°) to rise until double in bulk (about 1 hour). If oven with pilot light is not available, set bowl in oven over a pan of hot water. When double in bulk, punch to original size. Cut dough into 2 or 3 pieces, depending on pan size. Flatten dough with hands and roll out a bit wider than pan length, half-inch thick. Fold edges in and then roll dough tightly, jelly roll fashion. Place in buttered pans, oil will cause bread to stick. Cover bread pans. Let rise until dough reaches top of pan. Bake at 350° for 40-50 minutes. Remove bread from pans immediately and let cool on wire racks.

Pauline Ireland Carroll

Onion Cheese Bread

Yield 2-3 loaves

2 tablespoons dry yeast granules (El Molino) or 2 packages dry yeast
½ cup water
¼ cup honey
2 tablespoons safflower or olive oil
2 cups cottage cheese, well drained
1 cup grated onion
1 tablespoon dillweed
2 teaspoons salt
2 eggs, beaten
7-9 cups whole wheat flour

Soften the yeast in the water. When the yeast mixture bubbles (after about 15 minutes), add all ingredients except flour. Add 4 cups unsifted flour and beat with electric mixer at low speed 5 minutes. If dough is not beaten sufficiently, the bread will be heavy. Add and stir well 3 cups more flour or enough to make a stiff dough, cleaning the bowl. Sprinkle approximately 1 cup flour over bread board and turn dough on to it. Knead 10 minutes until dough is smooth and elastic. Use more flour if necessary to prevent sticking. It is essential to knead thoroughly. The elastin in whole wheat flour dough takes longer to develop than with white flour. Put into oiled bowl smooth side down, and turn so greased side is up, cover with clean cloth, and set in a warm place (85°) to rise until double in bulk (about 1 hour). If oven with pilot light is not available, set bowl in oven over a pan of hot water. When double in bulk, punch down to original size. Cut dough into 2 or 3 pieces, depending on pan size. Flatten dough with hands and roll out a bit wider than pan length, half inch thick. Fold edges in and then roll dough tightly, jelly roll fashion. Place in buttered pans, oil will cause bread to stick. Cover bread pans. Let rise until dough reaches top of pan. Bake at 350° for 40-50 minutes. Remove bread from pans immediately and let cool on wire racks.

Pauline Ireland Carroll

Kathryn's Bread

Yield: 2 regular loaves or 4 smaller loaves

3½ cups boiling water
2-3 tablespoons butter or margarine
1½ cups cracked wheat
1 cup dry milk
3 tablespoons brown sugar
3 teaspoons salt
1 package dry yeast
¼ cup lukewarm water
6 or 7 cups white flour (varies with weather)
1 cup whole wheat flour
Oil or shortening

Pour boiling water over butter, cracked wheat, milk, sugar, and salt. Let cool to lukewarm. Suspend yeast in ¼ cup of water. When first mixture is lukewarm, add yeast and stir well. Add white flour and whole wheat flour cup by cup, stirring until you have workable dough. Put on board or marble and knead 10 minutes. Add flour as needed to keep dough from sticking. Must knead 10 minutes. Place in greased bowl (about 3-quart size or larger) and let rise. Cover bowl with cloth. Allow to double in size, about 2 hours. Punch down and let double again, about 1 hour. Divide into 2 parts. Roll out and fold opposite sides to center, tucking ends under. Place in bread pans which have been greased and floured. Let rise for about 45 minutes. Bake at 350° about 30-40 minutes. Cooking time depends on size of pans. Makes 2 loaves in regular size loaf pans or 4 loaves in 8″ x 4″ loaf pans.

Variations: Doubles well. Omit cracked wheat and add 1½ cups more flour to make cinnamon raisin bread. Just roll out, brush with melted butter, sprinkle heavily with sugar, cinnamon, and raisins. Roll up, tuck ends under and place in pans.

Tandy Sweeney Graves

Sprouted Wheat Bread

Yield: 2 loaves

4-5 cups unbleached white flour or stone ground whole wheat or combination
2 packages yeast
⅛ cup brown sugar
1 tablespoon salt
½ cup non-instant nonfat dry milk solids
¼ cup wheat germ
½ stick butter or margarine
2 cups hot water
½ cup wheat berries, soaked for 1 day, washed and left to sprout 1 day.

In large bowl combine 3 cups flour, yeast, sugar, salt, milk, and wheat germ, stirring well. In second bowl combine butter and hot water. Stir to melt and add to flour mixture. Stir in wheat berries and mix well. Gradually add flour, a cup at a time, stirring well after each addition until dough leaves sides of bowl clean. Turn onto well-floured board and knead about 10 minutes until smooth and elastic. Cover with plastic wrap and towel and let rise until double, about 2 hours. Punch down and divide into 2 parts. Roll each into a rectangle. Roll up each rectangle and place in greased 8½″ x 4½″ x 2½″ loaf pan. Let rise again for several hours. Bake at 400° for 35-40 minutes. Brush with melted butter.

Dill Bread

Yield: 1 loaf

1 (13½ ounce) package hot roll mix
½ cup cottage cheese
1 tablespoon sugar
1 teaspoon onion, minced
2 teaspoons dill weed or seed
1 teaspoon salt

Prepare hot roll mix as directed, but instead of stirring in egg as label directs, add cottage cheese, sugar, onion, dill weed or seed, and salt. Knead until smooth and elastic. Cover with towel and let rise in warm place (80° to 85°) away from draft. On floured board shape dough into loaf, and place in greased 7″ x 5″ loaf pan. Cover with towel and let rise until double. Preheat oven to 375° and bake 50 minutes. Cool in pan 5 minutes.

Mrs. Alvin A. Biggio

Parmesan Wine Bread

Serves 8-10

2 cups self-rising flour
¼ cup shortening
1 tablespoon sugar
1 small onion, grated
1 teaspoon oregano, crushed
½ stick butter, melted
¼ cup white wine
1 egg, beaten
½ cup milk
¾ cup Parmesan cheese

Preheat oven to 400°. Cut shortening into flour and combine with sugar, onion, and oregano. Add butter, wine, egg, milk, and stir until well blended. Put in greased 8-inch cake pan. Sprinkle heavily with Parmesan cheese. Bake for 20- 25 minutes. Serve warm. *This is good as an appetizer with wine or served with salad for lunch.*

Trudy Rogers Evans

English Muffin Bread

Yield: 2 loaves

1 cup milk
2 tablespoons sugar
1 teaspoon salt
3 tablespoons butter
1 package yeast
1 cup warm water (110°)
5½ cups flour
Corn meal

Scald milk. Stir in sugar, salt, and butter. Cool to lukewarm. In large bowl, dissolve yeast in water. Add milk mixture, then 3 cups flour. Beat until smooth. Add remaining flour to make soft dough. Turn on floured board and knead about 2 minutes until dough can form ball (will be sticky). Place in greased bowl. Cover and let rise until doubled, about 1 hour. Punch down. Divide in half. Shape into rectangle and roll up like jelly roll. Turn ends under. Roll each loaf in cornmeal. Place in 2 greased 9″ x 5″ loaf pans, seam side down. Cover. Let rise until doubled, about 1 hour. Bake 400° for 25 minutes. Remove from pans. Cool on wire racks.

Melbarized Pita Bread

1 package pita or unleavened pocket bread
Melted butter
Celery salt
Garlic salt

Open pita bread and spread with melted butter. Sprinkle with celery salt and garlic salt. Place in 200° oven for about 2 hours or until crispy. Break into chunks to use with dips.

Garland Cook Smith

Monkey Bread

Children love to help make this!

Yield: 2 loaves or 1 Bundt pan

2 packages yeast
1 cup lukewarm water
1 cup shortening
¾ cup sugar
1½ teaspoons salt
1 cup *boiling* water
2 beaten eggs
6 cups flour
2 sticks butter, melted

Dissolve yeast in lukewarm water. Mix shortening, sugar, and salt. Add boiling water slowly to mixture. Add beaten eggs and dissolved yeast to the mixture. Add flour about 1 cup at a time. Let rise in warm place until dough is double in size. Push dough down. Can be refrigerated at this point. Roll out dough on floured board to about ¼-½ inch thick. Cut into various shapes—squares, triangles, rounds. Dip shapes in melted butter and lay pieces in layers in Bundt pan or loaf pan until pan is half full. Pour extra butter over loaf. Let rise to top of pan. Bake at 350° for about 45 minutes or until brown. Pull apart to eat. *May be prepared ahead. May be frozen after cooking.*

Mushroom Bread

Serves 10

1 long, narrow loaf of French bread
1 tablespoon chopped shallots
½ stick butter, melted
1 pound fresh mushrooms, sliced
1 teaspoon lemon juice
Salt and pepper to taste
2 tablespoons Madeira wine
¾ cup whipping cream
1 tablespoon chopped parsley
1 cup grated Gruyère cheese

Preheat oven to 350°. Slice bread in half lengthwise and pull out the middle of the halves. Sauté shallots in butter for 1 minute. Add mushrooms, lemon juice, salt and pepper. When moisture is gone, add Madeira and let evaporate. Add cream, stirring constantly on low heat until cream has reduced and absorbed into mushrooms. Stir in parsley. Fill French bread halves with mushroom mixture and top with grated cheese. May be frozen at this point. Bake 20 minutes, then brown under broiler. Slice into finger-sized pieces and serve hot. *This may be served as an appetizer or with a salad for lunch.*

Judy Toronto Rotenstreich

Mom's Cinnamon Bread

I made my reputation as a mother with this recipe for cinnamon bread. Many long hours on the phone; many days of meetings at the Junior League Building were forgiven when the children came home from school and found that Mom had stayed home long enough to make bread.

Yield: 3 loaves

1 package yeast
½ cup lukewarm water
1 tablespoon sugar
1 egg
½ cup melted butter
2 cups lukewarm water
2 teaspoons salt
½ cup sugar
8 cups sifted flour
1 cup sugar
3 tablespoons cinnamon
Melted butter

Dissolve the yeast in water. Add the sugar and let this mixture stand in a warm place for 45 minutes. (A sponge should develop.) Using a mixmaster, set on medium speed, beat in the next 5 ingredients. Add 4 cups of the flour gradually—mixture will be runny. Slowly add as much of the remaining flour as possible, until the mixture is too stiff to beat. Turn out onto a floured board and knead in the rest of the flour. Knead until smooth. The entire kneading process should take about 10 minutes. Place the dough in a well-greased bowl and let it stand until double in bulk (about 1 hour). Knead the edges in, turn the dough, and let it stand in a warm place until double in size again, about 1 more hour. Cut the dough into 3 portions. Roll each out in a rectangle, spread with melted butter and sugar/cinnamon mixture. Roll up like a jelly roll, turning in the edges when rolled and sealing the ends. Place each loaf in a well-greased, 8-inch loaf pan and permit them to rise until double in bulk (1 more hour). Place them in a cold oven. Turn the heat to 400°. After 15 minutes reduce the heat to 375° and bake the bread 25 minutes longer. Remove the loaves from the oven and place on a rack to cool.

Sheila S. Blair
PAST PRESIDENT

Moravian Sugar Bread

Yield: 3 loaves

2-3 potatoes, cooked and mashed, about 1 cup
1 package dry yeast
⅔ cup warm water
1 cup milk, scalded and cooled
½ cup sugar
1½ teaspoons salt
1 stick butter or margarine
2 eggs, slightly beaten
7 cups sifted flour
2 cups light brown sugar
1 stick butter, divided
Cinnamon

Dissolve yeast in warm water. To scalded milk add sugar, salt, and butter, stirring until dissolved. Cool until lukewarm. Combine mashed potatoes, yeast, and eggs, beating mixture until smooth. Add milk mixture. Add flour 1 cup at a time, kneading after each addition. Place dough in buttered bowl. Turn dough over, buttering all sides. Cover and let rise at 80° for 1-1½ hours or until doubled in bulk. Turn raised dough out on floured board and divide into 3 parts. Roll each part into a 11″ x 5″ piece and place on cookie sheet. Cover and let rise to ¾- to 1-inch thickness. Sprinkle with light brown sugar and punch holes in dough about 1 inch apart. In each hole put a pat of butter. Melt the last 2 tablespoons of butter and spread over dough with pastry brush. Sprinkle with cinnamon and bake at 350° for 20-25 minutes. Cool.

Marjorie Longenecker White

Almond Breakfast Bread

Serves 8-10

1 cup butter
¾ cup sugar
1 egg, separated
½ cup almond paste
1 teaspoon vanilla
2 cups sifted flour
¼ cup sliced almonds

Preheat oven to 350°. In a large bowl, cream butter and sugar until fluffy. Beat in egg yolk. Add almond paste and vanilla, and beat until smooth. At low speed, stir in flour just until well combined. Press into ungreased 8″ x 8″ pan. Beat egg white until frothy, brush over top, sprinkle with almonds and bake 30 minutes or until golden brown. Cool completely.

Joan Boblasky

Blueberry Bread

Yield: 2 loaves

3 cups flour
1 teaspoon salt
1 teaspoon soda
1 tablespoon ground cinnamon
2 cups sugar
3 eggs, well beaten
1¼ cups salad oil
2 pints blueberries
1¼ cups chopped pecans

Preheat oven to 350°. Combine flour, salt, soda, cinnamon, and sugar. Make a well in center of dry ingredients. Add eggs and oil, stir only until dry ingredients are moistened. Stir in blueberries and pecans. Spoon batter into 2 lightly-greased 8″ x 4″ loaf pans. Bake for 1 hour. Let stand overnight before slicing.

Pat Casey Gillepsy

Healthy Banana Bread

Yield: 1 large loaf

¾ cup brown sugar
½ cup margarine
1 egg
3 or 4 ripe bananas, mashed
1 cup whole wheat flour
½ cup white flour
1 teaspoon baking soda
¼ cup plain yogurt
1 cup chopped pecans

Preheat oven to 350°. Cream sugar and margarine. Add egg and mashed bananas. Then add remaining ingredients except pecans and mix well. Stir in pecans after mixture is well beaten. Pour into a large greased loaf pan and bake for 30-40 minutes.

Martha Smith Vandervoort

Cranberry Bread

Yield: 1 loaf

1 cup sugar
2 cups flour
1 teaspoon salt
1½ teaspoons baking powder
½ teaspoon soda
1 orange, juice and grated rind
2 tablespoons butter, melted
1 egg, beaten
2 cups fresh cranberries, chopped or halved
½ cup chopped pecans or walnuts

Preheat oven to 350°. Sift together sugar, flour, salt, baking powder, and soda. Combine orange juice and rind. Add butter and enough water to make 1 cup of orange juice. Stir in egg. Pour liquid mixture into the dry ingredients, mixing just enough to dampen. Fold in cranberries and nuts. Pour into greased 9″ x 5″ x 3″ loaf pan. Bake for 50-60 minutes. Remove from oven and cool. Store in refrigerator for best flavor and easiest slicing. For gift loaves, bake in 2 or 3 small pans for 30-45 minutes.

Quick Lemon Bread

Yield: 1 loaf

2½ cups flour
3 teaspoons baking powder
1 teaspoon salt
5½ tablespoons butter
1 cup sugar
Grated peel of 1 lemon
2 eggs
1 cup milk
½ cup chopped walnuts

Syrup

¼ cup sugar
⅓ cup lemon juice
Grated peel of 1 lemon

Preheat oven to 325°. Mix flour, baking powder, and salt. Set aside. Cream butter, sugar, and lemon peel. Add eggs, beating well after each. Add flour mixture and milk, alternately, half at a time, to egg mixture. Stir until batter is smooth. Fold in nuts. Grease loaf pan and pour in batter. Bake 60 minutes or until tester comes out clean. Glaze with syrup and let cool in pan 30 minutes. Remove from pan and cool on rack 2 hours before slicing. *May be prepared 2 days ahead.*

Pumpkin Bread

Make small muffins for lunch or snack.

Yield: 2 loaves

3 cups sugar
1 cup salad oil
3 eggs
2 cups fresh pumpkin, cooked (may substitute 2 cups canned pumpkin)
3 cups flour
½ teaspoon salt
½ teaspoon baking powder
1 teaspoon cinnamon
1 teaspoon nutmeg
1 teaspoon baking soda

Preheat oven to 350°. Mix sugar, oil, and eggs. Add remaining ingredients. Pour into two 8½" x 4½" x 2⅝" ungreased loaf pans and bake for 45 minutes. *May be prepared ahead. May be frozen.*

Joan Gerbec Ellis

Sugar Plum Ring

Serves 16

1 package active dry yeast
¼ cup warm water
½ cup milk, scalded
⅓ cup sugar
⅓ cup shortening
1 teaspoon salt
3¾-4 cups sifted flour
2 eggs, beaten
¾ cup sugar
1 teaspoon cinnamon
½ stick butter, melted
½ cup whole blanched almonds or chopped pecans
Red cherries, optional
⅓ cup dark corn syrup

Preheat oven to 350°. Dissolve yeast in water. Set aside. Combine milk, sugar, shortening, and salt. Cool to lukewarm. Stir in 1 cup flour, blending well. Add yeast mixture and eggs. Add remaining flour to make soft dough. Mix thoroughly. Place in greased bowl, turning once to grease surface. Cover and let rise about 2 hours in warm place until double in size. Punch dough down and let rest about 10 minutes. Divide dough into 4 parts. Cut each part into 10 pieces and shape into balls. Mix sugar and cinnamon together. Dip each ball into melted butter and then sugar mixture. Arrange ⅓ of the balls in a well-greased, 10-inch tube pan. Sprinkle with almonds and cherries. Repeat with 2 more layers. Mix corn syrup with remaining sugar/cinnamon mixture and drizzle over the top. Cover and let rise in warm place about 1 hour or until doubled in size. Bake for 35 minutes. Cool 5 minutes. Invert pan and remove ring.

Jackie Stevens Hall

Cinnamon Biscuit Coffee Cake

Remarkably easy to prepare

Serves 8-10

1½ sticks butter or margarine
1½ cups sugar
4 heaping teaspoons cinnamon
½-1 cup chopped pecans
3 cans (10 each) Hungry Jack Buttermilk Biscuits

Preheat oven to 300°. Grease a tube pan. Melt butter over low heat. Mix together sugar, cinnamon, and nuts in bowl. Take biscuits from can and dip them 1 at a time first in butter, then in sugar mixture, so that all sides of biscuits are covered. Line sides of pan with biscuits touching edge to edge. Repeat rows of biscuits moving toward center. Make as many layers as necessary to use all biscuits. Bake for 1 hour. Let cool 5-10 minutes and remove from pan by turning pan upside down on platter. The coffee cake ring can be garnished with fresh or candied fruits to look festive. Biscuits pull off easily, so there is no need to slice. *If making ahead of time or freezing, wrap in foil so it can be reheated. It is best served hot.*

Mimi Presley Cranz

Apple Coffee Cake

Serves 12

½ cup shortening
1 cup sugar
1 teaspoon salt
1 teaspoon vanilla
2 eggs
2½ cups flour
1 teaspoon soda
1 teaspoon baking powder
1 cup sour cream
2 cups chopped apples

Topping

1 cup brown sugar
2 teaspoons cinnamon
1 stick butter, melted
1 cup chopped pecans

Preheat oven to 350°. Cream together shortening and sugar. Add salt, vanilla, and eggs, mixing well. Combine the dry ingredients in separate bowl. Add dry ingredients alternately with the sour cream to the creamed mixture. Stir in apples. Pour batter into greased 13″ x 9″ pan. Combine brown sugar, cinnamon, butter, and pecans. Pour over the top of the coffee cake. Bake for 25 minutes.

Peggy McLean Monroe

Oatmeal Banana Cupcakes

Yield: 24 cupcakes

½ cup sugar
1 stick butter
2 eggs
3 ripe bananas, mashed (1 cup)
¾ cup honey
1½ cups flour
1 teaspoon baking powder
1 teaspoon baking soda
¾ teaspoon salt
1 cup quick cooking rolled oats

Preheat oven to 375°. In mixer, cream together sugar and butter. Beat in eggs, bananas, and honey. Stir together flour, baking powder, soda, and salt. Add to creamed mixture, beating just until blended. Stir in oats. Line muffin tins with baking cups and fill ⅔ full with batter. Bake for 18-20 minutes. Remove from pans and cool on wire rack.

Sharon Mann Piper

Blueberry Coffee Cake

Good for gifts. Nice for Christmas morning.

Serves 16

1 stick butter or margarine, softened
1 cup sugar
2 eggs
1 (8 ounce) carton sour cream
1 teaspoon vanilla
2 cups flour
½ teaspoon baking powder
½ teaspoon baking soda
¼ teaspoon salt
1 (16 ounce) can blueberries, drained

Topping

⅓ cup sugar
½ cup chopped pecans
3 teaspoons cinnamon

Preheat oven to 350°. Cream together the butter and sugar. Add the eggs, beating at moderate speed on the mixer. Add sour cream and vanilla. Sift together the flour, baking powder, soda, and salt. Add to the batter. Carefully fold in the drained blueberries. Combine topping ingredients. Using a greased and floured Bundt pan, pour in half the batter, spread half of the topping on this, and then add the rest of the batter. Spread on the remaining topping. Swirl with a knife. Bake for about 50 minutes. When doubling recipe, use 5 eggs instead of 4. *May be prepared ahead. May be frozen.*

Caroline Johnson Abele

Cranberry Coffee Cake

Good for coffees–especially pretty at Christmas time.

Serves 16

1 stick butter or margarine
1 cup sugar
2 large eggs
1 teaspoon or more almond extract
2 cups flour
1 teaspoon baking powder
1 teaspoon baking soda
½ teaspoon salt
1 cup sour cream
1 (17 ounce) can whole berry cranberry sauce
½ cup chopped pecans

Frosting

¾ cup powdered sugar
2 tablespoons warm water
½ teaspoon almond extract

Preheat oven to 350° for tube pan; 325° for Bundt pan. Grease and flour pan. Cream butter and sugar; add eggs one at a time and beat well. Add flavoring. Sift dry ingredients together and add about ½ cup at a time alternately with some sour cream, until all is blended. Put ⅓ batter in pan. Spoon half cranberry sauce over and swirl through batter. Spoon another ⅓ of batter into pan; layer remainder of sauce; top with remaining batter and sprinkle with nuts. Bake about 50-60 minutes in tube pan; about 45-55 minutes in Bundt pan. Cool thoroughly before removing from pan. Combine frosting ingredients and drizzle over cake. *Flavor improves if made day ahead. Wrap in foil and warm to serve. Freezes well.*

Ann Adams Pritchard

Sour Cream Coffee Cake

Serves 16

2 sticks butter or margarine
2 cups sugar
2 eggs
½ teaspoon vanilla
2 cups flour
1 teaspoon baking powder
½ teaspoon salt
1 cup sour cream
½ cup chopped pecans
3 tablespoons cinnamon
4 tablespoons brown sugar
3 tablespoons sugar

Preheat oven to 350°. Cream butter, sugar, eggs, and vanilla. Sift flour, baking powder, and salt. Add to creamed mixture. Fold in sour cream. Pour half mixture into greased and floured Bundt pan. Top with half mixture of nuts, cinnamon, brown sugar, and sugar. Repeat these layers. Swirl the batter with knife. Bake 50-60 minutes.

Becky Herren Bashinsky

Cinnamon Apricot Ring

Good Gift

Serves 12

1 (13½ ounce) package hot roll mix
¾ cup apricot preserves
1 stick butter
1 teaspoon cinnamon

Prepare hot roll mix as package directs. Let rise once and roll out in a rectangle 16″ x 10″. Spread with preserves, dot with butter, and sprinkle with cinnamon. Starting at long end, roll up jelly roll fashion and seal edges. Place seam-side down in circle on greased cookie sheet. Let rise in warm place until doubled, about 1 hour. Bake in a preheated 400° oven 25-30 minutes. *May be prepared ahead.*

Kappy Mills Hamilton

DESSERTS

Desserts

Praline Angels

Serves 12

4 egg whites, room temperature
¼ teaspoon cream of tartar
Pinch of salt
1 cup sugar
1 cup chopped pecans
1 teaspoon vanilla
½ gallon pralines and pecan ice cream or French vanilla

Preheat oven to 275°. Beat together egg whites, cream of tartar, and salt. When foamy, gradually add sugar. Beat until stiff peaks form. Fold in nuts and vanilla. Shape into individual meringue shells with bottom of spoon and place on greased cookie sheet. Bake for 1 hour until light brown and crisp.

Sauce

1 teaspoon baking soda
1 cup buttermilk
2 cups sugar
1 stick butter
4 tablespoons white Karo syrup
2 teaspoons vanilla

Dissolve baking soda in buttermilk. Combine remaining ingredients and place all in large heavy skillet and stir. Bring to boil and allow to boil gently for 5-10 minutes, until medium thick. *May be kept at room temperature for a day or indefinitely in refrigerator.*

To serve, scoop ice cream into meringue shells and top with sauce.

Ann McMorries Smith

Strawberry Torte

Serves 12

9 egg whites
3 cups sugar
¼ teaspoon cream of tartar
1 teaspoon vinegar
1 pint whipping cream, whipped and sweetened to taste
2 quarts strawberries, sliced and sweetened to taste

Preheat oven to 250°. Beat egg whites until stiff, adding sugar gradually. Add cream of tartar and vinegar. Bake in 2 shallow cake pans (spring form pans are best) for 1 hour, or until slightly browned. Remove from pans and let cool. Put a thick layer of strawberries on 1 cake layer, add a layer of whipped cream. Place other cake layer on top of whipped cream. Add more berries. Ice torte completely with whipped cream, then decorate top with whole or half berries. *Fresh peaches may be used instead of strawberries.*

Lella Clayton Bromberg
PAST PRESIDENT

Grandmother's Wine Jelly Dessert

Serves 8-10

3 tablespoons gelatin
2¾ cups boiling water
2 cups sugar
Juice of 5 lemons
Grated rind of 2 lemons
½ teaspoon mace
1 stick cinnamon
10 cloves
2 egg whites, beaten
1¼ cups red wine
½ pint whipping cream

Soften gelatin with 1 cup cold water in a saucepan. Pour boiling water, sugar, lemon juice, and grated rind over gelatin mixture. Add mace, cinnamon, cloves, and egg whites. Boil 5 minutes. Strain. Add wine. Put in refrigerator to congeal (takes several hours). Before serving, top with whipped cream. *This is light, refreshing, and unusual.*

Susan Nabers Haskell

Frozen Lemon Mousse

Serves 12

30 lemon thins or vanilla wafers
4 egg yolks
½ cup fresh lemon juice
¼ cup sugar
1½ tablespoons grated lemon rind
4 egg whites
⅛ teaspoon cream of tartar
Pinch of salt
¼ cup sugar
1½ cups whipping cream
½ cup sugar

Line the bottom and sides of a 9-inch spring form pan with wafers. Combine egg yolks, lemon juice, ¼ cup sugar, and lemon rind in a large bowl. Let stand at room temperature. Beat egg whites until foamy. Add cream of tartar and salt. Continue beating until soft peaks form. Gradually add remaining sugar, beating constantly until stiff and glossy. Whip cream with ½ cup of sugar until stiff. Gently fold whites and cream into yolk mixture. Carefully spoon into pan. Cover with foil and freeze for 8 hours. Let soften 1 hour in refrigerator before serving. *This is excellent for brunches or after Oriental food.*

Betty Clark Meadows

Lemon Cake Top Pudding

Serves 4-6

1 tablespoon butter or margarine
1 cup sugar
2 tablespoons flour
2 eggs, separated
1 lemon, juice and rind
1 cup milk
½ pint whipping cream, whipped

Preheat oven to 300°. Cream butter and sugar. Stir in flour, egg yolks, lemon, and milk. Beat egg whites until stiff and fold into mixture. Pour into greased custard cups or ramekins. Place cups in pan with ½-1 inch of water. Bake 45 minutes. Serve at room temperature or cold. Top with whipped cream.

Margaret Gresham Livingston

Lemon Curd

Delicious in a tart shell or as a filling for a cake

Yield: 2 cups

2 large lemons
½ pound lump sugar (48 hostess tablets)
¾ stick butter
3 eggs

Extract lemon oil by rubbing uncut lemon over sugar lumps. Be careful to get as much as you can. Put sugar and butter into top of double boiler and melt. Add the juice of both lemons. Beat eggs well and pour through a strainer into sugar mixture. Cook over moderately high heat until good and thick. Stir constantly. Store covered in refrigerator. Mixture thickens when cool.

Mary Dorman Mullervy
CLAYGATE, SURREY, ENGLAND

Charlotte

Serves 12-14

2 envelopes gelatin
½ cup cold water
1 pint whipping cream, whipped
6 large eggs, separated
10 tablespoons sugar
10 tablespoons cream sherry
2 packages lady fingers (total of 24)

Dissolve gelatin in cold water. Beat egg yolks until light. Add sherry and half of sugar to yolks. Stir in the gelatin, mixing well. In a large bowl, beat egg whites until they form peaks. Add remaining sugar to egg whites. Fold whipped cream into the egg yolk mixture until it is all the same color. Fold egg yolk mixture into egg whites until evenly blended. Pour into large glass bowl or spring mold pan lined with halves of lady fingers. Chill well.

Ann Rosamond Patton
DALTON, GEORGIA

Amaretto and Cream Mold

Serves 12-15

1 envelope gelatin
¼ cup cold water
3 eggs, separated
½ cup sugar, divided
Salt to taste
½ cup Amaretto liqueur
1 cup whipping cream, whipped
Slivered almonds, optional

Sprinkle gelatin over water in cup. In medium saucepan, beat egg yolks, ¼ cup sugar, and salt. Add gelatin and water. Mix well. Place over medium heat and stir until gelatin and sugar are dissolved and mixture coats spoon, about 5 minutes. Remove from heat and add Amaretto. Cool, stirring occasionally, until mixture gels slightly. Beat egg whites until they form soft peaks, then add ¼ cup sugar gradually while beating until stiff. Fold egg whites into gelatin mixture, then fold whipped cream into above mixture. Pour into serving bowl and chill in refrigerator. Before serving, sprinkle top with slivered almonds. *One recipe fills 2 shallow pie crusts or, for best results, 2 recipes fill Bundt pan for lovely mold.*

Salinda Taylor Bewley

Kentucky Tombstone Pudding

Serves 8

6 egg yolks
1 cup sugar
1 teaspoon flour
1 cup dessert sherry
2 dozen almond macaroons
4 egg whites
Pinch of salt
Pinch of cream of tartar
4 tablespoons sugar
½ cup whole almonds
2 (1 ounce) squares semi-sweet chocolate, optional

Beat yolks until thick and lemon colored. Mix sugar and flour and beat into yolks. Add sherry and cook over low heat, stirring constantly until thickened. Pour over macaroons which have been arranged in a shallow, ovenproof baking dish. Beat egg whites and add salt and cream of tartar. Spread over the custard, covering it completely. Stud with almonds and bake for 20 minutes or until lightly browned at 300°. Sprinkle with shaved or grated chocolate slivers. Serve hot or at room temperature. *Recipe can be doubled.*

Eleanor Bridges Griffin

Bisque Tortoni

Serves 10

Must be prepared ahead.

1 (12 ounce) carton cottage cheese
1 (3 ounce) package cream cheese
3 eggs, separated
1 cup sugar
1½ teaspoons almond extract
½ teaspoon vanilla
½ pint whipping cream, whipped
18 almond macaroons, crumbled

Cream the cheeses together. Add egg yolks one at a time beating well after each addition. Add sugar and mix thoroughly. Add flavorings and fold in whipped cream. Beat egg whites until stiff and fold into mixture. Line bottom of loaf pan with waxed paper. Put half of macaroons into loaf pan. Pour in dessert mixture and top with remaining macaroons. Freeze.

Grace Brewer Hunter

Chocolate Mousse

Serves 8-10

- **¼ cup sugar**
- **4 tablespoons Grand Marnier liqueur**
- **½ cup semi-sweet chocolate morsels**
- **3 talbespoons whipping cream**
- **2 tablespoons strong coffee**
- **2 egg whites, stiffly beaten**
- **2 cups whipping cream, whipped**

Cook sugar and Grand Marnier over very low heat until sugar is dissolved. Melt chocolate in top of double boiler. When chocolate has cooled, add the 3 tablespoons of whipping cream and coffee. Add sugar/Grand Marnier mixture to melted chocolate mixture and stir until smooth. When the mixture is cool, fold in egg whites. Gently fold in whipped cream. Pour into individual molds or dish and chill at least 2 hours before serving.

Norma Jean McClanahan Bueschen

Cold Chocolate Soufflé

Serves 8

- **2 (1 ounce) squares unsweetened chocolate**
- **½ cup confectioner's sugar**
- **1 cup milk**
- **1 envelope gelatin, softened in ¼ cup cold water**
- **¾ cup granulated sugar**
- **1 teaspoon vanilla extract**
- **¼ teaspoon salt**
- **2 cups whipping cream, whipped**

Combine chocolate and confectioner's sugar in double boiler. Gradually add milk, stirring constantly. Place over low heat and stir until mixture just reaches boiling point. DO NOT BOIL. Remove from heat and stir in softened gelatin, sugar, vanilla, and salt. Chill until slightly thickened. Fold in whipped cream. Pour in 2-quart serving dish. Chill 2-3 hours.

Prudy Willis Yeates

Chocolate Rum Bombe

Serves 8

½ gallon vanilla ice cream, softened
1 (12 ounce) package semi-sweet chocolate morsels
2 tablespoons rum
6 eggs, separated (yolks beaten, whites whipped)
4 teaspoons vanilla
1 cup whipping cream, whipped

Place 12-cup bowl in freezer until thoroughly chilled. Using a cold spoon, spread ice cream evenly on sides and bottom, leaving center hollow. Freeze 1 hour or until firm. Melt chocolate in top of double boiler. Add rum. Remove from heat; gradually add beaten egg yolks and vanilla, beating constantly. *Fold* in stiffly beaten egg whites, then whipped cream. Pour chocolate mixture into ice cream-lined bowl. Cover with wax paper, then foil. Freeze at least 4 hours. To serve, dip in hot water for 30 seconds, then turn onto serving plate and serve immediately.

Molly Liles Carter

Chocolate Crumb Dessert

Serves 12

2 cups vanilla wafer crumbs
1 cup chopped pecans
2 sticks butter or margarine
2 cups confectioner's sugar
6 egg yolks, well beaten
3 (1 ounce) squares unsweetened chocolate, melted
1 teaspoon vanilla
6 egg whites, stiffly beaten
½ pint whipping cream

Mix together vanilla wafer crumbs and pecans. Pour half of mixture in 9″ x 13″ pan. Cream butter and sugar well and add egg yolks, chocolate, and vanilla. Fold egg whites into batter mixture. Pour over crumbs and top with remaining half of crumb mixture. Refrigerate overnight. Cut into squares and top with whipped cream.

Jane Harsh Glasser

Chocolate Torte Supreme

Must be prepared ahead.

Serves 8-10

7 (1 ounce) squares Baker's semi-sweet chocolate
1 stick butter
1 cup sugar
7 egg yolks
7 egg whites
Sugar
Chocolate shavings
½ pint whipping cream, whipped and sweetened to taste

Preheat oven to 325°. Melt the chocolate and butter in a saucepan. Add sugar and egg yolks, and beat for 3 minutes with mixer at high speed. In a separate bowl, beat egg whites until stiff (add a little sugar to hold peaks). Fold egg whites *slowly* into the chocolate batter with a spatula. Pour only ¾ of the batter into an ungreased spring form pan. Bake for 35 minutes. Let torte cool and fall. Then run knife around edge and remove frame. Pour the remaining uncooked batter over the top and chill. Garnish with chocolate shavings and serve with whipped cream.

Gordon Balch Lanier

Pôts de Crème

Serves 4

6 ounces Nestle's semi-sweet chocolate chips
3 tablespoons sugar
1 egg
1 tablespoon rum
½ teaspoon instant coffee granules
¾ cup milk
Whipping cream, whipped and slightly sweetened

Combine chips, sugar, egg, rum, and coffee in a blender and blend well. Scald milk and add to blender. Blend 2-3 minutes at high speed. Pour into individual pots de creme or demi-tasse cups and refrigerate 4-6 hours. Top with whipped cream. *Recipe can be doubled.*

Ellen Cross Jackson

Mile-High Baked Alaska

Serves 12

2 (1 ounce) squares unsweetened chocolate
1 stick margarine
2 eggs
1 cup sugar
¾ cup flour
½ teaspoon baking powder
½ teaspoon salt
1 teaspoon vanilla
1 cup chopped pecans, optional
1½ quarts chocolate ice cream
1 quart vanilla or coffee ice cream
4 egg whites at room temperature
⅔ cup sugar

Melt chocolate and margarine in top of double boiler. Beat eggs, and add sugar. Beat in chocolate mixture, then add flour, baking powder, and salt. Blend in vanilla and nuts. Pour into greased round cake pan and bake about 25 minutes at 350°. Cool on rack. Line a 2-quart mixing bowl with foil. Spread a layer of chocolate ice cream about 1-inch thick on bottom and sides. Pack vanilla or coffee ice cream in center. Freeze until firm. Preheat oven to 500°. Beat egg whites until soft peaks form. Gradually add sugar, beating till stiff. To assemble, place brownie layer on oven-proof dish. Unmold ice cream, and place on top of cake. Ice with meringue. Bake 3-4 minutes at 500°. Serve at once; or freeze and serve straight from freezer.

Robin Hall Sulzby

Aunt Bene's Indian Pudding

Serves 6

3 cups milk
4 tablespoons yellow cornmeal
⅓ cup molasses
½ cup sugar
1 egg, beaten
1 tablespoon butter
¼ teaspoon salt
½ teaspoon ginger
½ teaspoon cinnamon
1 cup milk

Scald 3 cups milk. Mix meal and molasses and stir into hot milk. Cook until thickened, stirring constantly to prevent scorching. Remove from heat and add sugar, egg, butter, salt, ginger, and cinnamon. Mix thoroughly. Pour into buttered casserole dish and bake ½ hour at 300°. Pour 1 cup of milk over pudding and continue baking for 2 hours. *Serve with whipped cream and/or a light sprinkling of nutmeg.*

Edna Dexter Niederhauser

Fresh Peach Pudding Dessert

Serves 6-8

May prepare 1 day ahead.

6 peaches
1 cup sugar, divided
¼ teaspoon cinnamon
2 eggs, slightly beaten
½ cup flour
2 teaspoon baking powder
1 teaspoon vanilla
Pinch of salt
Butter
Whipped cream

Pare and slice peaches, then toss in small bowl with ½ cup sugar and cinnamon. Make a batter of ½ cup sugar, eggs, flour, baking powder, vanilla, and salt. Place fruit in a greased 8- or 9-inch square baking dish. Pour batter over fruit. Dot with butter and sprinkle with cinnamon. Bake at 350° for about 30 minutes or until brown and crusty on top. Serve warm with whipped cream.

Barbara Biglow Coyer

Grandma Wilde's Trifle

Custard may be prepared 1-2 days ahead.

Serves 12

Custard

2 eggs, beaten
½ cup sugar
⅛ teaspoon salt
2 tablespoons flour
2 cups scalded milk
1½ teaspoons vanilla

Beat eggs with sugar, salt, and flour. Slowly stir in milk and cook, stirring in a double boiler over low heat until it coats a metal spoon. Add vanilla when cool.

Assembly

2 sponge cake layers, commercial or homemade
¾ cup raspberry jam
½ cup blanched slivered almonds, reserve 1 tablespoon
8 almond macaroons, crumbled
½ cup sherry
2 cups boiled custard
1 cup whipping cream
¼ cup sugar
1 teaspoon vanilla
Garnish: crystallized cherries or shaved chocolate

Spread jam between sponge layers and place in attractive serving bowl. Push almonds into cake at frequent intervals. Top with the macaroons and pour sherry over the top. Then pour custard on top, piercing layers with a knife so mixture can soak through. Just before serving, whip cream with ¼ cup sugar and 1 teaspoon vanilla. Mound cream on top and garnish as desired, using reserved almonds, cherries, or chocolate.

Debby Hull-Ryde Tanner

Marie's Bread Pudding

Serves 8

½ cup apple jelly
4-5 cups day-old bread crumbs
4 cups milk
3 eggs
¾ cup sugar (½ cup for less sweet)
¼ teaspoon nutmeg
1 teaspoon vanilla
3 tablespoons butter
1 cup raisins

Preheat oven to 350°. Grease sides of 2-quart rectangular pyrex dish. Spread jelly ¼-inch thick on bottom of dish. (This jelly will bubble up through the pudding when it cooks. It will also keep the bottom from burning.) Tear bread into thumb-sized pieces and place in large bowl. Set aside. Scald milk. Beat eggs in small bowl and add sugar, nutmeg, and vanilla. Add butter and raisins to milk. When butter has melted, add this mixture to the bread and stir. Add egg mixture and stir. Using a cup, gently pour the pudding into the casserole. Bake for 1 hour. *Best served hot. For company serve with half-and-half poured over it.*

Marbury Rainer Ray

Praline Crunch

Yield: 3 cups

1 stick butter or margarine
1 cup brown sugar
½ cup pecan pieces
2½ cups corn flakes

Melt butter and sugar in pan. Bring to boil and immediately remove from heat. Add pecans and corn flakes and toss together with fork to coat mixture. Store in airtight container. Serve over ice cream.

Ann Rosamond Patton
DALTON, GEORGIA

Versatile Ice Cream Strata

Serves 16

1 (12 ounce) box vanilla wafers, crushed
1 stick melted butter or margarine
2 cups confectioner's sugar
1 stick butter or margarine, softened
2 (1 ounce) squares unsweetened chocolate, melted and cooled
1 teaspoon vanilla
3 egg yolks, beaten
3 egg whites, stiffly beaten
1 quart of your favorite ice cream, softened
1 cup chopped pecans, optional

Combine crushed wafers and melted butter. Press firmly and evenly in bottom of 13″ x 9″ x 2″ baking pan. Cream sugar and butter; add chocolate, vanilla, and egg yolks, beating well. Fold egg whites into chocolate mixture. Spread chocolate mixture evenly over crumb crust. Chill 2 hours or until firm. If using nuts, mix into ice cream and spread over chocolate mixture. Freeze 3-4 hours.

Betty Timberlake Knight
PAST PRESIDENT

Homemade Chocolate Mint Ice Cream

Must prepare at least 2 hours ahead.

Yield: 1 gallon

2 cups sugar
4 eggs, beaten
¼ teaspoon salt
5 (13 ounce) cans evaporated milk
1 (8 ounce) bar milk chocolate, grated
1½ teaspoons mint extract
Green food coloring

Gradually add sugar to eggs, beating until stiff. Stir in salt, evaporated milk, chocolate, and mint extract. Add food coloring to desired shade of green. Pour mixture into freezer can of ice cream freezer. Freeze until hardened (usually about 30-45 minutes in electric freezer). Let ripen at least 2 hours before serving.

Mary Evelyn Waits Smith

Poogan's Ice Cream á l'Orange

Serves 6

1 stick butter
2 teaspoons sugar
Juice of 1 orange
Juice of 1 lemon
1 tablespoon grated orange rind
1 tablespoon grated lemon rind
1 tablespoon chopped pecans
2 tablespoons Grand Marnier
1 tablespoon Kahlúa
Vanilla ice cream
6 peach halves

Combine first 7 ingredients and sauté until the mixture begins to bubble. Add Grand Marnier and Kahlúa. To complete this quick but gala dessert, place 1 large scoop of vanilla ice cream in a brandy snifter or over-sized glass. Top the ice cream with a peach half and spoon 2 tablespoons of the orange sauce over all.

Poogan's Porch
CHARLESTON, SOUTH CAROLINA

Old Fashioned Peach Ice Cream

Serves 10-12

6 cups chopped peaches
3 eggs, beaten
1 cup sugar
1½ cups sugar
2 tablespoons flour
½ teaspoon salt
1 quart whole milk or half-and-half
½ pint whipping cream, unwhipped
1 tablespoon vanilla

Add sugar to peaches and let stand. Stir eggs, sugar, flour, and salt together and blend well. Add milk and cook slowly in double boiler until slightly thickened. Let cool. Add whipping cream, vanilla, and sweetened peaches. Freeze in ice cream freezer.

Jean Bissell Willcox

No Cook Homemade Ice Cream

Serves 10-12

4 cups mashed peaches or strawberries
1 cup sugar
2 (14 ounce) cans sweetened condensed milk
2 tablespoons vanilla
5 cups milk
1 teaspoon salt

Mix fruit with sugar. Let stand 30 minutes. Combine fruit and sugar mixture with all other ingredients. Freeze in ice cream freezer.

Kay Blount Miles

Buttermilk Ice Cream

Yield: 3 quarts

1½ quarts buttermilk
2½ cups sugar
1 pint whipping cream
1 pint half-and-half
1 tablespoon vanilla
Juice of 5 lemons

Mix all ingredients together and freeze in ice cream freezer or refrigerator freezer. If using refrigerator, stir when half frozen.

Lynette Angell McCary

Strawberry Sherbet

Serves 6

2 pints fresh strawberries
2 cups sugar
2 cups buttermilk

Purée berries in blender. Add two cups of sugar (less if berries are sweet). Add buttermilk. Pour mixture into 2 ice trays or plastic freezer container. When mixture begins to freeze, beat with a mixer and refreeze.

Cynthia Adams Tappan

Apricot and Lemon Sherbet

Best prepared about 10 hours ahead.

Serves 8

2 cups water
1 (3 ounce) package lemon Jello
1 cup sugar
1 (17 ounce) can seeded apricots, mashed or processed
1 cup syrup from apricots
1 cup whipping cream

Boil water and add Jello. Cool and add sugar, apricots, apricot syrup, and whipping cream. Mix and put in freezer. When partially frozen, remove from freezer, and beat with electric mixer. Return to freezer.

Betty Timberlake Knight

Hot Fudge Sauce

Yield: 1 pint

½ stick butter or margarine
2 (1 ounce) squares unsweetened chocolate
⅛ teaspoon salt
1½ cups sugar
1 cup less 2 tablespoons evaporated milk
1 teaspoon vanilla

Heat butter and chocolate in top of double boiler over simmering water until melted. Stir in salt and add sugar in 4 or 5 portions, being sure to blend thoroughly after each portion. The mixture becomes thick, dry, and grainy. Add milk very slowly and cook 6-10 minutes until slightly thickened, stirring frequently. Remove from heat. Stir in vanilla. Keeps well in glass jar if tightly covered. Serve hot over ice cream or in chafing dish as a dip for strawberries, melon balls, pineapple chunks, apple wedges, or other fruits.

Dorothy Sarris McDaniel

Peanut Butter Fudge Sauce

Keeps for 2 weeks

Yield: 1½ cups

1 (6 ounce) package semi-sweet chocolate bits
⅓ cup milk
⅓ cup peanut butter
¼ cup corn syrup
½ teaspoon vanilla

Combine chocolate, milk, peanut butter, and corn syrup over low heat. Bring to full boil over medium heat. Add vanilla. Serve warm over ice cream.

Carol Perkins Poynor

Luscious Chocolate Cake

3 (1 ounce) squares unsweetened chocolate
1 stick butter (no substitute)
2½ cups firmly packed brown sugar (1 box plus ¼ cup)
3 eggs
½ teaspoon salt
2 teaspoons baking soda
2¼ cups cake flour, sifted
½ cup buttermilk
2 teaspoons vanilla
1 cup boiling water

Preheat oven to 375°. Grease 2 round cake pans and line with wax paper. Melt chocolate. Cream butter and sugar, then add eggs and melted chocolate. Stir in salt and baking soda. Alternately add flour and buttermilk, vanilla, and then boiling water. Bake for 45 minutes or until cake tester comes out clean. Check after 30 minutes.

Frosting

2 cups whipping cream
⅓ cup sugar
3 tablespoons cocoa
½ teaspoon vanilla
Chocolate shavings for garnish

Mix ingredients together and chill for at least 2 hours. Whip cream mixture and frost cool cake. Top with chocolate shavings and store in refrigerator.

Adele Redditt Williamson
BATON ROUGE, LOUISIANA

Mocha Torte

Serves at least 16

Cake

1½ tablespoons instant coffee granules
1 cup cold water
6 egg yolks
2 cups sugar
2 cups flour
3 teaspoons baking powder
¼ teaspoon salt
1 teaspoon vanilla
1 cup ground walnuts
6 egg whites

Dissolve coffee in water. Beat egg yolks until light and add sugar gradually. Beat until thick. Sift together flour, baking powder, and salt; gradually add to egg mixture, alternating with coffee. Add vanilla and walnuts. Beat egg whites until stiff and fold into batter. Pour into 3 buttered and floured 9-inch pans. Bake at 325° for 30 minutes. Cool 10 minutes and remove from pans. When layers are cool, cut in half horizontally to make 6 layers.

Filling

1 cup butter (no substitute), softened
2 cups confectioner's sugar
2 teaspoons cocoa
½ teaspoon instant coffee
2 tablespoons Grand Marnier
2 tablespoons orange juice

Cream butter. Gradually add sugar. Add remaining ingredients. Beat until smooth. Spread on all of the layers except the top.

Frosting

4 cups confectioner's sugar
4 teaspoons cocoa
1 teaspoon instant coffee granules
4 tablespoons Grand Marnier
4 tablespoons butter, melted
1 teaspoon vanilla
Chocolate leaves or walnuts for garnish

Combine sugar, cocoa, and coffee. Add liqueur, butter, and vanilla. Beat until smooth. Frost top and sides of torte. Garnish as desired.

To freeze, place unwrapped in freezer until firm; then wrap securely and return to freezer.

Nana's Pound Cake

8 eggs, separated
6 tablespoons sugar
2 sticks butter, no substitute
2 sticks margarine
2¾ cups sugar
3½ cups sifted flour
½ cup evaporated milk or half-and-half
1 tablespoon almond extract (may substitute vanilla, lemon, or coconut extract)

Preheat oven to 325°. Beat egg whites until stiff, slowly adding 6 tablespoons of sugar, then refrigerate. Cream butter, margarine, and remaining sugar until smooth. Add egg yolks and beat well. Add flour and milk alternately, beating well after each addition. Add extract. Fold in stiffly beaten egg whites by hand. Pour into a well-greased and floured tube pan. Bake approximately 1½ hours. Cool at least 20 minutes and turn out of pan. *May be prepared up to 1 week ahead, or may be frozen.*

Betty Clark Meadows

Bourbon Pound Cake

Serves 15

4 sticks butter, melted
3½ cups sugar
1 heaping teaspoon nutmeg
1 heaping teaspoon mace
¼ teaspoon salt
4 cups flour
8 eggs, beaten
2 teaspoons baking powder
2 teaspoons vanilla
6-7 tablespoons bourbon, brandy, or rum

Preheat oven to 350°. Mix all ingredients together by hand. Thoroughly grease and flour a large Bundt pan. Pour in batter. Bake 50-60 minutes or until surface springs back to the touch. Let cool before unmolding. *May be prepared ahead. Freezes well.*

Diana Rediker Slaughter

Ber's Dark Fruitcake

This is worth the effort as it is grandmother's favorite! This should be prepared weeks in advance. It may be doubled if you have a large enough bowl to mix it in.

Yield: 5-6 pounds or 3-4 small loaves

½ pound currants
½ pound raisins
½ pound dates, cut in thirds
½ pound citron
½ pound crystalized cherries, cut in half
½ pound crystalized pineapple, cut in wedges
¼ pound blanched almonds in halves
¼ pound pecans in pieces
2 sticks butter, softened
1 cup sugar
6 eggs, separated
1½ cups flour
⅛ teaspoon soda
¼ cup black molasses
1 tablespoon lemon extract
½ lemon, juice and grated rind
1 tablespoon cinnamon
½ cup red wine
½ tablespoon mace
½ tablespoon cloves
½ tablespoon allspice
5 ounces blackberry jelly

Preheat oven to 275°. Line greased pans with well-greased heavy brown paper. Mix all fruits and nuts and dredge with flour (in addition to amount of flour in batter). Cream butter, gradually adding sugar. Beat egg yolks and add to sugar-butter mixture. Stir in flour. Mix soda and molasses and combine with batter. Add extract, juice and rind of lemon, spices, jelly, and dredged fruits and nuts. Stir in wine. Beat egg whites and fold into batter. Pour into prepared pans, filling to within ½ inch of top. Bake for 3 hours. After cooling, seal well with foil and plastic bags or tins. *Flavor develops with aging.*

Susan Nabers Haskell

Mississippi Apple Cake

Serves 15

1 cup cooking oil
2 cups sugar
3 eggs
2½ cups flour
1 teaspoon baking soda
1 teaspoon salt
2 teaspoons baking powder
1 teaspoon cinnamon
1 teaspoon nutmeg
2 teaspoons vanilla
4 cups chopped, peeled apples
1 cup chopped pecans or walnuts

Preheat oven to 350°. Cream the oil and sugar well. Beat in eggs, 1 at a time. Sift together the dry ingredients and blend into creamed mixture. Add vanilla, then fold in apples and pecans. Pour into greased and floured Bundt pan. Bake for 1 hour or until done. When cool, remove from pan. Spoon on glaze. (Glaze is runny, so you must keep spooning it back onto the cake.)

Glaze

1 cup brown sugar
1 stick butter or margarine
¼ cup evaporated milk
1 teaspoon vanilla

Combine first 3 ingredients in a saucepan over low heat. Bring to a boil, stirring constantly. Remove from heat and stir in vanilla. Beat until glaze is cool.

Marie Taylor Roby
JACKSON, MISSISSIPPI

Grandmother's Banana Split Cake

We dare you to try this—you'll love it!

Serves 12

- **2 cups graham cracker crumbs**
- **1 stick butter or margarine, softened**
- **½ cup Hershey's chocolate syrup**
- **2 cups confectioner's sugar, sifted**
- **1 stick butter or margarine, softened**
- **2 eggs**
- **3 or 4 bananas, sliced**
- **1 (1 pound, 4 ounce) can crushed pineapple, drained**
- **1 (12 ounce) container Cool Whip**
- **⅔ cup chopped nuts**

Combine crumbs and 1 stick butter in bowl and mix well. Pat mixture in 13" x 9" x 2" pan. Drizzle chocolate syrup evenly over crumb mixture. Combine sugar and remaining stick of softened butter in large mixing bowl. Beat well. Add eggs and beat until light and fluffy. Spread evenly over chocolate syrup. Arrange banana slices to cover butter/sugar mixture. Top with drained pineapple. Cover with Cool Whip and sprinkle with chopped nuts. Chill until ready to serve. Cut into squares.

Sarah Oliver Walsh

Lane Cake Filling

To be used with your favorite 3-layer yellow or white cake

- **1 stick margarine**
- **1 cup sugar**
- **7 egg yolks, well beaten**
- **1 teaspoon vanilla**
- **1 cup raisins**
- **1 cup chopped pecans**
- **1 cup coconut, canned or fresh**
- **2 ounces bourbon**

Cream margarine and sugar. Add egg yolks and cook in top of double boiler for 10-12 minutes. Remove from heat and add all other ingredients. Use as filling between 3 layers and frost cake with divinity frosting.

Praline Oatmeal Cake

Serves 16

Cake

1½ cups oatmeal
2 cups hot water
3 eggs
1½ cups sugar
1½ cups brown sugar
1 cup cooking oil
2 cups flour
Pinch of salt
1½ teaspoons cinnamon
1½ teaspoons soda

Soak oatmeal in hot water while beating eggs and sugars. Add oatmeal mixture and oil to sugar mixture. Batter will be thin. Add flour, salt, cinnamon, and soda to batter and mix well. Pour into a tube pan lined with greased waxed paper. Bake at 350° for 15 minutes, then turn down to 325° and continue baking for 1 hour.

Icing

1 stick butter (no substitute)
1 tablespoon milk
1 cup brown sugar
½ cup chopped pecans
½ cup coconut

Bring first 3 ingredients to a boil. Add pecans and coconut. Leave cake in pan and spoon warm icing over cake. Put in 325° oven for 10-15 minutes. Let cake cool for 30 minutes and then remove from pan carefully. *Freezes well.*

Dottie Haynes Miller

Oatmeal Pie

Serves 6 *Don't let the name put you off—this is delicious!*

⅔ cup regular oats, uncooked
⅔ cup light corn syrup
2 eggs, beaten
⅔ cup sugar
1 teaspoon vanilla
¼ teaspoon salt
⅔ cup butter, melted
8-inch pie shell, unbaked

Combine oats, corn syrup, eggs, sugar, vanilla, and salt. Add butter and mix thoroughly. Pour into pastry shell and bake at 350° for 1 hour. Let cool before serving.

Allison Comer Murray

Quick Processor Pie Crust

Yield: 9-inch pie crust

1 stick cold butter
1⅓ cups flour
¼ cup ice water

Preheat oven to 425°. Cut butter into 5 or 6 pieces and put in work bowl with flour. Process with steel blade until consistency of coarse meal. With machine running, pour in ice water. A ball of dough will form. Roll out dough on wax paper and place in a 9-inch pie pan. Bake at 425° for 12-15 minutes or until brown. *Dough will keep in refrigerator for several days.*

Carol King Nolen

Surprise Pie

Serves 6-8

9-inch pie shell, baked
3 egg yolks
1 cup sugar
Juice of 1 large lemon
4 tablespoons self-rising flour
1 stick margarine, cut up
2 cups buttermilk
3 egg whites
1 cup sugar

Beat egg yolks at medium speed. Continue mixing while adding next 5 ingredients in order. Pour into top of double boiler over boiling water. Cook, stirring until thickened. Set aside to cool. Beat egg whites until stiff. Mix in 1 cup sugar. Pour slightly cooled filling into pie crust. Top with meringue. Run under broiler to brown when ready to serve.

Margie Thompson
REDSTONE CLUB KITCHEN

French Chocolate Pie

Serves 6

¼ teaspoon cream of tartar
½ cup (3) egg whites
½ cup sugar
½ cup sugar
¼ cup cocoa
¼ cup chopped pecans
1 cup whipping cream, whipped
3 tablespoons sugar
1 tablespoon cocoa

Scatter cream of tartar over egg whites in small but deep mixing bowl and beat until stiff. Add ½ cup sugar gradually. Mix together in separate bowl, ½ cup sugar, ¼ cup cocoa, and chopped pecans. Stir this into egg white mixture and turn into *well-greased* pie pan. Bake at 350° for 30 minutes. Cool thoroughly. Fill center with mixture of whipped cream, sugar, and cocoa. Chill until ready to serve.

Jane Skinner Webb

Frozen Toffee Cream Pie

Serves 6

1½ cups chocolate wafer crumbs
6 tablespoons butter
1 cup whipping cream
⅔ cup sweetened condensed milk
¼ cup strong cold coffee
½ teaspoon vanilla
2 chocolate-covered toffee bars, crushed (2⅛ ounce total)

In a small bowl, combine crumbs and butter. Press into 9-inch pie plate. Chill. Meanwhile, combine cream, milk, coffee, and vanilla with mixer on low speed. Beat on high speed 4 minutes or until thickened. Stir in candy, reserving 2 tablespoons for topping. Pour into crust. Sprinkle with reserved candy, and freeze until firm.

Anne Moore Vogtle Baldwin

Chocolate Chess Pie

Serves 6-8

1½ cups sugar
3¼ tablespoons cocoa
1 stick margarine, melted
2 eggs, beaten
1 (5.33 ounce) can evaporated milk
1 teaspoon vanilla
9-inch pie shell, unbaked

Preheat oven to 325°. Mix together all ingredients and pour into pie shell. Bake 40-45 minutes. Refrigerate for 4 hours to set. Do not slice warm. *May be frozen.*

Cynthia Scott Ard

German Sweet Chocolate Pie

Yield: 1 large or 2 small pies

1 (4 ounce) package Baker's German Sweet Chocolate
1 stick butter
1 (14½ ounce) can evaporated milk
1½ cups sugar
3 tablespoons cornstarch
⅛ teaspoon salt
2 eggs
1 teaspoon vanilla
10-inch pie shell, unbaked or 2 8-inch pie shells, unbaked
1⅓ cups Baker's Angel Flake Coconut
½ cup chopped walnuts or pecans

Melt chocolate with butter over low heat. Gradually blend in milk. Mix sugar, cornstarch, and salt thoroughly. Beat in eggs and vanilla. Gradually blend in chocolate mixture. Pour into pie shell. Combine coconut and nuts and sprinkle over filling. Bake at 375° for 45 minutes. Filling will be soft but will set while cooling. Cool at least 4 hours before cutting.

Jane Kaul Morgan

Mocha Buttercrunch Pie

Serves 6-8

Crust

½ package pie crust mix
1 (1 ounce) square unsweetened chocolate
¼ cup light brown sugar, firmly packed
¾ cup chopped walnuts and pecans, mixed (chop by hand, not in food processor)
1 teaspoon vanilla
1 tablespoon water

Line 9-inch glass pie plate with foil, pressing down well. Preheat oven to 375°. Place pie crust mix in bowl. Add chocolate which has been ground in food processor or nut grinder. Stir in sugar and nuts. Mix vanilla and water and drizzle over pie crust mixture. Stir and toss with fork. Mixture will be lumpy. Press into pie plate. Bake 15 minutes and cool.

Filling

1 (1 ounce) square unsweetened chocolate, melted and cooled
1 stick butter
¾ cup light brown sugar, firmly packed
2 teaspoons instant coffee granules
2 eggs

Cream butter, add sugar, and beat on high speed for 2-3 minutes. Mix in chocolate and coffee. Add eggs 1 at a time, beating 5 minutes each time. Pour filling into pie crust. Refrigerate 5 or 6 hours or overnight. *Pie can be frozen at this point.* Before serving prepare topping.

Topping

1 cup whipping cream
1 tablespoon instant coffee granules
¼ cup confectioner's sugar
Chocolate shavings

Whip cream with coffee and sugar until it holds shape but is not stiff. Spread over filling. Decorate with chocolate shavings. Refrigerate. *May be prepared 1 day ahead.*

Catharine Comer Crawford

Chocolate Pecan Pie

Serves 8-10

3 eggs, lightly beaten
1 cup light corn syrup
½ cup brown sugar
1 cup pecan pieces
¼ teaspoon salt
½ teaspoon vanilla
1 (6 ounce) package semi-sweet chocolate morsels
10-inch pie shell, unbaked

Preheat oven to 450°. Mix all ingredients and turn into shell. Bake for 10 minutes. Reduce heat to 350° and bake for 35 minutes more. Serve chilled with whipped cream or vanilla ice cream.

Joan Barrett Veenschoten

Black Bottom Pie

Serves 6-8

Pie crust

22-25 ginger snaps
½ stick margarine, melted

Crush ginger snaps and mix with margarine. Press in 9-inch pie pan and bake 10 minutes at 200°.

Filling

3 eggs, separated
1½ cups milk
1½ cups sugar
1 tablespoon cornstarch
1 tablespoon gelatin
1½ (1 ounce) squares unsweetened chocolate, melted
1 teaspoon vanilla
A pinch of nutmeg
3 tablespoons bourbon
½ pint whipping cream, whipped
Grated chocolate for garnish

Cook eggs yolks, milk, sugar, and cornstarch until mixture thickly coats a spoon. Dissolve gelatin in 4 tablespoons of water and add to custard. Take out ⅓ of custard mixture (about 1 cup) and mix with chocolate. Flavor with vanilla and spread in ginger snap crust. Cool remaining custard. Whip egg whites and fold in bourbon and nutmeg. Pour over chocolate layer. Cool and top with whipped cream and grated chocolate. Refrigerate until ready to serve.

Katherine Parker Reed

Fudge Pie

Serves 6-8

2 (1 ounce) squares unsweetened chocolate, melted
1 stick butter, melted
2 eggs
¼ cup flour
1 cup sugar
1 teaspoon vanilla
½ cup chopped pecans

Combine chocolate, butter, and eggs. Stir until creamy. Add flour, sugar, vanilla, and pecans. Pour ingredients into a buttered pie plate. Bake at 375° for 25 minutes. Serve warm with vanilla or mocha ice cream or serve cool with whipped cream. *May also be baked in a pie shell.*

Anne Cumbee Wilson

Sam's Praline Pumpkin Pie

Yield: 1 large or 2 small pies

Crust

⅓ cup finely chopped pecans
⅓ cup packed light brown sugar
3 tablespoons softened butter
10-inch pie crust or 2 8-inch pie crusts

Preheat oven to 450°. Combine crust ingredients and press into bottom of pie shell. Bake for 10 minutes. Cool.

Filling

3 eggs, slightly beaten
½ cup sugar
½ cup packed light brown sugar
2 tablespoons flour
¾ teaspoon salt
¾ teaspoon cinnamon
½ teaspoon ground ginger
¼ teaspoon ground cloves
¼ teaspoon mace
1½ cups canned pumpkin
1½ cups half-and-half

Combine all filling ingredients except pumpkin and half-and-half. Add pumpkin and mix thoroughly. Heat half-and-half and gradually add to filling mixture and pour into pie shell. Bake 350° for 50-60 minutes or until a knife comes out clean. *If making 2 pies, double the crust ingredients. Can be frozen.*

Joan Gentry Price

English Pie

Serves 6

1 stick butter
1 cup sugar
2 egg yolks
½ teaspoon cinnamon
½ teaspoon cloves
½ teaspoon allspice
1 teaspoon vanilla
1 cup chopped pecans
1 cup raisins
2 egg whites
9-inch pie shell, unbaked

Preheat oven to 350°. Combine butter and sugar. Add egg yolks, spices, vanilla, nuts, and raisins. Beat egg whites until stiff and fold into mixture. Pour into pie crust and bake for 30 minutes.

Pat McCabe Forman

Fresh Fruit Pie *(Peach, Strawberry or Blackberry)*

Serves 6-8

Pie Crust

1 stick butter, softened (no substitute)
1 cup flour
3½ tablespoons confectioner's sugar

Preheat oven to 350°. Mix butter, flour, and sugar. Work into soft dough. Press into metal pie pan. Bake for 20 minutes or until lightly brown.

Filling

1 cup sugar
1 cup water
3 tablespoons cornstarch
4 tablespoons fruit flavored gelatin (peach for peach pie, etc.)
Pinch of salt
2 cups fruit
½ teaspoon lemon juice
1 tablespoon sugar
½ pint whipping cream, whipped

Bring sugar, water, cornstarch, gelatin, and salt to a rolling boil. Set aside to cool. Cut up fruit and sprinkle with a few drops of lemon juice and sugar. Add to cooled gelatin mixture. Pour into baked pie crust, and cover with whipped cream. *Should be refrigerated.*

Joan Gentry Price

Sour Cream Apple Pie

Serves 6

2 tablespoons flour
¾ cup sugar
¼ teaspoon salt
¼ teaspoon ground nutmeg
1 egg, slightly beaten
1 (8 ounce) carton sour cream
1 teaspoon vanilla
2 cups very thinly sliced apples
9-inch deep dish pie shell, unbaked

Crumb Topping

½ cup sugar
⅓ cup flour
1 teaspoon ground cinnamon
½ stick butter, melted

Preheat oven to 400°. Sift flour, sugar, salt, and nutmeg into a large bowl. Stir in beaten egg, sour cream, and vanilla. Fold in apples; spoon into pastry shell. Bake for 15 minutes. Lower heat to 350° and bake 30 minutes longer. Mix crumb topping ingredients. Remove pie from oven. Reset oven to 400°. Sprinkle pie with topping and return to oven. Bake 10 minutes longer or until topping is browned. Cool slightly on wire rack before serving. *Refrigerate and reheat individual pieces later in microwave or regular oven.*

Margaret Marks Porter

Shirley's Brownies

Yield: 2 dozen

2 sticks margarine
5 (1 ounce) squares unsweetened chocolate
2 cups sugar
2 teaspoons vanilla
4 eggs
1 cup flour, sifted
Confectioner's sugar

Preheat oven to 350°. Grease 9″ x 13″ pan. Melt margarine, then add chocolate. Cool. Add sugar, vanilla, and eggs, mixing well. Stir in flour. Pour into pan and bake 30 minutes. Cut into squares while warm. Sprinkle with confectioner's sugar.

Lee White Van Tassel

Chocolate Mint Brownies

Yield: 4 dozen

Brownies

2 (1 ounce) squares unsweetened baking chocolate
1 stick butter or margarine
2 eggs, well beaten
1 cup sugar
¼ teaspoon peppermint extract
½ cup flour, sifted
⅛ teaspoon salt
½ cup chopped pecans

Melt chocolate and butter over boiling water or low heat. Cool completely. Add remaining ingredients. Pour into a well-greased 9-inch square pan. Bake at 350° for 20-25 minutes.

Mint Frosting

2 tablespoons butter, softened
1 cup confectioner's sugar, sifted
1 tablespoon evaporated milk
½ teaspoon peppermint extract
3 drops green food coloring

Mix together until creamy and spread over brownies. Refrigerate pan while preparing the glaze.

Glaze

1 (1 ounce) square semi-sweet chocolate
1 generous tablespoon butter

Melt over *low* heat and stir. Drizzle over green icing. Tilt pan to cover surface. Refrigerate to set glaze. Cut into *tiny* squares.

Betty Clark Meadows

Chocolate Caramel Bars

Yield: 6 dozen small bars

1 (14 ounce) bag caramels
⅔ cup evaporated milk, divided
1 (18½ ounce) package regular German Chocolate cake mix *or* Duncan Hines Swiss Chocolate Deluxe II cake mix
1½ sticks butter or margarine, melted
1 cup chopped nuts
1 (6 ounce) package semi-sweet chocolate chips

Preheat oven to 350°. In top of double boiler over medium heat, combine caramels and ⅓ cup of evaporated milk, stirring constantly until melted and smooth. Remove from heat. Combine cake mix, melted butter, and remaining milk in mixer until well blended. Press half of cake mixture into a greased 9″ x 13″ pan. Bake 6 minutes. Sprinkle chocolate pieces and nuts over crust. Pour caramel mixture evenly over chips and nuts. Dollop rest of cake mixture over caramel. Return to oven and bake another 15 to 18 minutes. Cool, then chill 30 minutes. Cut into small bars. *Store at room temperature or freeze.*

Carol King Nolen

Caramel Squares

Yield: 2 dozen

2 cups graham cracker crumbs
1 can Eagle Brand milk
1 (6 ounce) package butterscotch chips
1 cup chopped pecans

Preheat oven to 325°. Butter and flour 9-inch square pan. Combine all ingredients and spread in pan. Bake for 20-25 minutes. Cut before cool.

Nikki Partlow Naftel

Toffee Cookies

Yield: 2½ dozen

2 sticks margarine
1 cup brown sugar
½ cup white sugar
1 egg, separated
1 teaspoon vanilla
2 cups flour
1 teaspoon salt
2 teaspoons cinnamon
½ cup chopped pecans

Cream butter and sugars. Add egg yolk and vanilla. Add flour, salt, and cinnamon. Thinly spread mixture onto greased jelly roll pan. Pour unbeaten egg white over mixture and spread over all, tilting pan to cover evenly. Pour off excess. Sprinkle with nuts. Bake 30 minutes at 275°. Cookies should be thin and crisp. Cut into squares while warm.

Lynn Otey Tutwiler

Chess Squares

Yield: 2 dozen cookies

1 box yellow cake mix with pudding
1 stick butter, softened
½ cup chopped pecans
1 (8 ounce) package cream cheese, softened
1 (1 pound) box confectioner's sugar
2 eggs
½ teaspoon vanilla

Preheat oven to 350°. Cream butter and cake mix by hand. Press mixture into 9″ x 11″ pan. Sprinkle with pecans. Mix remaining ingredients with electric mixer until smooth. Pour this mixture over cake mixture. Bake for 40 minutes or until top is golden brown. Let cool and cut into squares. *Best if made a day ahead, and can be frozen.*

Vivian Ferguson Perry

Blonde Brownies

Yield: 30 brownies

1 stick butter or margarine
2 cups packed light brown sugar
2 eggs
1½ cups flour
2 teaspoons baking powder
1 teaspoon salt
1 teaspoon vanilla
1 cup coarsely chopped nuts

Preheat oven to 350°. Melt butter over low heat. Remove from heat. Add brown sugar and stir until well blended. Cool. Add eggs and mix well. Stir in dry ingredients, then add vanilla and nuts. Spread in well-buttered 9″ x 13″ baking pan and bake 25 minutes. Cool in pan. Cut into squares.

Barbara Derr Chenoweth

Pumpkin Bars

Bars

4 eggs
2 cups sugar
2 cups cooked, puréed pumpkin (or *Libby's* canned)
1 cup oil
2 cups flour
½ teaspoon salt
1 teaspoon soda
2 teaspoons baking powder
2 teaspoons cinnamon

In mixing bowl beat eggs. Add sugar and beat well. Add pumpkin and oil, then stir in dry ingredients. Pour into ungreased 15½″ x 10½″ x 1″ jelly roll pan. Bake at 350° for 30 minutes.

Frosting

1 (3 ounce) package softened cream cheese
½ cup butter
1 tablespoon cream
1 teaspoon vanilla
½-¾ box (1 pound) of confectioner's sugar

Cream together cream cheese and butter. Add cream and vanilla. Beat in confectioner's sugar till frosting is spreadable. Frost bars when cool.

Mary Dorman Mullervy
CLAYGATE, SURREY, ENGLAND

Cinnamon Apple Bars

Yield: 4 dozen bars

Crust

1 stick butter, softened
¼ cup shortening
¾ cup confectioner's sugar
1½ cups flour

Cream butter, shortening, and sugar. Cut in flour. Pat onto 10″ x 15″ jelly roll pan. Bake at 350° for 10-12 minutes or until lightly browned.

Filling

2 or 3 apples
½ stick butter
¾ cup brown sugar
1 egg, beaten
1 teaspoon vanilla
1¾ cups flour
1 teaspoon baking powder
⅓ teaspoon salt

Peel and chop apples. Melt butter in a saucepan. Blend in apples, brown sugar, egg, and vanilla. Sift flour, baking powder, and salt. Stir into apple mixture. Spread over baked crust. Bake at 350° for 25 minutes.

Icing

1½ cups confectioner's sugar
¼ teaspoon cinnamon
2 or 3 tablespoons milk

Sift sugar and cinnamon for easy blending. Whisk in the milk until smooth. Glaze while warm. Cut into bars.

Marie Taylor Roby
JACKSON, MISSISSIPPI

Apple Hill Treats

Serves 20 generously

2 cups sugar
½ cup oil
2 eggs
4 cups finely diced apples
2 cups flour
1 teaspoon salt
2 teaspoons cinnamon
1 teaspoon nutmeg
2 teaspoons baking soda

Preheat oven to 350°. Combine sugar, oil, eggs, and beat well. *Stir* in apples. Sift dry ingredients together and add to apple mixture. Pour into a greased and floured 9″ x 13″ cake pan. Bake 1 hour. Serve warm or cold, plain or topped with your favorite frosting, whipped cream, or ice cream.

Gay Edwards

John's Favorite Cookie Bars

Yield: 5 dozen

Crust

1 stick butter
¼ cup confectioner's sugar
1¼ cups flour

Preheat oven to 350°. Cut butter into flour and sugar with pastry blender. Press mixture into a 9″ x 12″ pan. Bake for 12-15 minutes or until mixture leaves the sides of the pan and is slightly brown.

Filling

2 eggs
2 tablespoons flour
½ teaspoon salt
1 cup chopped dates
1½ cups brown sugar
¼ teaspoon baking powder
1 cup chopped pecans
1 teaspoon vanilla

Mix the filling ingredients and spread over the crust. Bake at 350° for 20-25 minutes. Remove from oven and let cool in pan.

Frosting

1½ cups confectioner's sugar
2 tablespoons orange juice
2 tablespoons melted butter
1 tablespoon lemon juice

Blend frosting ingredients until smooth and spread over cool filling. When frosting is firm, cut into squares.

Jan Roby Wofford

Old Fashioned Date Nut Bars

Yield: 30 bars

1 cup flour, sifted
½ teaspoon baking powder
½ teaspoon salt
1 stick butter
1 cup sugar
2 eggs
1 teaspoon vanilla
1 (8 ounce) box chopped, sugared dates
1 cup pecans, chopped
Confectioner's sugar

Preheat oven to 375°. Sift together flour, baking powder, and salt. Cream butter and gradually blend in sugar. Add eggs, 1 at a time, beating well after each addition. Beat until light and fluffy. Add vanilla. Gradually add dry ingredients, beating after each addition. Fold in dates and nuts. Spread evenly in a greased rectangular 7″ x 11″ x 1½″ pan. Bake 30 minutes. Cool completely before removing from pan. Cut into bars and sprinkle with confectioner's sugar. A 9″ x 13″ pan may be used for thinner bars.

Evelyn Payne Brooks

Yummy Almond Bars

Yield: 2-3 dozen

1½ sticks butter
1½ cups sugar
2 eggs
1½ cups sifted flour
Pinch of salt
1 teaspoon almond flavoring
1 (2¼ ounce) package slivered almonds
Sugar

Preheat oven to 350°. Melt butter and combine with sugar. Beat in eggs 1 at a time. Add flour, salt, and flavoring, mixing well. Pour batter into 9″ x 11″ greased pan. Cover top with slivered almonds. Sprinkle with sugar. Bake 30-40 minutes. Remove from oven, cool, and cut into squares.

Harriet Hicks Gee

Mrs. Reese's Sugar Cookies

Cookieland Cookies

For cut cookies, prepare dough a day ahead.

Yield: 75 cookies

1 stick butter
1 stick margarine
1 cup sugar
1 egg
1 teaspoon vanilla
3 cups flour
1 teaspoon baking powder
⅛ teaspoon salt

Combine butter, margarine, and sugar in a mixing bowl. Beat with an electric mixer until foamy (at least 5 minutes). Add egg and vanilla. Beat well. Put flour, baking powder, and salt in sifter and sift into other mixture. Beat well. These can be rolled out, used with a cookie press or dropped and garnished with a nut on top. If rolled out, put dough in refrigerator overnight. Take out a little at a time and roll on a pastry cloth. If used with a cookie press or dropped, DO NOT put in refrigerator. Bake at 350-375° until light brown, about 10 minutes. Decorate as desired.

Colored Sugar

1 cup sugar
5 drops food coloring

Mix sugar and coloring with spoon until sugar is all colored. Let dry making sure there are no lumps, and put in a jar. This will keep indefinitely. This is the quickest decoration for cookies. Sprinkle sugar on the cookies on cookie sheet before baking.

Shiny Icing

½ cup confectioner's sugar
1 drop vanilla
About 1 tablespoon water
A few drops food coloring

Mix sugar with a drop or so of vanilla and enough water to make it spreadable. Spread on cookies when they *come out* of the oven, while they are still on the cookie sheet. This makes a shiny icing on the cookies.

Icing for Piped Decorations

(for tube decorators)

1 stick butter softened
1 box confectioner's sugar
1 tablespoon milk
A few drops of vanilla
A few drops of food coloring

Mix butter, sugar, milk, and vanilla. Add colors desired. Have fun decorating cookies with a tube decorator.

Icing for Painted Cookies

1 egg white
A drop of food coloring

Mix egg white and food coloring. Amount of coloring depends on how deep you want the color. Use a *small* brush—test by painting the inside of your wrist. One egg can be put in different saucers and used to make different colors. This is cute used on round cookies painted like faces.

Martha Sanford Reese

Old Fashioned Sugar Cookies

Yield: 70 cookies

1 cup granulated sugar
1 cup confectioner's sugar
2 sticks margarine
1 cup salad oil
2 eggs
4½ cups sifted flour
1 teaspoon cream of tartar
1 teaspoon soda
2 teaspoons vanilla

Preheat oven to 350°. Mix first 4 ingredients. Beat in eggs, then add flour sifted with cream of tartar and soda. Add vanilla. Roll into balls the size of a walnut. This is a soft dough and is easier to handle if chilled before rolling into balls. Place on greased cookie sheet. Flatten with the bottom of a glass (buttered and dipped in sugar). Bake for 10-12 minutes.

Martha Dick McClung

Healthy Oatmeal Cookies

Yield: 3 dozen

2 cups Quick Quaker Oats
1 cup Brownulated brown sugar
½ cup oil
1 egg, beaten
1 teaspoon vanilla
¼ teaspoon salt
½ cup chopped pecans

Preheat oven to 300°. Mix oats, brown sugar, and oil. Add other ingredients and stir until well blended. Drop tablespoons of mixture immediately onto 2 greased cookie sheets. Bake for 8 minutes with 1 pan on each oven rack. Switch pans from upper to lower racks and bake 5-8 more minutes. Cookies will burn easily. Let cool 10 minutes. For crispier cookies, turn off heat and leave in oven an additional 15 minutes.

Rachel Kracke Drennen

Potato Chip Shortbread Cookies

These buttery cookies are delicious.

Yield: 5 dozen

4 sticks butter (no substitute)
1 cup sugar
1 teaspoon vanilla
3½ cups flour
1 cup chopped pecans
2 cups crushed potato chips

Preheat oven to 350°. Cream butter and sugar. Add vanilla and gradually add flour. Stir in nuts and potato chips. Drop by teaspoonfuls onto greased cookie sheet. Bake for 15 minutes.

Mary Adelia Rosamond McLeod
ATHENS, ALABAMA

Peanut Butter Surprises

These freeze well and are delicious!

Yield: 36 cookies

1 roll Pillsbury Sugar Cookies or Pillsbury Peanut Butter Cookies
1 box bite-size Reese's Peanut Butter Cups

Preheat oven to 350°. Slice cookie dough into 9 sections and then quarter each section. Grease a miniature muffin tin and place each quarter into muffin sections. Cook according to directions or until slightly brown. Remove from oven and immediately push one small Reese's into center of hot cookie leaving the top showing. Let cool thoroughly before removing from tins.

Grace Mandeville Christian
TUSCALOOSA, ALABAMA

Millionaires

Yield: 3½ dozen

1 (14 ounce) package caramels
4 tablespoons milk
2 cups chopped pecans
Buttered waxed paper
¼ (1¾ ounce) bar paraffin
12 ounces semi-sweet chocolate chips

Melt caramels with milk over very low heat. Add pecans. Drop by teaspoonful onto buttered waxed paper. Chill. Melt paraffin and chocolate chips over low heat. Dip candy in chocolate and return to waxed paper. Chill.

Mary Phelps Mellen

Martha Washington Candy

Yield: 70 pieces

2 (1 pound) boxes confectioner's sugar, sifted
1 stick margarine or butter
1 (14 ounce) can sweetened condensed milk
1 teaspoon vanilla
4 cups chopped pecans
1 (½ pound) package bitter or semi-sweet chocolate squares
¼-½ block paraffin, 1 or 2 ounces

Cream first 5 ingredients. Chill. Roll into balls the size of walnuts, and place in refrigerator. Melt the chocolate and paraffin over *low, low* heat or use a double boiler. Dip chilled balls into chocolate mixture, 1 piece at a time, holding each with a toothpick. Drop onto wax paper. *May be frozen.*

Susie Hand Denson

English Toffee Candy

Yield: 1 pound

2 sticks butter
1 cup sugar
1 tablespoon dark Karo syrup
3 tablespoons water
1½ cups coarsely chopped almonds or pecans, divided
6 ounces semi-sweet chocolate bits
2 ounces unsweetened chocolate, melted

Melt butter in 2-quart pan. Gradually stir in sugar. Add syrup and water. Cook to 290° on candy thermometer. Add 1 cup nuts. Cook 3 minutes more. Pour candy onto greased cookie sheet and let cool. Melt chocolates together. Spread with ½ of melted chocolate mixture and top with ½ of remaining nuts. Cool until chocolate is set. Turn over and cover other side with remaining chocolate and nuts. Chill and break into pieces.

Susie H. Wetzel

Candied Almonds

½ pound whole, raw almonds with the skin (1⅓ cups)
⅔ cup sugar
⅓ cup water

Stir sugar and water together in large heavy skillet. Bring to a boil; add almonds, and continue cooking until all liquid has been absorbed. Turn heat to medium low and stir almonds until sugar dissolves and an amber coating covers each nut. Be careful not to burn! Turn out on buttered cookie sheet and separate with buttered fork. Cool and store in airtight container.

Carolyn Markstein Frohsin

Plantation Pecan Pralines

Yield: 36 small pralines

2 cups sugar
1 cup light brown sugar
1 cup half-and-half cream
2 tablespoons light Karo syrup
2 cups pecans
1 stick butter
1 teaspoon vanilla

Butter wax paper. Place sugars, cream, Karo, and pecans in a saucepan. Stir to mix. Place candy thermometer in saucepan. Cook over medium-high heat to soft ball stage. Remove from heat immediately. Stir in butter and vanilla. *Do not beat.* Place in a pan of ice water. Do not stir or beat. Remove pan of candy from ice water when pan is cool enough to touch. Beat candy with wooden spoon or whisk until it loses its gloss. Spoon onto buttered wax paper. If candy gets hard to manage, place pot back into a skillet of hot water. It will melt the candy enough to spoon it out. Let candy become firm. Store in an airtight tin. Best eaten the day made, but delicious for 2-3 days. *These are not hard, just pay attention and do not answer the phone and forget the candy!*

Adele Williamson Scielzo

GIFTS FROM THE KITCHEN

Gifts from the Kitchen

Apricot Liqueur

1 quart vodka
1 pound dried apricots
1 pound rock candy or 4 cups sugar

Combine all ingredients in a glass jar, seal, and leave for 6 weeks. The longer it sets the better the apricot flavor. *Pretty and delicious on ice cream or custard.*

Martha Fletcher Brodnax

Kahlúa

Yield: ½ gallon

2 cups water
2 cups sugar
2 ounces instant coffee
1 pint brandy or vodka
1 vanilla bean

Boil water, sugar, and coffee. Stir until dissolved. Cool. Add brandy or vodka and pour in ½-gallon bottle. Add vanilla bean. Age in cool dark place for 30 days.

Mike Casey Vann

Homemade Vanilla

Yield: 1 pint

1 whole pod of vanilla beans, broken into 1-inch lengths
1 pint brandy

Combine and place in sterilized jar. Let sit for 3 weeks. *This makes a great present if you put it in pretty jars.*

Martha Fletcher Brodnax

Blueberry Cordial

A gourmet touch to pancakes and waffles, and simply divine over vanilla ice cream or lemon sherbet.

Yield: 10 half-pint jars

7 cups blueberries
9 cups sugar
4 sticks cinnamon, broken in half
3 tablespoons lemon juice
¼ cup slivered lemon peel
¼ cup brandy
Paraffin

Mix sugar and blueberries in kettle and allow to sit 8-10 hours. Add cinnamon, lemon juice and peel to berries and place on medium-high heat. Cook for 20 minutes, or until syrup is relatively thick. Stir and watch constantly, being sure fruit does not stick on bottom. Skim foam from top. Remove from heat and cool. Add brandy; stir and seal in sterilized jars with paraffin. *Try to include a piece of cinnamon in each jar. Flavor mellows with aging.*

Curried Almonds

Yield: 2 cups

2 cups blanched whole almonds
1½ tablespoons butter, melted
1 tablespoon curry powder
2 teaspoons salt

Preheat oven to 300°. Mix ingredients together. Pour into 8-inch cake pan. Toast in oven 30 minutes, stirring occasionally. *This is very easy, different, and good! May be prepared ahead and frozen.*

Lucie Mason Bynum

Boursin Spread

Wonderful for gift giving!

1 (8 ounce) package cream cheese, softened
½ stick butter, softened
½ teaspoon Beau Monde seasoning
1 clove garlic, crushed
½ teaspoon Herbs of Provence spice
1 teaspoon parsley
1 teaspoon water
¼ teaspoon red wine vinegar
¼ teaspoon Worcestershire sauce

Mix all ingredients and pour into any type container (small crocks are perfect). Allow to mellow at least 12 hours, 24 hours is even better. Serve with crackers of your choice. *Keeps 1 month in refrigerator.*

Katherine Kennedy Jefferson
LITTLE ROCK, ARKANSAS

Strawberry Butter

Yield: 2½ cups

¾ cup finely chopped fresh strawberries
3-5 tablespoons confectioner's sugar
1 pound sweet whipped butter

Combine all ingredients in food processor with steel blade. Process until light. Serve with warm biscuits or use as a spread for thin white bread cut in rounds or shapes. *This is pretty to use for coffees, showers, or brunches.*

Karen Valentine Sanders

Cheese Covered Dates

Wonderful for the Christmas holidays

Yield: About 80 dates

½ pound extra sharp Cheddar cheese, grated, at room temperature
1 stick margarine, room temperature
2 cups sifted flour
¼ teaspoon red pepper
2 (1 pound) packages pitted dates
80 pecan halves, toasted

Blend cheese and margarine. Combine flour and red pepper, and slowly add to cheese mixture until a soft dough is formed. Stuff each date with pecan half. Pinch off small amount of dough and wrap a thin layer around each date, covering it completely. Bake in 375° oven 12-15 minutes or until slightly brown. Store in tins.

Elizabeth Landgrebe
PAST PRESIDENT

Granola

A healthy snack your children will love.

Yield: 3 quart jars

½ cup oil
¾ cup honey
1 tablespoon vanilla
1 (18 ounce) box Quaker oatmeal
Your favorite combination:
1 cup chopped pecans
1 cup walnuts
1 cup unsalted peanuts
1 cup raisins
1 cup chopped dates
1 cup sunflower seeds
½ cup sesame seeds
½ cup wheat germ

Preheat oven to 350°. Heat oil and honey together. Add vanilla. Pour over oatmeal in shallow roasting pan. Cook in oven stirring often until toasty brown. Allow to cool, then add any or all of the suggested ingredients. Store in refrigerator. Serve with sliced bananas and milk.

Sherry Moore Wilson

Old Fashioned Lemon Jelly

Yield: 1½ cups

¾ cup fresh lemon juice
Grated rind of 4 lemons
2 cups sugar

Place juice, rind, and sugar in a heavy 4-quart saucepan. Cook until mixture comes to a boil on medium-high heat. Cover with a lid and boil 1 minute to wash down crystals. Uncover and cook until 2 drops fall together from wooden spoon. Let stand 5 minutes. Put in sterilized jars. Seal with paraffin. Allow to set 1 day before storing.

Judith Tomme Fackler

White Wine Jelly

Keeps about 3 months

Yield: 8 half-pint jars

6 cups Chablis or champagne
4 cups sugar
2 tablespoons fresh lemon juice
1 bottle Certo
Paraffin

Heat wine, sugar, and lemon juice in top of 3-quart double boiler. Stir with wooden spoon and cook until sugar is dissolved. Do not allow wine to reach boiling point. Remove from heat and immediately add Certo. Stir well. Skim foam from top. Seal in hot sterilized jars with paraffin. Allow 1 day to set.

For Minted Chablis Jelly put 4-5 springs of fresh mint in wine while cooking. Remove before adding Certo.

Pattie Perry Robinson Finney

Chris' Fig Preserves

5 pounds peeled, ripe, firm figs (peeled weight)
5 pounds sugar
10 thin slices lemon
Paraffin for sealing

Cover figs with sugar and let stand until sugar is half melted (1-2 hours). Add lemon slices and put pot on low heat. Cook slowly until all sugar is dissolved, stirring occasionally. Increase heat to medium high. Stir frequently and skim foam from top. Do not let figs stick to bottom of pot. Cook until syrup is thick, about 1 hour. Seal in sterile jars.

Chrissie Davis Redditt
COLUMBIA, LOUISIANA

Pear Chutney

Yield: 6-8 half-pints

½ teaspoon mustard seed
½ teaspoon whole allspice
½ teaspoon whole cloves
10 cups sliced (about ¼ inch thick), peeled, pared pears (4-5 pounds or 15 pears)
1½ cups seedless raisins
½ cup finely chopped green pepper
2 cups brown sugar
2 cups white sugar
½ cup crystallized ginger (found in Chinese food department)
3 cups cider vinegar
½ teaspoon salt
2 (2 inch) sticks cinnamon

Tie mustard seed, allspice, and cloves in double thickness of cheese cloth or clean tea towel. Combine all ingredients in large saucepan and leave uncovered. Bring to a boil; reduce heat and simmer slowly for 1 hour, or until thick. Discard spices. Spoon into hot sterilized jars.

This is delicious served with pork or lamb and any curry. Also makes a nice accompaniment when spooned inside a canned peach half and broiled about 5 minutes or until bubbly.

Jane Powell Goings

Grandmother Ida's Pear Relish

A natural accompaniment to ham and garden vegetables

Yield: 10-12 half-pint jars

1 dozen large sand pears*, peeled
1 dozen green peppers
2-3 hot peppers, optional
8 large yellow onions, peeled
3 tablespoons plain salt
2 cups vinegar
2 cups sugar

**Sand pears are large brown cooking pears that mature in late summer in the South. Any tart cooking pear could be substituted.*

Wash, core, and remove all seeds from pears and peppers. Cut onions into chunks. Grind pears, peppers, and onions. Place ground fruits and vegetables in non-aluminum bowl, add 2 tablespoons salt, and cover with boiling water. Let sit 10 minutes. Drain. In cooking vessel place ground mixture, vinegar, sugar, and 1 tablespoon salt. Boil 10 minutes. Seal in hot sterile jars.

Ida Stewart Webb
ATMORE, ALABAMA

Onion Ring Pepper Relish

Yield: 6-7 pints

12 red bell peppers
12 green bell peppers
5-6 hot red peppers (optional—use only if hot relish is desired)
5 pounds onions, thinly sliced and separated
Boiling water
5 cups sugar
6 cups cider vinegar
4 tablespoons non-iodized salt

Carefully remove seeds from peppers. Grind peppers. Place peppers in small bowl and fill with boiling water. Let stand 10 minutes. Drain *well* in a colander. Place onion rings in another bowl. Pour boiling water over onions and let stand 10 minutes. Drain *well* in a colander. Make a syrup of sugar, vinegar, and salt. Add peppers and onions. Cook 10 minutes. Put in hot sterile jars and seal.

Martha Sanford Reese

Upside Down Pickles

Yield: 1 gallon

1 gallon jar of sour pickles
5 pounds sugar
1 (1¼ ounce) box pickling spice
3 garlic cloves
3 tablespoons oil

Empty pickles out of jar and pour off juice. Slice crosswise. Fill the gallon jar with pickles, sugar, spices, and garlic in layers repeating layers to the top. On top put 3 tablespoons of oil. Seal tightly (it will all fit in if you are determined). Turn upside down for 3 days, then right side up for 3 days, then upside down for 3 more days. Pickles should sit for 3 weeks before serving. Refrigerate after opening. *May pack in smaller sterilized jars if desired.*

Joyce Robinson McGraw

Jerusalem Artichoke Relish *(Sunchokes)*

Yield: 5-6 pints

1 quart Jerusalem artichokes
1 pint onions
1 pint green peppers
1 gallon water
1 cup non-iodized salt
1 pound sugar (2 cups)
1 quart cider vinegar
2 tablespoons mustard seed
1 tablespoon turmeric

Scrape and clean artichokes. Peel and slice onions. Remove seed from peppers and cut peppers into pieces. Soak vegetables overnight in a solution of water and salt. Next day drain vegetables well in colander. Grind vegetables and drain again. Make a syrup of sugar, vinegar, mustard seed, and turmeric. Add vegetables to syrup and boil 15 minutes. (Taste-test amount of salt—you may want a bit more). Put into hot sterile jars. Seal.

Martha Sanford Reese

Bread And Butter Pickles

Yield: 16 half-pints

1 gallon cucumbers, thinly sliced
10 medium onions, thinly sliced
2 green peppers, sliced in thin strips lengthwise
½ cup non-iodized salt
2 trays ice cubes
5 cups cider vinegar
5 cups sugar
½ teaspoon turmeric
½ teaspoon ground cloves
2 tablespoons mustard seed
1 teaspoon celery seed

Put cucumbers, onion, and peppers in pan. Sprinkle with salt and ice cubes. Cover and let stand 3 hours. Drain, removing ice and water. Put all ingredients except cucumbers, onions, and peppers in large pot and stir. Add vegetables and cook on low heat until just under a boil is reached-do not let boil! Pour into sterilized jars and seal.

Jane Hill Head
PAST PRESIDENT

Mrs. B's Green Tomato Pickle

4 cups pickling lime
2 gallons water
7 pounds green tomatoes, sliced (I like small tomatoes that will fit into a ½ pint jelly jar)
7½ pounds sugar
4½ pints vinegar
1½ teaspoons whole cloves
1½ teaspoons powdered ginger
1½ teaspoons whole allspice
1½ teaspoons celery seed
1½ teaspoons ground mace
1½ teaspoons ground cinnamon

Combine lime and water. Place tomatoes in a crock, pour on lime water, and soak tomatoes for 24 hours. Drain and wash each tomato under cool running water. Soak 4 hours in fresh water, changing water every hour. Handle with care as the tomatoes will become brittle. Mix remaining ingredients and bring this syrup to a boil. Place tomatoes in a large pot. Pour syrup over tomatoes and let stand overnight. Next day, boil 1 hour and seal in sterilized jars.

Louise Byler
JACKSON, MISSISSIPPI

Bouquet Garni for Soups and Stews

Yield: 1 bouquet

Each bundle contains:

1 tablespoon dried parsley
1 clove garlic
1 teaspoon dried basil
1 teaspoon dried rosemary
1 teaspoon dried oregano
2 bay leaves
6 whole peppercorns

Tie bundles with colored cord or ribbon in a cheesecloth bag.

Sally Morrison Payne

Special Mustard

Men love this. Once tried, it is hard to settle for commercial mustard. Delicious on eggrolls.

Yield: 1½ cups

2 (2 ounce) cans Coleman's dry mustard
1 cup cider vinegar
2 eggs
¾ cup sugar

Mix mustard and vinegar; cover, and let stand overnight at room temperature. Next day, beat eggs and add sugar. Combine sugar/egg mixture with mustard in top of double boiler. Cook, stirring, until desired thickness, about 4 minutes. Put in jar and keep indefinitely in refrigerator.

Mary Elizabeth Thuston

Measurements of Food Before and After Preparation

INGREDIENT	AMOUNT BEFORE PREPARATION	AMOUNT AFTER PREPARATION
Apples	3 medium (1 pound)	3 cups sliced
Bacon	8 slices cooked	½ cup crumbled
Bananas	3 medium	2½ cups sliced or 2 cups mashed
Biscuit mix	1 cup	6 biscuits
Butter	1 pound	2 cups, 4 sticks, or 16 ounces
Bread	1 pound loaf	12-16 slices
	1½ slices	1 cup soft crumbs
Cabbage	1 pound head	4¼ cups shredded
Cereals and Grains		
Macaroni	4 ounces (1 cup)	2¼ cups cooked
Noodles	4 ounces	2 cups cooked
Quick cooking oats	1 cup	1¾ cups cooked
Regular long grain rice	1 cup (6½ ounces)	3-4 cups cooked
Precooked rice	1 cup	2 cups cooked
Spaghetti	7 ounces	4 cups cooked
Cheese American or Cheddar	1 pound	4-5 cups shredded
Chocolate	1 square	4 tablespoons grated
Coconut	1 medium	1 cup milk and grated flesh
Coffee	1 pound	40 cups perked
Corn	2 medium ears	1 cup kernels
Crab, in shell	1 pound	¾-1 cup flaked
Crackers		
Chocolate wafers	19 wafers	1 cup crumbs
Graham crackers	14 squares	1 cup fine crumbs
Saltine crackers	28 crackers	1 cup finely crushed
Vanilla wafers	22 wafers	1 cup finely crushed
Cream, whipping	1 cup (½ pint)	2 cups whipped
Dates, pitted	1 pound	2-3 cups chopped
Eggs		
Whites	5 large	1 cup or 2 ounces
Yolks	12-14	1 cup
Flour	1 pound	4 cups
Gelatin	¼ ounce	1 tablespoon
Green pepper	1 large	1 cup diced
Herbs	1 tablespoon fresh	1 teaspoon dried
Lettuce	1 pound head	6¼ cups torn

INGREDIENT	AMOUNT BEFORE PREPARATION	AMOUNT AFTER PREPARATION
Lemon	1 medium	2-3 tablespoons juice and 2 teaspoons grated rind
Lime	1 medium	1½-2 tablespoons juice
Mushrooms	3 cups raw (8 ounces)	1 cup sliced, cooked
Nuts, shelled		
Almonds	1 pound	3¼ cups chopped
Peanuts	1 pound	2-3 cups nutmeats
Pecans	1 pound	4½-5 cups halves
Walnuts	1 pound	4 cups chopped
Onion	1 medium	½ cup chopped
Orange	1 medium	⅓ cup juice and 2 tablespoons grated
Peaches	4 medium	2 cups sliced
Pears	4 medium	2 cups sliced
Potatoes,		
White	3 medium	2 cups cubed, cooked or 1¾ cups mashed
Sweet	3 medium	3 cups sliced
Shrimp raw in shell	1½ pounds	2 cups (¾ pound) cleaned and cooked
Strawberries	1 quart	4 cups sliced

EQUIVALENTS

	Equals	
Dash		Less than ⅛ teaspoon
3 teaspoons		1 tablespoon
4 tablespoons		¼ cup
5⅓ tablespoons		⅓ cup
8 tablespoons		½ cup
10⅔ tablespoons		⅔ cup
12 tablespoons		¾ cup
14 tablespoons		⅞ cup
16 tablespoons		1 cup
2 tablespoons (liquid)		1 ounce
8 ounces		1 cup (dry) or ½ pint (liquid)
16 ounces		1 pound (dry) or 1 pint (liquid)
2 pints		4 cups or 1 quart
4 quarts		1 gallon

Index

MAIL ORDER MAGIC

MAGIC

2212 Twentieth Ave., So.
Birmingham, AL 35223

Please send ________ copies of MAGIC @ $10.95 each $ ____________
Alabama residents add 7% sales tax @ .77 each $ ____________
Plus postage and handling @ $1.50 each $ ____________
Please gift wrap @ .50 each $ ____________
TOTAL $ ____________

Make checks payable to JUNIOR LEAGUE COOKBOOK.
Charge to Visa ( ) or Mastercard ( ) # ________________ Exp. Date ________________
Signature ____

Mail to: Name ____
Address ____
City ________________________________ State _____ Zip ____________

MAGIC

2212 Twentieth Ave., So.
Birmingham, AL 35223

Please send ________ copies of MAGIC @ $10.95 each $ ____________
Alabama residents add 7% sales tax @ .77 each $ ____________
Plus postage and handling @ $1.50 each $ ____________
Please gift wrap @ .50 each $ ____________
TOTAL $ ____________

Make checks payable to JUNIOR LEAGUE COOKBOOK.
Charge to Visa ( ) or Mastercard ( ) # ________________ Exp. Date ________________
Signature ____

Mail to: Name ____
Address ____
City ________________________________ State _____ Zip ____________

MAGIC

2212 Twentieth Ave., So.
Birmingham, AL 35223

Please send ________ copies of MAGIC @ $10.95 each $ ____________
Alabama residents add 7% sales tax @ .77 each $ ____________
Plus postage and handling @ $1.50 each $ ____________
Please gift wrap @ .50 each $ ____________
TOTAL $ ____________

Make checks payable to JUNIOR LEAGUE COOKBOOK.
Charge to Visa ( ) or Mastercard ( ) # ________________ Exp. Date ________________
Signature ____

Mail to: Name ____
Address ____
City ________________________________ State _____ Zip ____________